JUNG

Also in the Phoenix Introductions series

Depression: An Introduction
by Barbara Dowds

JUNG
An Introduction

Ann Casement

PHOENIX
PUBLISHING HOUSE
firing the mind

The account of Ovid's myth of Narcissus is taken from Schwartz-Salant, N. (1982). *Narcissism and Character Transformation: The Psychology of Narcissistic Disorders*. Toronto, Canada: Inner City. It is reprinted here with the kind permission of the author.

The version of the story of Parsifal is taken from Magee, B. (2000). *Wagner and Philosophy*. London: Penguin. Copyright © Bryan Magee, 2000.

First published in 2021 by
Phoenix Publishing House Ltd
62 Bucknell Road
Bicester
Oxfordshire OX26 2DS

British Library Cataloguing in Publication Data

A C.I.P. for this book is available from the British Library

ISBN-13: 978-1-912691-25-8

Typeset by Medlar Publishing Solutions Pvt Ltd, India

www.firingthemind.com

aletheia—satyagraha—truth

Photograph taken by the scholar Ernst Falzeder at the 2019 Vienna IAAP Congress. Featuring (l–r): Jianguo Feng, Ann Casement, Jingjing Xiang, Andreas Jung, Ainong Hu. Jianguo, Jingjing and Ainong are members of the IAAP Beijing Developing Group.

Contents

Acknowledgements

Firstly, I would like to give thanks to many friends and colleagues in the international Jungian psychoanalytic community who have contributed so much to that world as well as to my own life. And, a special thank you to analysands, patients, supervisees, and students, working with whom has been a lived experience of Jung's notion of *mutuality*. Given the strict confidentiality that rightly governs the profession of psychoanalysis, I am able to acknowledge them anonymously only but can at least say quite a number have gone on to be psychoanalysts, authors, and administrators themselves.

It makes me especially happy to have made many new Chinese friends and colleagues to add to my long-standing friends, Heyong Shen and Gao Lan Shen, and more recently, Beijing friends, Qin Nan, Yuan Lin, and Dangwei Zhou currently in London, each of whom has contributed entries to the last chapters of this volume.

As I have been allocated a finite number of words for the book, it has precluded any significant entries on Latin America (in which I have loved working), Australia, and New Zealand, where there is a flourishing analytical psychology community, and India which has a bourgeoning one.

For the same reason, many countries in Europe have, likewise, been excluded despite the fact I have worked in several of them.

My heartfelt thanks go to three people: Jason Armitage, a brilliant scholar, the scholar Dangwei Zhou, and my friend and colleague, Andrea Cone-Farran, each of whom took time to read the final manuscript and to feed back constructive critical comments on it.

Finally, my warm appreciation is due to the publishers of this book, Kate Pearce and Fernando Marques, who have started their own publishing house, Phoenix, after working with my friend, Oliver Rathbone at Karnac. My thanks go to them for the invitation to write this book, and for their help and guidance throughout the prolonged creative labour of love entailed by that enterprise.

About the author

Ann Casement LP, is an honorary professor at the Oriental Academy for Analytical Psychology; senior member of the British Jungian Analytic Association; associate member of the Jungian Psychoanalytic Association (New York); New York State licensed psychoanalyst; member of the British Psychoanalytic Council; member of the National Association for the Advancement of Psychoanalysis (New York); member of the British Psychological Society; founder member of the International Neuropsychoanalysis Association; and patron of the Freud Museum in London. She worked for several years in psychiatry from the late 1970s; chaired the UK Council for Psychotherapy (1997–2001); served on the Executive Committee of the International Association for Analytical Psychology (2001–2007), and the IAAP Ethics Committee (2007–2016), becoming its chair in 2010. For two years from 1999 she conducted research working with Lord Alderdice and other stakeholders in the profession on a Private Member's Bill in the House of Lords on the statutory regulation of the psychotherapy/psychoanalytic profession. She has been teaching and lecturing in China, starting in 2015 at the initial invitation of Professor Heyong Shen.

She has lectured and taught in many countries around the world, including the UK, China, Japan, Russia, USA, Canada, Israel, Lithuania, Switzerland, South Africa, Brazil, Mexico, and in several countries in Europe. She contributes to *The Economist*, and to psychoanalytic journals worldwide, being on the editorial board of some. She served on the Gradiva Awards Committee (New York) in 2013; gave the Fay Lecture in Texas in 2019; is a fellow of the Royal Anthropological Institute; a fellow of The Royal Society of Medicine; and was a member of the Council of the Metropolitan Opera in New York. She has produced many articles, reviews, and several chapters for books. Her published and forthcoming books are:

Post-Jungians Today (Routledge, 1998).
Carl Gustav Jung (Sage, 2001).
Who Owns Psychoanalysis? (Karnac, 2004) nominated for the 2005 Gradiva Award.
The Idea of the Numinous (Routledge, 2006) with David Tacey.
Who Owns Jung? (Karnac, 2007).
Thresholds and Pathways Between Jung and Lacan (Routledge, 2021).
Integrating Shadow: Authentic Being in the World (in press, Texas A&M.)

Preface

This new *Introduction* to the work of the Swiss psychiatrist and psychoanalyst, Carl Gustav Jung, shares some degree of overlap with the previous book I produced on the same subject in 2001. One of the many
differences between that volume and the current one is that I have had
even longer experience of functioning in the psychoanalytic world as a
practitioner, author, lecturer, and administrator. Furthermore, the previous book was written according to a formula dictated by the editor of the
series of which it was a part. Although the current volume is exploring
Jung's ideas from my standpoint, I trust that a newcomer to the field will
find it a useful introduction to the essential facts about his life and work.
Nevertheless, this volume is my own highly individual account of his
approach, for as Jung said: "… every psychology—my own included—
has the character of a subjective confession" (1961, p. 336).

What is incontrovertible is that Jung is a compelling, albeit controversial figure in depth psychology for a number of reasons, namely: for
some of his views; for his personal life; for his questionable dealings with
the Nazis in the 1930s, about which I have written extensively; and, in
recent times, for his attitudes to diversity that have been critically reas-
sessed by some members of the Jungian community.

My own stance vis-à-vis Jung is neither that of accuser nor apologist; the tone of this *Introduction* is at times critical in places though its overarching aim is to give a balanced account of Jung's psychoanalytical approach—theoretical and practical. Reading Jung is a mixed pleasure as his written work varies in style and content from sounding grandiose and appearing slipshod, as it is accompanied by frequent allusions to decontextualised mythological ramblings, countered by marvels of wisdom and insight (cf. Commentary on *"The Secret of the Golden Flower"* in *Alchemical Studies, Volume 13* of *The Collected Works* for just one example of the latter). All these different styles may feature in the same book as the volumes that make up the *Collected Works* include a selection of essays in each written over a considerable period of time. It should further be noted that, at frequent intervals, Jung carried out a cut-and-paste job on his various works; the hazards of functioning in this manner are evidenced in his vastly different views of Freud depending on the time of revision, instances of which will appear in this work.

The book starts with a brief commentary on Jung's early years in his natal home, then shifts focus to his professional life as an adult, in the course of which he created his own psychoanalytic tradition. In addition, the book represents my own ideas that have developed about psychoanalysis over more than fifty-five years, during which time I have been closely associated with that discipline. As an analytical psychologist, I am an adherent of the developmental approach, hence there is a certain bias towards that mode of theory and practice. Alongside this, I am drawn to Jung's *archetypal* theory, which will also feature prominently in this work. In my experience, the *developmental* approach needs the depths inherent in Jung's *archetypal* approach; whereas the latter needs to be grounded *clinically* in the *developmental* approach to analytical work in the consulting room with actual analysands and patients. The most significant event in the Jung world since 2001 is the 2009 publication of the *Red Book* which will, of course, feature in this work.

The following caveat needs to be borne in mind throughout, namely, that the psychological concepts touched on in this work are metaphors and have no ontic existence. Even the ubiquitous term *consciousness* that makes frequent appearances in the written output of the founders of psychoanalysis, Freud, Jung, Klein, and in their descendants' work, is itself being widely debated and has been called the *hard problem* by the philosopher and cognitive scientist, David Chalmers, who suggests it may well be fundamental like space and time, which cannot be analysed from an Archimedean Point. Prior to that, Heidegger had also questioned the use of the term *consciousness* in philosophy though, of course, the notion of *consciousness* has been central to philosophical thinking through the ages, and the quest for a scientific definition of its existence continues into the present time. Jung used it frequently, at the same time acknowledging that it is one of the great mysteries of life.

One other notion that warrants special mention here is what Jung calls the *soul*, also utilised by James Hillman and Wolfgang Giegerich, who will be featured later in this work. George Makari's account of the shift from the term *soul* to *mind* in *Soul Machine* is one of the essential books anyone interested in psychoanalysis should have on their shelves. It was the seventeenth-century philosopher Thomas Hobbes who initially substituted the term *mind* for *soul* when *mind* became equated with reason which lent itself to scientific inquiry; while *soul* remained an ecclesiastical concern that was not subject to scientific inquiry. Jung's frequent use of the term *soul* represents a return to the seventeenth century on his part along with his interest in *alchemy*, also featured in this volume.

A note on concepts. Dream material is central to Jung's psychological approach so rather than have a separate chapter on dreams, I have incorporated dream material in some of the chapters to illustrate how Jung's concepts appear in dreams and how they may be analysed. For Jung, the *manifest* contents of dreams were the focus of his approach, as well as the context in which the dreamer had the dream; furthermore, the dreamer's *associations* were needed in order to unravel the mysteries that are revealed in these illuminating messages. In my experience, dreams reveal everything and, for that reason, I remain in awe of them as they contain uncanny knowledge that is close to being magical. A practical point to note here is that I have used Jung's original language in depicting his concepts, that is, by reifying them with the definite article. The section in Chapter 4 on Wolfgang Giegerich's critique of this reification represents the way I currently think about them, but, in many instances, it reads better in grammatical terms to refer to them using Jung's original writing. In any case, I am trying to introduce readers to Jung first, followed by critical appraisal of his use of language or theory.

Two last points to note, one already evident in this *Introduction*, are that in the current book, technical terms are put into *italics* as many of them have ordinary usage in everyday language. The second is that there is some repetition of Jung's more esoteric ideas. This is done in order to facilitate new readers' grasp of highly complex theoretical constructs, in particular, *psychological alchemy*, to which Jung devoted the last thirty years of his life.

CHAPTER 1

Early life

Carl Gustav Jung (1875–1961), the psychiatrist and psychoanalyst, had a lonely, desperately poor childhood. He was born at Kesswil in Switzerland, as the fourth and first surviving child of Paul Achilles Jung, a country pastor, and his unhappy, unstable wife, Emilie Preiswerk. On both sides, there were many prominent ministers and doctors, professions that were to play an important role in Jung's own life. A sister, Trudi, arrived nine years later and, in the course of Jung's childhood, the family moved to different parsonages in Switzerland. These moves were accompanied by his mother's frequent hospitalisations brought about by her mental illnesses, although her condition improved following the birth of Trudi. The parental marriage was not a happy one, which led to the atmosphere in the house being *unbreathable* due to the tensions between Jung's mother and father.

In *Memories, Dreams, Reflections* (*MDR*), the book that is generally taken to be Jung's "autobiography", Jung displays a remarkable memory for the trivia of childhood, and often uses the word "defeat" (1963, p. 41) in relation to anything at which he did not excel in school, namely, mathematics, gymnastics, and drawing. In that book, the accounts of his No. 1 and No. 2 personalities are striking as they remained important for the whole of his life; the former was his actual youthful ordinary self; the latter was a wise old man from the eighteenth century. He made it clear these did not represent dissociations but, rather, insisted that these distinct personalities exist in everyone though most people are not aware of their No. 2 personality. The latter was of prime importance in Jung's life: "I have always tried to make room for anything that wanted to come to me from within" (1963, p. 55). From this statement, it may be deduced that Jung was an *introvert*, namely, someone who places greater value on the workings of the internal world of *objects* rather than on those of the external world. It could be further deduced that he was an *introverted intuitive* according to his own theory of typology, as he was a visionary with an intense inner life similar to Nietzsche, the latter being a huge inspiration for Jung's work as he was for psychoanalysis in general. There is Jung's own assessment of himself as an *intuitive* (that he was an *introvert* is exemplified in his writing and by descriptions of him by many people who knew him personally). In a case he wrote about at some length, which will be examined critically later in the book, he says of the *compensatory* projection onto him from a patient with strong *sensation* functioning and, hence, corresponding "inferior" *intuition*: "My own psychic peculiarity would make me a suitable projection in this respect" (1959a, p. 303).

This passing reference to Jung's work on *typology* needs to be further elaborated as follows. In my view, his theorising about what he calls the judging functions, *thinking* and *feeling*, which he situates diagrammatically along a vertical axis, owes a great deal to Kant's tripartite model of understanding, judgement, reason—the first of these relates to the faculty to conceptualise; the second allows for evaluation of those concepts; the third for drawing conclusions from them. The end result of this is that those situated along the vertical axis are rational beings; those situated along the horizontal axis of *sensation* and *intuition* are non-rational beings, whose strengths lie in the creative arts, chefs, visionaries (Nietzsche and Jung), technology wizards, and traders on the stock exchange among them. The above are the four main functions which are greatly impacted by the attitudes of *introversion* and *extraversion*; for example, Jung cites Kant exemplifying an *introverted thinker* as the *shadow* of Darwin exemplifying an *extraverted thinker*.

With regard to Jung's two personalities, it is important to note that he did not denigrate the No. 1 personality (any more than he did any of the four functions) which, with all its limitations, offered the light of *consciousness* (the greatest mystery for Jung) against the superior intelligence and timelessness of the No. 2 personality. At the age of twelve "… it came to me that I was actually two different persons" (1963, p. 45). No. 1 was a schoolboy who could not grasp algebra; the other was an important old man who lived in the eighteenth century, wore buckled shoes and a white wig, and was not to be trifled with. The latter appears to be Goethe, who was unknown to Jung at the time though there were rumours that his grandfather was a natural son of Goethe that Jung repeatedly denied. Later in life, Jung came to have the highest regard for that author's *Faust*.

To return to *Memories, Dreams, Reflections (MDR)* itself, there is a critical account of it in Sonu Shamdasani's *Jung Stripped Bare by His Biographers, Even* (2005), the title clearly an allusion to Marcel Duchamp's early twentieth-century work of art, *The Bride Stripped Bare by Her Bachelors, Even*. Shamdasani's book includes critiques of other biographies of Jung, a position with which I have every sympathy as I have expended a great deal of time writing critical reviews of biographies of Freud and Jung for *The Economist*, to the point where my editor suggested leaving one out of the paper as it did not exist to promote "bad" books. A revealing quotation about *MDR* is to be found in a letter Jung wrote as follows: "I have always vowed to myself that I would never write an autobiography and in this case … it is rather Frau Jaffé who is writing a biography of me to which I have made a few contributions" (Shamdasani, 2005, p. 37).

Sonu Shamdasani, who is the general editor and co-founder of the Philemon Foundation, says the following about *MDR*:

> Due to the involvement of another publisher, the book did not go down the same editorial channels as the rest of Jung's work, which was to have significant consequences for what ensued. Like Lucy Heyer, Jaffé undertook a series of regular interviews with Jung, which she noted in shorthand. These notes were later typed out. Copies of the notes of these interviews are currently in

the Library of Congress in Washington and at the ETH in Zürich (hereafter referred to as the "protocols").

Footnote 51: This copy of the protocols was donated by Helen Wolff to Princeton University Press, who in turn donated them to the Library of Congress in 1983, placing a ten-year restriction on them. I studied these in 1991, and they have been on open access since 1993. Bair stated that the copy in the Library of Congress, which is in the Bollingen collection, is restricted (2004, p. 657, n. 7). This is actually unrestricted and was moved to a separate collection. The copy at the ETH in Zürich is restricted. (Shamdasani, 2005, pp. 23–24)

As to the publication of the protocols, the following is taken from the website of the Philemon Foundation:

The literary executor of the estate of Aniela Jaffé, Robert Hinshaw, and the Foundation of the Works of C.G. Jung have agreed to a complete publication of Aniela Jaffé's protocols of Jung's recollections. The volume will be edited by Sonu Shamdasani with Thomas Fischer and Robert Hinshaw as consulting editors, appearing in English in the Philemon Series of the Philemon Foundation, published by Princeton University Press.

For the time being, only the current version of *MDR* is available so it is important to bear in mind the above caveats when reference is made to it. To proceed, Jung states in the book that his mother had two distinct personalities: "By day she was a loving mother, but at night she seemed uncanny" (1963, p. 59). From this it would appear that Jung's feelings for his mother were ambivalent, whereas he felt pity for his father as Jung could not discuss with him important questions he had about Christian teachings of an all good, kindly God; it appears that an unbridgeable abyss existed between father and son. The unsatisfactory nature of this interaction was there from an early age for Jung and was to have major repercussions throughout his lengthy existence. His lifelong religious quest has its origins in this relationship as his description of his preparation for confirmation with lessons from his father attests. In the course of those, he became interested in the Trinity but his father could not discuss it with him in any satisfying way, saying: "I can't make head or tail of it myself" (Jung, 1959a, p. 15).

Jung's attitude to his father was that the latter remained stuck in out-worn tradition, taking God as the Bible prescribed and from the teach-ings of his forefathers thus not having the freedom to "… know the immediate living God … omnipotent and free, above his Bible and his Church" (1963, p. 51). Jung kept these secret thoughts to himself and later, when he was eighteen years old, had many discussions with his father when he would try to explain them, to which his father responded: "Oh, nonsense, you always want to think. One ought not to think, but believe" (ibid., p. 53).

On reaching adulthood, Jung expressed his despair at the impover-ishment of Christian symbols:

> … we now try to cover our nakedness with the gorgeous trappings of the East, as theosophists do … A man does not sink down to beggary only to pose afterwards as an Indian potentate … we try to break into Oriental palaces that our fathers never knew. We have inherited this poverty from our fathers. (1959a, p. 15)

Alongside this beautifully written, hard-hitting denunciation, Jung could not come to terms with the fact that science and technology were the dominants of the world order but, instead, harked back to a bygone mythological age. Heidegger, equally pessimistic in *The Question Concerning Technology*, points to the fact that we live a certain tem-poral technical-way-of-being that draws us to a form of revealing—"Enframing"—where humans become resources. Enframing closes the path to a form of revealing where we might "experience the call of a more primal truth" (Heidegger, 1977, p. 28). He refused to stand up as a prophet "offering consolation" (Safranski, 1999, p. 153) any more than Freud did in *Civilization and Its Discontents*.

Jung's discomfort with the technological age was accompanied by his decrying of the rise of communism and fascism earlier in the first half of the twentieth century. He viewed their advent as a way of filling the void left by the decay of religious symbolism and warned of the dan-gers wrought by those two *isms*. This continues into the present time when identification with one or other *ism* easily possesses the susceptible: "… the mass man, the ever-ready victim of some wretched 'ism'" (Jung, 1960b, p. 219). The widespread use of social media facilitates this, accompanied by the facile proliferation of terms such as *elitism, racism,* and *sexism,* the kind of name-calling that reveals as much about the projector as it does about the object of such projections. The resort to ready-made labels leads to a lack of critical thinking as the former are far easier to reach for than the hard work entailed in reflecting on one's own *shadow.* An example of this is the frequent unquestioning usage of the derogatory term *participation mystique* that I am yet again exploring in my forthcoming book on *shadow.* For the monomaniacs of *isms* or *masked religions* the world shrinks: "In each and everything he finds only the confirmation of his opinion, which he defends with the fervor of faith against the world and against his own doubts" (Safranski, 1999, p. 153)—what Freud termed *reaction-formation.* A genuine religion, on the other hand, educates one for reverence of the inexplicability of the world. "In the light of faith, the world grows bigger, and also darker, because it retains its mystery, and Man sees himself as part of it" (ibid.). This evocation resonates with Jung's world view.

Childhood dream

To return to the relations between father and son, the growing estrangement between Jung and his father was exacerbated as a result of the following dream he had aged twelve. He later recounted this to E. A. Bennet, a close associate, who asserts it is the most significant dream of Jung's that remained fresh in his mind throughout his life.

> I was in the rather gloomy courtyard of the Gymnasium at Basel, a beautiful medieval building. From the courtyard I went through the big entrance where the coaches used to come in, and there before me was the Cathedral of Basel, the sun shining on the roof of coloured tiles, recently renovated, a most impressive sight. Above the Cathedral God was sitting on His throne. I thought: "How beautiful it all is! What a wonderful world this is—how perfect, how complete, how full of harmony." Then something happened, so unexpected and so shattering that I woke up. There the dream ended. I could not allow myself to *think* of what I had

seen, for had I done so I would be compelled to accept it, and this I couldn't possibly do. So I made every effort to put the thought from my mind. (Bennet, 1961, p. 16)

For several days, Jung was in torment and could not bring himself to think about the end of the dream, which Jung declared to Bennet was an experience of repression. Finally, he had to face it: "From his throne God 'dropped' a vast faeces on the Cathedral and smashed it to pieces" (ibid., p. 17).

Jung had a couple of sleepless nights during which he tried to repress any memory of the latter part of the dream as he was, at the time, a devout Christian following the religious teaching of his pastor father. He finally had to face the message explicit in the dream that God had poured scorn on the Church, his father's teachings, and his own beliefs. This dream has been interpreted countless times by Jung's followers and has come to be seen largely as his insight into the *shadow* side of Christianity.

The Jungian psychoanalyst, Michael Whan, has a different interpretation of Jung's reactions to the dream which he critiques through the lens of Wolfgang Giegerich who, in the view of the author of the current book, is the most thought-provoking Jung thinker of current times. According to Whan/Giegerich, the real *telos* of this moment of disillusionment was an initiation into disenchantment and an opening of the youthful Jung's mind "into the particular form of adulthood corresponding to the culture and spirit of the time" (Whan, 2018, p. 244). The acceptance of this rupture of his boyhood innocence would have been an initiation into a different, cultural-historical mode of being. Whan goes on to state:

But the *form* of consciousness (the religious form) remained immune from disenchantment. Jung's refusal to give up the notion of enchantment at the level of the form or syntactic level of consciousness carried over later into his very conception of psychology. (Ibid.)

Whan has encapsulated the essentials of Giegerich's thinking in these sentences, namely, that thenceforth Jung's conceptualising remained mostly on the level of the *contents* or *semantics* of *consciousness* or of experience. Giegerich's work will again be referenced in the chapter on *alchemy* as well as in the section of this book dedicated to his thinking.

In the end, the disappointment that existed at the heart of his feelings for his father had major repercussions for his later, crucially important relationship with Sigmund Freud, which will be examined further in this book. Whilst acknowledging different views by respected scholars that Freud's impact on Jung was less than has been claimed in the past, this writer sees Freud as *the* central figure in Jung's life for reasons that will be spelt out in this work. A vital *inner* figure for Jung was Goethe, who personified Jung's No. 2 personality from the eighteenth century.

CHAPTER 2

Psychiatry

This chapter attempts a succinct account of Jung's psychiatric work as it was his work with *dementia praecox* that laid the foundations for his later functioning as a psychoanalyst. It was the experience with seriously disorganised patients where one can observe him developing his method of listening to what they have to say, getting to know their case histories, and focusing on one patient at a time. I have a personal reason for writing at some length on Jung's time in psychiatry as I spent years working in that setting myself, eventually being offered a consultancy at the hospital where I practised. The one-to-one sessions I was conducting with psychiatric patients were supervised by a member of the British Psychoanalytical Society from whom I learnt a great deal, including the efficacy of using Kleinian technique in the here-and-now of the *transference–countertransference*, thus keeping the therapeutic relationship grounded in the room instead of *amplifying* it in a mythological haze or exploring dream material, which is counter-indicated when working with seriously disturbed patients. I thought of applying to the Institute of Psychoanalysis to do my analytic training, but, for a number of reasons, decided to remain in the Jungian world. My orientation since the late 1970s has been a process of incorporating the Jungian, Freudian, Kleinian, and Lacanian disciplines as every patient needs the benefit of an approach that matches his or her own needs not one that is an expression of the analyst's dogma. As a result of heading the UK Council for several years, I have also integrated other modalities into my way of thinking, for example, utilising *cognitive behavioural therapy* (*CBT*) when working with patients suffering from *obsessive compulsive disorder*. These different approaches, combined with the psychiatric training and my academic background in anthropology, have broadened my own psychoanalytic way of functioning. This experience has led me to the view that remaining fixated on the straight and narrow of one orientation leads to dogmatism and has been a major factor in contributing to the splits in the psychoanalytic profession. On that vexed subject, I was invited to contribute an article on Jungian splits in the UK for the fortieth anniversary edition of *The Journal of Analytical Psychology* titled "A Brief History of Splits in the United Kingdom" (Casement, 1995).

My experience of the London Jungian training I embarked on at the same time as I was working in psychiatry mirrored that of Michael Escamilla, who states the following about his Jungian training in Zürich: "I was a fish out of water—there were no other psychiatrists training in the program" (2016, p. 11). In this author's view, it is essential for a psychoanalyst to have experience of working in psychiatry. I was fortunate in the hospital I chose to work at as the two consultant psychiatrists who were consecutively head of department during my time there, Michael de Mowbray and Peter Rohde, were exemplary in their dedication to their patients. I was offered a consultancy by the latter as it appeared that my therapeutic work with highly disturbed patients, combined with the relevant medication, was helping to maintain them as outpatients, which was saving the national health service money.

To revert back to Jung himself, in early adulthood he finally decided on a career in medicine and was initially inclined to surgery though, eventually, in keeping with his interest in the phenomenon of *double identity disorder* which was fashionable in the nineteenth century, he decided to specialise in psychiatry. He remained fascinated by the phenomenon of *dissociation* for the rest of his life. In 1900 he took up his post at Burghölzli Mental Hospital in Zürich, which was under the directorship of the celebrated psychiatrist, Eugen Bleuler. Burghölzli was founded in 1870, linked to the University of Zürich though financed by the Canton of Zürich, which this writer was fortunate to be taken around some years ago and shown where Bleuler and Jung worked. It is now an acute unit with the forensic work being conducted at a sister hospital further out of Zürich. It was at Burghölzli that both Bleuler and Jung undertook research into the *psychoses*, in particular, *dementia praecox*—a term coined by Emil Kraepelin, the eminent nineteenth-century German organic psychiatrist—that was renamed *schizophrenia*, or, more accurately, the *schizophrenias*, by Bleuler. It was Kraepelin who founded psychiatry based on scientific lines in the nineteenth century and in "1900 the positivist medical model was in full operative mode in Swiss Germany and Europe" (Escamilla, 2016, p. 34).

Kraepelin, Bleuler, and Jung were drawn to the word association test, a discovery of Francis Galton but developed by the German experimental psychologist, Wilhelm Wundt. This method was used at Burghölzli for the treatment of *psychosis*, and Bleuler had drawn up a list of 156 stimulus words, using a stopwatch to time a patient's response to each. Bleuler was interested in comparing *psychotic* patients with "normal" people by using this method and asked Jung to test several women and men in this way. The latter, in turn, discovered that individuals were susceptible to internal distractions as well as to external ones, the internal distractions being of particular interest to Jung, namely, *complexes*.

Theodor Ziehen, the German psychiatrist, discovered the feeling-toned *complex* in 1898; a brief definition of this is that it is a combination of images and ideas clustered around an emotional core. At Burghölzli, Jung became interested in the work Bleuler was doing in applying the word association tests to *complexes*, having first become interested in them through attending Pierre Janet's seminars at the Salpêtrière Hospital in Paris. Janet had followed in the footsteps of the great neurologist, Jean-Martin Charcot, "the Napoléon of the Neuroses", who died suddenly in 1893. Janet's importance for Jung lay in his work on *subconscious fixed ideas* and the lowering of the *conscious* level though, later, Jung had no hesitation in criticising Janet in defence of Freud whom Janet accused of plagiarising his own ideas.

The work over eleven years of the three Burghölzli psychiatrists, Bleuler, Franz Riklin, later to be honorary secretary to Jung as first president of the International Psychoanalytical Association, and Jung himself, brought together four separate lines of intellectual thought as follows:

> 1) the "brain" centered research approach of Kraepelin and the German school; 2) the dissociative and proto-psychodynamic approach of the French school; primarily represented by the work of Janet; 3) the psychoanalytic approach of Freud and his group from Vienna; and 4) the experimental psychology approach of Wilhelm Wundt. (Escamilla, 2016, p. 58)

It was Bleuler who first drew Jung's attention to Freud's *The Interpretation of Dreams* which was to be of such importance to Jung's own development. Furthermore, Freud's approach to the study of *histology* followed a similar path to his own interest in hypnotism, hugely influenced by the French psychiatrists and neurologists working in that area. Freud enthusiastically conducted microscopic examinations of brain tissue, which in turn proved unavailing in enlightening him about the intruders of the mind, as he called mental disturbances such as *hallucinations* and *delusions*. This kind of scientific research was common practice among psychiatrists in the nineteenth century conducted by such luminaries as Alzheimer, Kraepelin, and Meynert.

At the time Jung arrived at Burghölzli Hospital in 1900, it had gained a considerable reputation in the world of psychiatry for the enlightened approaches of its practitioners to psychiatric disorders compared to the barbaric practices of psychiatry that preceded this in the nineteenth century. A book I reviewed in 2018 by the eminent London psychoanalyst, Brett Kahr, for the San Francisco *Jung Journal: Culture and Psyche*, paints a horrifyingly medieval picture of psychiatry practised at the Narrenturm (the Fools' Tower), the special building for the incarceration of mental patients at the Allgemeines Krankenhaus in Vienna. This grim fortress was full of barbaric practices such as chaining patients to iron rings on the walls and floors, where they slept on straw and were refused any bathing rooms, books, music, or places of worship. These practices were described in a book "written in 1853 by the American physician, Dr Pliny Earle" (Kahr, 2018, p. 37).

In contrast to this was the humane approach to insanity to be found at Burghölzli that led to Jung's growing recognition of the valuable contents of the inner worlds of *psychotic* patients, encapsulated in the following: "We healthy people, who stand with both feet in reality, see only the ruin of the patient in *this* world, but not the richness of that side of the psyche which is turned away from us" (Escamilla, 2016, p. 164). This was echoed many years later in the British psychoanalyst Donald Winnicott's realisation that we are poor indeed if we are only sane.

Auguste Forel, the Swiss French predecessor of Bleuler, had worked with Janet and Bernheim in France on hypnotism, which Jung likewise practised for a while. He quickly came to see it as being superficial, as he thought it useful only in the elimination of symptoms though not in shedding light on the underlying causes of those symptoms. "The influence of Janet and the French school on the Burghölzli from the mid-1890s throughout the 1900–1911 period ... can thus be traced back to this interest of Forel's" (Escamilla, 2016, p. 55). Forel's other activities also had an impact on Jung: for instance, he put together a combined social, psychological, and anthropological study on sexuality, and was a devotee of eugenics, the study of human improvement by genetic means. In that, he was more extreme than the English eugenicist, Francis Galton; and Jung's later Larmarckian (inheritance of acquired characteristics) theorising on a racial *psyche* may relate back to Forel's interest in eugenics.

Two significant figures for Jung were also first encountered by him during his time at Burghölzli, namely, the brilliant though erratic Austrian, Otto Gross, and the Russian, Sabina Spielrein. The Jungian psychoanalyst, Gottfried Heuer, has produced a well-researched work on Gross entitled *Freud's 'Outstanding' Colleague/Jung's 'Twin Brother'*, and is co-founder of the International Otto Gross Society that holds regular conferences around the world. Spielrein, Jung's first psychoanalytic patient at Burghölzli, will appear further in the book in her role as an *anima* figure for Jung though she later developed into a psychoanalyst in her own right. Her thinking on *creative destruction* bears some resemblance to the Austrian political economist Joseph Schumpeter's thinking on this phenomenon in economics, still a feature of that discipline to this day.

Psychiatric case material

In addition to his overtly scientific work at the hospital, Jung spent a great deal of time talking with patients in the wards, hoping in this way to discover something about the origins of their illness and what their symptoms meant to them. The accounts of these case histories are taken from *Psychiatric Studies* which makes up *Volume 1* of *The Collected Works*, and the dates of the cases are given as and when they appear in that volume. Jung was a gifted psychiatrist and his work with these patients took place between 1900 and 1909 during his time there as assistant to the director, Eugen Bleuler.

One female patient, who had been an inmate for forty years, was treated as just another senile patient by the nursing staff. She was in the habit of moving her hands up and down and shovelling food into her mouth in this way, which the medical students diagnosed as *catatonic schizophrenia*. Jung discovered that there was some connection with shoemaking and he was struck by the resemblance between the patient's hand movements and those he had seen made by cobblers at work. When the patient died, her brother came to the hospital, at which point Jung asked him why the patient had been admitted to the hospital. The brother replied that the patient had gone mad when she had been jilted by a shoemaker, which led Jung to propose there was a *psychogenic* element in the onset of *dementia praecox/schizophrenia*.

Jung was also elaborating his work on the word association test, using it to time the response to each stimulus word, at the same time recording the rate of heart-beat and respiration, as well as the psycho-galvanic reaction—a change in the electrical properties of the skin in response to stress or anxiety. The graph of such a test showed a correspondence between the verbal response and the respiration rate which, in turn, demonstrated that the mind and body worked in unison and that the test depended on the emotional not the intellectual state of the participant. Jung published a paper in 1907 with a colleague entitled "Psycho-physical Investigations with the Galvanometer and Pneumograph in Normal and

Insane Individuals", which set out to show that the influence of emotion can be demonstrated physiologically as well as psychologically.

Another paper on a female patient suffering from *paranoid dementia* illustrated how Jung used the word association test. She was an unmarried dressmaker who had heard voices slandering her for years before she was admitted as an inpatient. These voices told her she was a doubtful character, that her child had been found in a toilet, and that she had stolen a pair of scissors in order to poke out a child's eye. As a result, the patient thought of drowning herself and was subsequently admitted as an inpatient in 1887. This patient produced vivid coherent delusions such as that she had a fortune of many millions and that her bed was full of needles. Gradually these delusions became less coherent and more grandiose; for instance, she claimed to be Noah's Ark and an empress. Over two years, Jung took simple word tests from her with each stimulus word followed by a prolonged silence lasting up to fourteen seconds. The following are some examples of her associations.

To the stimulus word "pupil" she responded "Socrates"; to "love", "great abuses"; to "ring", "bond", "alliance", or "betrothal". Jung suggested the long time in responding could be explained by the continual interference of the *complexes*, which assimilate everything that comes within their orbit. With this patient, three *complexes* can be deduced from the association tests as follows: *the complex of personal grandeur; the complex of injury;* and *the erotic complex*. The summary of the long case history Jung wrote on her pointed to the fact that the confused and senseless fantasies the patient had constructed in her *psychosis* had similarities with "dream-thoughts" in their symbolic imagery. "The patient describes for us in her symptoms, the hopes and disappointments of her life, just as a poet might who is moved by an inner, creative impulse" (1960a, p. 144). He continued: "In dreams she remoulds her complexes into symbolic forms, in a disconnected, aphoristic manner, and only seldom do the dream-formations assume broader, more coherent structure, for this requires complexes of poetic—or hysterical—intensity" (ibid.). These symptoms expressed symbolically became more understandable once the patient's life-history was taken into account. What Jung was at pains to show in his psychiatric work was how dream formations developed out of *complexes* and how a patient's conscious *psychic* activity may be limited to a systematic creation of fantasies that *compensate* for a wretched life. For Jung, the *psyche* works in a compensatory way to balance the attitude of the waking state.

There were several important, long-lasting results of the lengthy research Jung conducted with the word-association test. First, it confirmed his hypothesis about *complexes*, which evolved into one of his central theories. Another was to show that *complexes* were located in what Jung called the *personal unconscious* and were not part of the realm of the *collective unconscious.* The tests also demonstrated the autonomous character of *complexes*, which can affect persons and objects in the person's vicinity. Jung's term *constellate* refers to a psychologically charged moment when the contents of a *complex* manifest in *consciousness.* This may be experienced as exhilarating or disturbing depending on the *affect* with which the *complex* is imbued.

A recent study done on the word association test by Escamilla, Sandoval, Calhoun, and Ramirez published in *The Journal of Analytical Psychology* "confirmed that the human brain responds differently to words which generate complexes (unconscious reactions, as measured in the word association test) from the way it does to neutral words (words which do not generate complexes)" (2018, p. 494). Functional magnetic resonance imaging was used in the experiments to study neuropsychological mechanisms operative in brain areas that "should help guide the development of both analytic psychology theory and practice" (ibid., p. 504).

In the past, the most important outcome of the word association tests was the part they played in bringing Freud and Jung into collaboration with each other. From Jung's point of view, Freud's theory of *repression*, one of the cornerstones of the latter's theory, confirmed the outcome of the tests. Similarly, for Freud, the association tests conducted by Jung provided a scientific underpinning to important parts of his work. Ultimately, Jung came to find the paraphernalia surrounding the tests cumbersome and increasingly boring, as well as being a hindrance to the patient–doctor relationship. He used them less frequently and eventually abandoned them altogether.

CHAPTER 3

Freud

From this author's viewpoint, the most significant professional relationship for Jung was the one he had with Freud. The former's interest was piqued by *The Interpretation of Dreams*, the contents of which helped in linking the thought-formations produced by *schizophrenics* with dream-formations. Their friendship and collaboration lasted for seven years from 1907 to 1913, with the first meeting taking place on 3rd March 1907 at Freud's home in Vienna. Dangwei Zhou, the scholar doing his PhD with Sonu Shamdasani at University College London, has informed me that Ernest Jones was mistaken in stating, in his three-volume biography of Freud, that their meeting took place on Sunday 27th February that year. To begin with, that date was a Wednesday not a Sunday. This erroneous dating can be found in Jones's three-volume biography of Freud in Volume 2, page 36, paragraph 3. The correct date was Sunday 3rd March, confirmed by William McGuire in the *Correspondence* between Freud and Jung from which there are several extracts in the following pages.

Although their collaboration ended acrimoniously, Jung remained president of the International Psychoanalytical Association until 1914. The impact of this parting of the ways on psychoanalysts of different persuasions is still felt up to the present day, not only between *"Freudians"* and *"Jungians"* but within their own communities as destructive splits continue unabated.

Volume 4 of Jung's *Collected Works* is titled *Freud and Psychoanalysis*, and incorporates his writings on Freud from 1906–1916, with the earlier papers showing Jung ardently defending classical Freudian concepts such as the sexual aetiology of *neurosis* and the theory of dreams, including *manifest* and *latent* content, *wish-fulfilment*, *condensation*, and the dream *censor* though, even at the outset, Jung expressed doubts with regard to the sexual theory in a letter to Freud in 1907 as follows:

> Do you regard sexuality as the mother of all feelings? Isn't sexuality for you merely one component of the personality (albeit the most important), and isn't the sexual complex therefore the most important and most frequent component in the clinical picture of hysteria? Are there not hysterical symptoms which, though co-determined by the sexual complex, are predominantly conditioned by a sublimation or by a non-sexual complex (profession, job, etc.)? (McGuire, 1974, p. 79)

The later papers in *Volume 4* increasingly show Jung's growing criticism of Freud's theory and, in particular, of the sexual theory. In a paper on the *Oedipus Complex* and the problem of incest, Jung puts forward his own theory as follows:

> Here religion is a great help because, by the bridge of the symbol, it leads his libido away from the infantile objects (parents) towards the symbolic representatives of the past. (1961, p. 156)

The paper ends on a note of complete rejection of Freud's *Oedipus Complex*:

> He therefore takes the tendency towards incest to be an absolutely concrete sexual wish, for he calls this complex the root-complex, or nucleus, of the neuroses and is inclined, viewing this as the original one, to reduce practically the whole psychology of the neuroses, as well as many other phenomena in the realm of the mind, to this one complex. (Ibid.)

In *Memories, Dreams, Reflections* Jung stated he had doubts from the beginning about Freud's theory that sexual *repression* and *trauma* were the cause of all *neuroses*. As he felt at the time that Freud had opened up a new path of investigation, Jung tried to suppress his own misgivings, though when he did attempt to air them, Freud would attribute these to Jung's lack of experience. On one occasion in 1910, Jung recalled Freud saying to him: "My dear Jung, promise me never to abandon the sexual theory. That is the most essential thing of all. You see, we must make a dogma of it, an unshakable bulwark against the black tide of mud of occultism" (1963, p. 173). He felt that for Freud sexuality was a sort of *numinosum*, namely, a tremendous and compelling force akin to a religious experience. "Freud who had always made much of his irreligiosity, had now constructed a dogma; or rather, in the place of a jealous God whom he had lost, he had substituted another compelling image, that of sexuality" (p. 174).

In the early 1900s, when Jung was first coming into contact with Freud's ideas, the latter was still *persona non grata* in academic and scientific circles. Jung himself had mixed feelings about the fact that his association experiments were in agreement with Freud's theories and was tempted to publish his conclusions without mentioning Freud's name. At that point, he heard the No. 2 personality telling him that would be a piece of trickery and he would be basing his life on a lie.

Heir apparent

From that time, Jung became an open advocate of Freud and in 1906 published a supportive paper on Freud's theory of hysteria. He was warned that he was endangering his own academic career but nevertheless went on defending Freud. In 1907, the latter invited Jung and Emma Jung to visit him in Vienna. As this was one of the great historical meetings of minds of the twentieth century, two brief accounts of it are given—the first from a Jungian perspective, the other from a Freudian.

> Jung in his turn was eager to know Freud, and he records that he was the most remarkable person he had then met. Their first talk, in Freud's house, lasted for thirteen hours! … According to Jung, the talk was protracted because he continued to question

Freud, hoping to get beyond … Freud's insistence on the importance of the infantile sexual trauma as a settled unalterable basis
of his work. (Bennet, 1961, p. 33)

In July 1967 at the International Congress of Neurology in Amsterdam,
the Freudian, Ernest Jones presented the following:

Jung gave me a lively account of his first interview (with Freud).
He had very much to tell Freud and to ask him, and with intense
animation he poured forth in a spate for three whole hours. Then
the patient, absorbed listener interrupted him with the suggestion that they conduct their discussion more systematically. To
Jung's great astonishment, Freud proceeded to group the contents of the harangue under several headings that enabled them
to spend the further hours in a more profitable give and take.
(Jones, 1955, p. 36)

Their mutual admiration was unbounded after this first meeting when
Jung declared that Freud was handsome and asked the latter's wife,
Martha, to send him a photograph of her husband. To continue with
Jones's account, Jung regarded this meeting as the high point of his life
(confirmed by the Jungian Bennet) and said that "whoever had acquired
a knowledge of psychoanalysis had eaten of the tree of Paradise and
attained vision" (ibid, p. 37).

Freud, for his part, was equally inspired and grateful to have the support of an Aryan as he wanted psychoanalysis to be opened up to the
non-Jewish world. He claimed that Jung had one of the only two original
minds among his followers.

He soon decided that Jung was to be his successor and at times
called him his "son and heir" … Jung was to be the Joshua des-
tined to explore the promised land of psychiatry which Freud,
like Moses, was only permitted to view from afar. Incidentally,
this remark is of interest as indicating Freud's self-identification
with Moses, one which in later years became very evident.
(Ibid., p. 38)

There were strong undertones of an idealised father/son *transference-countertransference* in all this, in which both men appeared to have been swept up at the moment of their first meeting.

> Freud and Jung were to come together on nine or ten further occasions, including four Congresses and the journey to America together, but the freshness of the first meeting could never be experienced again. The last time they saw each other was at the Munich Congress in September 1913. (Ibid., p. 38)

Freud, Jung, and Jones were in agreement in being unimpressed by the followers with whom Freud surrounded himself in Vienna, as testified by the following.

> Jung had told me in Zürich what a pity it was that Freud had no followers of any weight in Vienna, and that he was surrounded there by a "degenerate and Bohemian crowd" who did him little credit. (Jones, 1959, pp. 169–170)
>
> The reader may perhaps gather that I was not highly impressed with the assembly. It seemed an unworthy accompaniment to Freud's genius, but in the Vienna of those days, so full of prejudice against him, it was hard to secure a pupil with a reputation to lose, so he had to take what he could get. (Ibid., pp. 169–170)
>
> I (Freud) no longer get any pleasure from the Viennese. I have a heavy cross to bear with the older generation, Stekel, Adler, Sadger. (Jones, 1955, p. 78)

Jones imputes the antagonism between Jung and the Vienna Group to the former's anti-Semitic streak. John Kerr in his book *A Most Dangerous Method*, the title of which derives from the eminent American philosopher and psychologist, William James, says this charge is unfair.

> At the time of his first visit, Jung was still in the grip of what can best be described as his Jewish romance. He was positively attracted by the Jewishness of psychoanalysis ... Having earlier abandoned Swiss Calvinism, the faith he was raised in, Jung was

> without a church of his own; for him Judaism, like occultism, was
> an intriguing church next door. (Kerr, 1994, p. 133)

In actual fact, Jung did not belong to *Swiss Calvinism* as Kerr has it in the above quotation but was, instead, a member of the *Swiss Reformed Church* founded by Zwingli.

Freud came to rely on Jung increasingly and made him the editor of *The Yearbook for Psychoanalysis*, which had its first edition in 1909. At the second Psychoanalytic Congress held at Nuremberg in 1910, the International Psychoanalytical Association (IPA) was founded and Freud's initial idea was to appoint Jung as the president in perpetuity, with complete power to appoint and remove analysts. Fritz Wittels's biography entitled *Sigmund Freud* gives a glimpse of how the Viennese analysts reacted to this; for instance, Alfred Adler and Wilhelm Stekel were utterly dismayed as it meant that from then on analysts would have to submit their scientific writings to Jung for approval before publication. Furthermore, the future development of psychoanalysis would lie in Jung's and not Freud's hands.

The Viennese analysts held a private meeting in the Grand Hotel at Nuremberg to discuss the new situation and Freud made an unexpected appearance. He burst into an excited speech as follows:

> Most of you are Jews, and therefore you are incompetent to win friends for the new teaching. Jews must be content with the modest rôle of preparing the ground. It is absolutely essential that I should form ties in the world of general science. I am getting on in years and am weary of being perpetually attacked. We are all in danger. [Seizing his coat by the lapels, he said:] They won't even leave me a coat on my back. The Swiss will save us—will save me, and all of you as well. (Wittels, 1934, p. 12)

The furore this appointment caused, particularly among the Viennese, resulted in a modification of the original proposals. Jung was made president for two years and the official seat of the IPA was to be in Zürich for the duration of his presidency. Alfred Adler was made president of the Vienna Society. The organisational birth of the psychoanalytical movement was fraught with difficulties on all sides and even Bleuler refused to join. He was to be an increasingly important figure in the ongoing relations between Freud and Jung. By August 1910, Freud had expressed doubts but was reassured by Jung in such a heartening way that the founding of the IPA had one positive outcome, that of reconciling them to each other after the tensions engendered by the American trip, a description of which follows.

America

Jung came to see the year 1909 as a decisive one for his relationship with Freud. The two had been invited to lecture at Clark University in Worcester, Massachusetts, and decided to travel together accompanied by Sándor Ferenczi. They met in Bremen and, according to Jung, this was where Freud's famous fainting fit occurred. It was provoked by a discussion of the prehistoric peat-bog corpses found in Northern Germany during which Freud became agitated and suddenly fainted. He later interpreted Jung's fascination with corpses as a death wish against himself.

The other time Freud fainted in Jung's presence was during the Psychoanalytic Congress in Munich in 1913. On this occasion the discussion centred on the monotheistic Egyptian Pharoah, Akhenaten. Jung was disputing the interpretation of Akhenaten's monotheism as a personal resistance to his father because he had obliterated his father's name from statues. At this point, Freud slid off his chair in a faint and Jung picked him up and carried him to a sofa. Both instances of fainting are attributed by Jung to Freud's phantasy of father-murder. Although Freud made frequent allusions to Jung as his heir, the latter declared he was not enamoured of the idea as it would mean sacrificing his intellectual independence.

Freud and Jung spent seven weeks in the USA, during which time they were together every day analysing each other's dreams, but on one occasion Freud had a dream for which Jung asked for information about his private life. At that point, Freud declared he could not risk his authority by disclosing this, which led to Jung feeling Freud was placing himself above the truth. Jung, in his turn, had a dream that culminated in two human skulls being discovered. Freud repeatedly asked for Jung's associations, as he appeared to be thinking again about Jung's death wish against himself.

Freud's dream alluded to above was apparently one in which he, Martha, and Minna (Freud's sister-in-law) featured, that Jung later mentioned in an interview in 1957 with a John M. Billinsky. In the course of that interview, Jung asserted that Minna Bernays had told him in 1907, at the time of his first visit to Freud in Vienna, that she and Freud were conducting an affair. It strains credibility to believe she would have disclosed such intimate details to a complete stranger ten years her junior; nevertheless, this rumour has been doing the rounds since that time, even being given credence by the award-winning historian of psychoanalysis, George Makari, in his book *Revolution in Mind*. The interested reader is directed to the ever-reliable Zvi Lothane's account of this alleged affair, full details of which are to be found in the References section of this volume. My thanks are due to John Beebe for his help in locating this information.

These incidents were indicative of a growing rift between Freud and Jung, made worse by the fact that the United States represented the unknown for both men. A. A. Brill, one of the first to foster psychoanalysis in the United States, took them around New York City, and then to Worcester for the Congress. Their host was Stanley Hall, who had been William James's star pupil at Harvard in the study of psychological psychology, and Ernest Jones, who established psychoanalysis in the UK, bringing with him James Jackson Putnam, holder of the first American chair in neurology at Harvard.

Freud and Jung had a huge success at the Congress and their American audiences were enormously interested to hear more about psychoanalysis and the experiments with complexes. Freud's conflict theory, namely, *libido* versus *repression*, was seen as shedding much-needed light on Janet's constitutional theory of hereditary weakness combined with moral degeneration as progenitors of hysterical symptoms. Freud and Jung were gratified at the adulation with which such sophisticated audiences greeted their lectures and they were both awarded honorary degrees at the end of the Congress.

Correspondence

The voluminous correspondence between Freud and Jung from 1906 to 1914 was put together in a single volume in the 1970s by their architect sons, Ernst Freud and Franz Jung. Key moments from Freud and

Jung's interaction are illustrated through these letters with Jung always addressing the older man with the respectful "Dear Professor Freud", and being addressed by Freud more familiarly as "Dear Colleague" or "Dear Friend". Jung was living at Burghölzli in the early years of the correspondence so his letters are addressed from there until 2nd June 1909 when they are sent from Küsnach (as it is spelt in the Correspondence), where he and Emma had built their house on the lake. The letters are fascinating in the way they express the close collegial as well as warm personal relations between the two men, and incorporate the exploration of ideas in the early days of the psychoanalytic movement, including the arrival at Burghölzli of such psychoanalytic luminaries as Karl Abraham from Berlin and Ernest Jones from London. In relation to the latter, Freud cites Shakespeare's description of Cassius as having a lean and hungry look. There are also intriguing morsels of information such as Jung sharing the same birth date—26th July—with Freud's wife, Martha Bernays. From the start, one sees Jung writing of his doubts of the sexual aetiology of all the neuroses as follows:

> Jung (23rd October 1906)
> It is possible that my reservations … are due to a lack of experience. But don't you think that a number of borderline phenomena might be considered more appropriately in terms of the other basic drive, (predominantly *hunger*) … Two complexes existing at the same time are always bound to coalesce psychologically, so that one of them invariably contains constellated aspects of the other. (McGuire, 1974, p. 7)

Though there exists a telling letter from Jung to Freud that points to the former adhering strongly to the latter's sexual theory as follows:

> Jung (5th May 1910)
> Germany and America! The contortions of the latter are priceless. The so-called freedom of research in the land of the free has indeed been well guarded—the very word "sexual" is taboo. (McGuire, 1974, p. 316)

It is ironic to think that if the word "death" were substituted for "sexual" today, the same sentiments expressed by Jung would still apply as death is now the taboo word in the USA , from where it has travelled and been taken up in other parts of the world, being replaced by euphemisms such as "passed away". In this way, Freud's famous *death drive* may shortly be renamed the "passing away" *drive* by those of delicate disposition, who need to be shielded from and to remain in denial of the stark reality of every living organism's ultimate destination.

> Jung (24ᵗʰ May 1907)
> Your *Gradiva* is magnificent. I gulped it at one go ... Often I have to transport myself back to the time before the reformation of my psychological thinking to re-experience the charges that were laid against you. I simply can't understand them any more ... So you may be absolutely right when you seek the cause of our opponents' resistance in affects, especially sexual affects. (Ibid., p. 49)

> Freud (6ᵗʰ June 1907)
> I am very much surprised to hear that I am the rich man from whose table you glean a few crumbs. (Ibid., p. 58)

> Jung (19ᵗʰ August 1907)
> Do you regard sexuality as the mother of all feelings? Isn't sexuality for you merely one component of the personality (albeit the most important) ... Are there not hysterical symptoms which, though co-determined by the sexual complex, are predominantly conditioned by a sublimation or by a non-sexual complex (profession, job, etc.). (Ibid., p. 79)

> Freud (27ᵗʰ August 1907)
> For the present I do not believe that anyone is justified in saying that sexuality is the mother of all feelings ... I regard (for the present) the role of sexual complexes in hysteria merely as theoretical necessity. (Ibid., p. 80)

> Jung (28ᵗʰ October 1907)
> Actually—and I confess this to you with a struggle—I have a boundless admiration for you both as a man and as a researcher, and I bear you no conscious grudge. So the self-preservation

complex does not come from there; it is rather that my venera-
tion for you has something of the character of a "religious" crush.
Though it does not really bother me, I still feel it is disgusting and
ridiculous because of its undeniable erotic undertone. This abominable feeling comes from the fact that as a boy I was the victim of
a sexual assault by a man I once worshipped. (Ibid., p. 95)

Freud (2nd January 1910)
It has occurred to me that the ultimate basis of man's need for
religion is *infantile helplessness*, which is so much greater in man
than in animals. After infancy he cannot conceive of a world without parents and makes for himself a just God and a kindly nature;
the two worst anthropomorphic falsifications. (Ibid., p. 284)

Freud (3rd March 1911)
Since the day before yesterday I have been the chairman of the
Vienna group. It had become impossible to go on with Adler; he
was quite aware of it himself and admitted that his chairmanship
was incompatible with his new theories. Stekel, who now sees eye
to eye with him, followed suit ... I now feel that I must avenge
the offended goddess Libido ... I see now that Adler's seem-
ing decisiveness concealed a good deal of confusion. I would
never have expected a psychoanalyst to be so taken in by the
ego. (Ibid., p. 400)

Freud (15th March 1912)
I have pointed out to you that the Association cannot prosper
when the president loses interest in it over a period of months,
especially when he has so unreliable an assistant as our friend
Riklin. You seem to recognize that I am right ... You make it
clear to me that you don't wish to write to me at present, and I
reply that I am trying to make the privation easy for myself ...
You speak of the need for intellectual independence and quote
Nietzsche in support of your view ... But if a third party were
to read this passage, he would ask me when I had tried to tyran-
nize you intellectually, and I should have to say: I don't know.
(Ibid., p. 492)

Jung (2ⁿᵈ August 1912)

In certain circumstances, indeed as a general rule, the fantasy object is *called* "mother". But it seems to me highly unlikely that primitive man ever passed through an era of incest. Rather, it would appear that the first manifestation of incestuous desire was the prohibition itself. (Ibid., p. 512)

Jung (3ʳᵈ December 1912)

Our analysis, you may remember, came to a stop with your remark that "you could not submit to analysis *without losing your authority*". These words are engraved on my memory as a symbol of everything to come. (Ibid., p. 526)

Freud (5ᵗʰ December 1912)

For the present I can only suggest a household remedy: let each of us pay more attention to his own than to his neighbour's neurosis. (Ibid., p. 529)

Jung (18ᵗʰ December 1912)

I would, however, point out that your technique of treating your pupils like patients is a *blunder*. In that way you produce either slavish sons or impudent puppies ... You go around sniffing out all the symptomatic actions in your vicinity, thus reducing every-one to the level of sons and daughters who blushingly admit the existence of their faults. Meanwhile you remain on top as the father, sitting pretty. (Ibid., p. 535)

Freud (3ʳᵈ January 1913)

It is a convention among us analysts that none of us need feel ashamed of his own bit of neurosis. But one who while behav-ing abnormally keeps shouting that he is normal gives ground for the suspicion that he lacks insight into his illness. Accord-ingly, I propose that we abandon our personal relations entirely. (Ibid., p. 539)

Jung (6ᵗʰ January 1913)

I accede to your wish that we abandon our personal relations, for I never thrust my friendship on anyone. You yourself are the best

judge of what this moment means to you. "The rest is silence."
(Ibid., p. 540)

Eugen Bleuler

A key figure in the relations between Freud and Jung was the psychiatrist, Eugen Bleuler, alluded to earlier in this chapter. Jung's working
relationship with Bleuler preceded that of the one with Freud. "Bleuler
had handpicked Jung to join the staff, and had offered him a position as an assistant physician" (Falzeder, 2007, pp. 343–368). In their
Correspondence, Freud and Jung make frequent mention of Bleuler,
often in an unflattering light as the following quotations exemplify.

Jung (8th November 1907)
My chief (Bleuler) is the most notable example of a brilliantly
successful pseudo-personality. (Ibid., p. 97)

Jung (2nd January 1908)
Bleuler really is a psychoanalytical curiosity. (Ibid., p. 106)

Freud (19th April 1908)
I am rather annoyed with Bleuler for his willingness to accept
a psychology without sexuality, which leaves everything hanging in mid-air. In the sexual processes we have the indispensable
"organic foundation" without which a medical man can only feel
ill at ease in the life of the psyche. (Ibid., p. 140)

Jung (19th June 1908)
Bleuler, sad to say, is festooned with complexes from top to
bottom. (Ibid., p. 157)

There is more in the same vein though the crucial point here is that
the presence of Bleuler was of such importance in bestowing credibility
on the new psychoanalytic movement that Freud and Jung had a press-
ing need for him to join the newly formed IPA. This he duly did, as
acknowledged in Jung's letter of 19th January 1911 but, later that year, in
a letter dated 24th November, Jung had to inform Freud that "Bleuler has
suddenly announced his resignation" (ibid., p. 466).

The fact is that despite his early enthusiasm for Freud's *Interpretation of Dreams*, Bleuler remained *ambivalent*, coined by Freudians borrowing Bleuler's own term, about Freud's discovery and, in particular, about its scientific credentials. Decades later this was echoed by the magisterial philosopher of science, Adolf Grünbaum, in his (constructive) critique of the scientific foundations claimed by Freud for psychoanalysis. Bleuler decided to test its clinical efficacy by having an analysis with Freud via correspondence, which failed.

> His enduring interest in psychoanalysis sat alongside his criticism of its claim to objective truth underpinning, for example, libido theory as well as the increasing sectarian character of the movement (Shamdasani in Casement, 2016, *IAAP 2016 Newsletter*, p. 249).

Psychology of the Unconscious

The *Psychology of the Unconscious* has been mythologised as the nail in the coffin of the Freud/Jung close relationship so that a brief account of its contents would seem appropriate at this juncture. It first appeared in 1916 in a translation when it was renamed *Psychology of the Transference* by a young American follower of Jung, Beatrice Hinkle. It was republished in 1991 with an Introduction by William McGuire, who was the instigator of its reappearance under its original title *Symbols of Transformation* (personal communication William McGuire). He starts his Introduction saying that this "… may have been the most influential work by C. G. Jung" (p. xvii). The reason being because "… it was his entirely individual attempt to find a coherence among ideas in religion, psychoanalysis, philosophy, cultural history, literature" (ibid.). Jung went on to describe the book as consisting of fragments strung together in an unsatisfactory manner, a statement with which any discerning reader will readily agree.

Furthermore, Jung's choice of thinkers from the world of anthropology leaves much to be desired; for example, James Frazer, who though entertaining to read was a library-bound scholar whose "… very few 'conjectures' seem in the least plausible and, on the rare occasions when they can be tested, almost invariably prove to be wrong" (Leach, 1965, p. 560).

In his excoriating critique of Frazer, Leach was comparing the latter unfavourably with Malinowski, who pioneered field work amongst anthropologists in the early twentieth century. On the other hand: "Frazer believed that first-hand experience of primitive peoples is a discomfort which the more intelligent anthropologist can well afford to do without" (ibid.). Thus, Leach concludes that the "Frazerian manner may be linked with a deep-seated contempt for nine-tenths of the human race" (ibid.)

The philosopher Wittgenstein claimed that Frazer was more savage than most of his "savages" because lacking an inward knowledge of his own spiritual experiences he did not understand that he understood nothing about the spiritual experiences he obstinately attempted to understand (Wittgenstein, 1933, p. 137). Notwithstanding increasing criticism of Frazer as a serious anthropologist throughout the twentieth centruy, Jung continued to take Frazer's work seriously as the many references to it in the *Collected Works* testify. The following is just one instance of this: "Thus the understanding of primitive psychology would have remained an almost insoluble task without the assistance of mythology, folklore, history, and comparative religion. Sir James Frazer's work is a splendid example of this composite method" (1977, p. 562).

It remains puzzling as to why Jung relied on the likes of Frazer while scarcely acknowledging the well-grounded empirical anthropological work done by some of the great practitioners of the twentieth century in the field, Bronislaw Malinowski, Claude Lévi-Strauss, and Edmund Leach. This is especially so in Malinowski's case as his approach was based on two notions that Jung frequently claimed carried equal weight in his own thinking—*context* and *empirical science*.

Equally baffling are Jung's frequent references to Leo Frobenius in the book, the latter being an arch exponent of *diffusionism*, a branch of ethnology that holds to the hypothesis that every phenomenon originates in one place and is diffused throughout the world through conquest or trade. The hypothesis favoured by *diffusionists* was that *the* place of origin was Ancient Egypt from where all culture descended, which would more appropriately be cited in support of *mimesis*, currently enjoying a renaissance, partly due to the important work of the late Franco-American anthropologist, René Girard. On the other hand, it seems a shaky foundation for Jung to choose to support his budding theory of *archetypes* expounded in *Psychology of the Unconscious*. The central thesis of that book was to demonstrate that sex, *à la* Freud, is not the origin of everything but, instead, it is what Jung came to call the *collective unconscious*.

Although the book is an indigestible mishmash of mythologies from around the world, the purpose behind that was Jung's lifelong quest to found an interdisciplinary *psychology of complexities*, namely, one that would encompass all human functioning. With this in mind, he thought of calling his own discipline *complex psychology* following the split with Freud in 1913.

Psychology of the Unconscious, while not living up to the claim that it was the death knell of the Freud–Jung collaboration, nevertheless provides a fascinating account of Jung's transition from being a Freudian trying his utmost to remain true to the master while, at the same time, developing his own theory of *libido*. The latter is renamed *psychic energy* in the book, wherein Jung is following his own path on the way to the discovery of the realm of *archetypes* and the *collective unconscious*. The book also includes Jung's claim that there are two kinds of thinking, *directed* and *fantasy* thinking, the latter to be found particularly in dreams. In their written account of what led to the final rupture, both Jung and his close colleague E. A. Bennet cite the publication of Jung's book *Psychology of the Unconscious*, later extensively revised and re-titled *Symbols of Transformation* (its original title), *Volume 5* of the *Collected Works*. This work was also published in 1956 by Princeton University Press as Bolingen Series XX.

In the chapter on Freud in *Memories, Dreams, Reflections*, Jung put forward his own hypothesis of *libido* and incest, which portrayed them as having a spiritual meaning:

> Sexuality is of the greatest importance as the expression of the chthonic spirit. That spirit is the "other face of God", the dark side of the God-image. The question of the chthonic spirit has occupied me ever since I began to delve into the world of alchemy. Basically, this interest was awakened by that early conversation with Freud, when, mystified, I felt how deeply stirred he was by the phenomenon of sexuality. (1963, p. 163)

Stepansky's hypothesis

The *intellectual historian*, Paul Stepansky, takes a different view of *Psychology of the Unconscious* and of the final cause of the parting of the ways between Freud and Jung. In his paper "The Empiricist as Rebel: Jung, Freud and the Burdens of Discipleship", he scrutinises the supposed controversial parts of the book and concludes that these could in no way have given cause for the contentious split. The move away from a narrow formulation of the libido concept was instigated by Freud himself in his analysis of paranoia in the Schreber case history where Jung had stated that Freud here demonstrates that the paranoiac's longing for the reality principle cannot be traced to the withdrawal of libido alone. "Freud as well as myself, saw the need of widening this conception of libido" (Stepansky, 1992, p. 177).

Stepansky also points to Freud as the original source of Jung's exploration of the *collective unconscious* as the realm of myth-making and symbolism, for instance, in his study of Leonardo da Vinci. After reading Freud's 1910 essay, Jung wrote to him as follows: "*Leonardo* is wonderful. The transition to mythology grows out of this essay from inner necessity, actually it is the first essay of yours with whose inner development I felt perfectly in tune from the start" (McGuire, 1974, p. 329).

Stepansky further suggests that: "However extensive the classical and philological themes contained in the Miller fantasies, Miss Miller's 'vision of creation' remains first and foremost a function of an 'erotic impression'; the source of her symbolical productions is 'an erotic conflict'" (1992, p. 176). Most significantly of all, he points out that in the chapter on "Symbolism of the Mother and Rebirth", Jung's hypothesis that incestuous desire signifies the wish to return to the mother in order to be reborn is similar to Freud's concept of primal narcissism. As early as 1910, the latter had given his blessing to an early draft of the work.

Stepansky's aim in revisiting the account of the Freud–Jung split is to pave the way for his own hypothesis about what took place. He questions why Freud, for whom the sexual aetiology of neuroses was the central tenet of psychoanalysis, would have named as "his heir apparent a disciple whose ruthless empiricism undercut the social and clinical crusade that was already under way" (ibid., p. 187). The answer to this lies in a letter of 1908 to his Berlin disciple, Karl Abraham, in which Freud tries to assuage the former's qualms over Jung's silence on sexual theory. Freud says it is easier for Abraham to accept this as they are racial kinsmen while Jung "as a Christian and a pastor's son finds his way to me only against great inner resistance. His association with us is the more valuable for that analysis escaped the danger of becoming a Jewish national affair" (ibid., p. 191).

Freud also pinned his hope on Jung to take his work further in applying it to the psychoses as well as the neuroses. For these reasons:

> Freud ... consciously deceived Jung in allowing him to believe his conditional appropriation of dream mechanics and energetics constituted full-fledged loyalty to the movement ... The entire episode ... is a long and ominous testimony to Freud's emotional investment in the institutionalized movement his work had created. (Ibid., p. 192)

Freud's view of the rupture is different to this as he demonstrated in a scathing attack on Jung and what he terms the "Neo-Zürich" school in his *On the History of the Psycho-Analytic Movement*. As he says there about them:

> Suppose—to make use of a simile—that in a particular social group there lives a *parvenu*, who boasts of being descended from a noble family living in another place. It is pointed out to him that his parents live in the neighbourhood, and that they are quite humble people. There is only one way of escape and he seizes on it. He can no longer repudiate his parents, but he asserts that they themselves, are of noble lineage and have merely come down in the world, and he procures a family-tree from some obliging official source. It seems to me that the Swiss have been obliged to behave in the same way ... [i]f ethics and religion were not allowed to be sexualized but had to be something "higher" from the start, and if nevertheless the ideas contained in them seemed undeniably to be descended from the Oedipus and family-complex ... (1914d, p. 73)

In this manner, Freud made it clear that Jung's modification of the sexual theory represented both an abandonment of psychoanalysis and a secession from it. This was formalised in the UK when the British Medical Association (BMA) set up a committee that included Ernest Jones to investigate psychoanalysis. The BMA Report of 1928 defined psychoanalysis as "the technique devised by Freud, who first used the term, and the theory which he has built upon his work" (King & Steiner, 1991, p. 12). The Report went on to recognise the distinction between "psychoanalysts" and "pseudo-analysts". In this way, Jones enabled psychoanalysts to differentiate themselves from other forms of psychotherapeutic practice and to be treated like any other form of specialism in medicine. "This was the first time an official national body of the medical profession from any country had recognized the distinction between 'psychoanalysts' and 'pseudo-analysts', as well as the qualifications established by membership of the International Psychoanalytical Association" (ibid., p. 13).

Aftermath

Up to the point of the professional rupture between Freud and Jung, Zürich had been the second most important centre of psychoanalysis after Vienna. There was a flourishing Psychoanalytical Association which was initially attached to both Burghölzli Hospital and the University of Zürich. In 1912 this separated from Burghölzli and became an independent institution in its own right. In 1914, after Freud published his *On the History of the Psycho-Analytic Movement*, the Zürich Psychoanalytical Association voted to leave the International Psychoanalytical Association. This group consisted mainly of medical doctors that met regularly until 1918 when it became absorbed into the newly formed Analytical Psychology Club.

The emotional impact of the rupture on both men was profound and Jung developed what Henri F. Ellenberger in his magisterial work *The Discovery of the Unconscious* calls a *creative illness* for a few years after the break with Freud, during which time he was working on the *Red Book* (Ellenberger, 1970, p. 672). The background to the relationship with Freud was that it was fuelled by *wish-fulfilment* for the idealised father, namely, one who had the courage to face the dark side of life. As the idealisation, like all idealisations, began to break down, Jung experienced Freud as one-sided and dogmatic and his father *complex* resurfaced with renewed energy as he tried to *redeem* Freud from the error of his ways, which resulted in Freud ejecting Jung from the psychoanalytic movement.

There is an *archetypal*, even tragic, feel to the decline of the relationship that existed for a few years between the two men. Their last meeting was at the fourth International Psychoanalytical Congress in September 1913 in Munich. Jung was again put forward as president of the IPA when Freud's close followers—Abraham, Ferenzci, Jones, Rank among them—handed in twenty-two blank ballot papers. On the other hand, fifty-two analysts voted in favour of Jung so he was reinstated in office. Over the following months there was consternation among Freud's close followers about Jung's continuing role at the IPA and as editor of the *Jahrbuch für psychoanalytische und psychopathologische Forschungen*, but on 29th October 1913, he stood down as editor, followed in April 1914 by his resignation as president of the IPA. At the Munich 1913 Congress, the atmosphere became so poisonous that the poet Rainer Maria Rilke, who attended with his close friend, the psychoanalyst Lou Andreas-Salomé, had to go outside for a walk in the fresh air when he could bear it no longer (personal communication from the distinguished Freud scholar and former director of the Freud Museum, Michael Molnar).

The eminent analytical psychologist, the late Michael Fordham, in his obituary on Jung in 1961 stated the following:

> His name is still almost automatically linked with that of Freud as most nearly Freud's equal, and if his main life's work was in the end to be founded on a personal and scientific incompatibility with Freud, there are those who believe, like myself, that this was a disaster, and in part an illusion, from which we suffer and will continue to do so until we have repaired the damage. (Astor, 1995, p. 182)

Apart from Freud, there were other significant male figures in Jung's life, for example, C. A. Meier, James Kirsch, Erich Neumann, Gerhard Adler, R. F. C. Hull, Peter Baynes, Michael Fordham, Franz Riklin, Richard

Wilhelm, and Father Victor White. Equally significant were many female figures, for example, his wealthy wife of fifty-two years, Emma, who was the most important of them (personal communication, Sonu Shamdasani). In addition, there were Barbara Hannah, Sabina Spielrein, Toni Wolff, Marie-Louise von Franz, Yolande Jacobi, Aniela Jaffé, Olga Fröbe-Kapteyn, Cary Baynes, and Edith Rockefeller McCormick, the US heiress, amongst others. Cameos of many of these people will feature further in this work.

CHAPTER 4

Archetypes and the collective unconscious

Some of the content in this section is based on material I contributed on Jung's theory of *archetypes* to *The Encyclopedia of Psychology and Religion* (2010), edited by David Leeming, Kathryn Madden, and Stanton Marlan.

The theories of *archetypes* and the *collective unconscious* are Jung's two signature concepts closely linked the one to the other. As the *collective unconscious* is the realm of *archetypes* it would not make sense to treat them separately and they are presented together in this chapter. Jung describes *archetypes* as "... archaic ... universal images that have existed since the remotest times" (1959a, p. 5). In contrast to the *collective unconscious*, Jung also describes a *personal unconscious*, the latter being the realm of the *complexes* already defined in the chapter on psychiatry.

I suggest Schopenhauer as a likely contender to be the most important influence on Jung's discovery of the *collective unconscious* through his writings on the *will*. Both thinkers acknowledged the misery and suffering of worldly existence which, for them, was illusory and from which an individual should separate him- or herself; particularly Schopenhauer, who basically viewed the world as a concentration camp (personal communication, Paul Bishop). At the same time, Schopenhauer described the *will* as the true motivator in life, albeit blindly, as in the following: "Thus the bird builds a nest for the young it does not yet know" (1819, paragraph 191). He equates the *will* with Kant's *thing-in-itself*, both of which underpin Jung's thinking in the production of his linked notions of *archetypes* and of the *collective unconscious*. Kant applied his notion of the *thing-in-itself* to everything that is unknown and boundless, which is, indeed, often cited by Jung as *the* inspiration for his own notion of *archetypes*. Further in this chapter, several authors' analyses will be featured of the undifferentiated way in which Jung brought together a variety of sources in the creation of his notion of *archetypes*.

According to Jung's thinking, the *collective unconscious* is also the realm of *symbols* which are "… the best possible expression for an unconscious content whose nature can only be guessed, because it is still unknown" (1959a, p. 6). As these concepts are closely involved in Jung's basic theory of *individuation*, according to which a person becomes a separate, indivisible unity and achieves wholeness, a critique of Jung's study illustrating the *individuation* process will be given later in the book.

Jung describes the *collective unconscious* as the part of the *psyche* that can be negatively distinguished from a *personal unconscious* as it does not owe its existence to personal experience. Whereas Jung's notion of the *personal unconscious* consists for the most part of *complexes*, the content of the *collective unconscious* "is made up essentially of *archetypes*" (ibid., p. 42). This realm is the *container* of the ancient and universal thought-forms which are common to all humans, and Jung asserts that *archetypes* are "*patterns of instinctual behaviour*" (p. 44). He goes on to say the concept of the *collective unconscious* is neither a speculative nor a philosophical but an empirical matter—*archetypes* exist *a priori* as biological norms of *psychic* activity.

It is important to differentiate between the *personal unconscious* and the *collective unconscious*, as *archetypes* of *the* mother and *the* father need to be viewed separately from the experience of the personal mother and father. In the course of analysis, the latter will usually be activated early in the process and may be projected onto the analyst in the form of a negative mother or father *transference* linked to the childhood experience of the *analysand*/patient. One would then speak of the *analysand/*

patient having a negative mother or father *complex*. *Transferences* are loaded with *affect* and can have a powerful impact on both *analysand/* patient and analyst. This kind of *transference* derives from unresolved childhood deprivations and desires that are still alive in the adult *analysand/*patient that need to be *worked through* by way of *regressions* to infantile states. In this way, the *analysand* is guided by the analyst along the developmental path.

The term *countertransference* applies to the feelings that are *introjected* by the analyst as a result of the analysand's *transference* projections. In this instance, one is dealing with what may be termed the *personal transference–countertransference* where the analyst is largely in control and the *analysand* is being analysed with a view to enabling him to come to terms with outer reality; this is known as the *transference work*.

Archetypal transference–countertransference

On the other hand, "… there is no lunacy people under the domination of an *archetype* will not fall prey to" (Jung, 1959a, p. 48). To illustrate this, he cites the revival in Germany in the 1930s of the medieval persecution of the Jewish people, of Europe trembling before the Roman eagles and the tramp of legions giving the Roman salute. According to Jung, that was the result of the possession of a whole people by the *archetype* of the Germanic God of war and death, *Wotan*. *Archetypal* possession is the reason the masses are breeding grounds for *psychic* epidemics; on a more positive note, it may also engender feelings of human solidarity.

There are as many *archetypes* as there are typical situations in life and the way their existence can be proved is by the above example and also by their appearance in dreams, which are involuntary spontaneous products of the *unconscious psyche*. Dreams are the ways in which *archetypal* contents display themselves in the course of psychoanalysis. In addition, they manifest through another kind of *transference–countertransference*, which is not aimed at helping the *analysand* to *grow up*, that may occur in the course of in-depth analysis, namely, *archetypal transference–countertransference*. This gives rise to a dialectical process that involves both *analysand* and analyst in an immersion in contents from the *collective unconsciousness* that can result in the *mutual* transformation of each. This is termed the *transference process* when both *analysand* and analyst share the same goal of bringing *unconsciousness* into *consciousness*. For Jung, this latter procedure is exemplified by what he called the *alchemical process*, which he worked on from 1929 when he was first introduced to Chinese *alchemy* by the Sinologist, Richard Wilhelm, until his death in 1961. Jung claimed that *alchemy* and his own approach to analysing *unconscious* material had much in common and he saw *alchemy* as giving an historical grounding to his way of working with *psyche*. There is a lengthy elaboration of the *psychological alchemical* process later in the book.

Ego–self axis

It is in the course of the latter *alchemical* work that the so-called *ego–self axis* may be constellated in the alchemical *container* of the analysis, the term *self* denoting, for Jung, the essence of individuality and the unity of the whole personality. In this way, it stands out from the other *archetypes*, which are universal and belong to the generality. If *archetypal* contents erupt into *consciousness*, they take possession of *ego consciousness* as happens in *psychosis* or experiences of the *numinous*, akin to awesome religious experiences. The Israeli Jungian psychoanalyst Erich Neumann pioneered the notion of an *ego–self axis*, which is a conceptual tool for exploring the creative interaction between the two realms.

According to the American Jungian psychoanalyst Edward Edinger, following in the footsteps of Neumann, the integrity of the *ego* depends on a living connection with the *self*. If that fails, the *ego* loses its vital connection with the *self*, which is the origin and source of its energy and stability.

> Since *ego* cannot exist without the support of the *self* and the *self*
> apparently needs the *ego* to realize it, psychic development can
> be considered a continuous process of dialectic between *ego* and
> *self* leading paradoxically to both greater separation and greater
> intimacy. (Edinger, 1960, p. 51)

According to this mode of thinking, the beginning of the infant's life is marked by a primitive inflated identity of *ego* and *self* (what Freud called "*primary narcissism*") deriving from the original infantile state of wholeness. Neumann's so-called *ego–self axis* refers to what he saw as the vital connecting link between *self* and *ego* which maintains the latter's functional autonomy.

Archetype and instinct

Jung first used the term *"archetype"* in 1919 in "Instinct and the Unconscious". In that paper, he claims there is good reason for supposing that *archetypes* are the *unconscious* images of the instincts themselves; in other words, they are *"patterns of instinctual behaviour"* (Jung, 1959a, p. 44). He goes on to say: "There are as many archetypes as there are typical situations in life" (p. 48). In Jung's model, *unconsciousness* rests on a spectrum with the *archetype* at the ultraviolet end and instinct at the infrared end. The two struggle and intermingle with each other in *unconsciousness* to form units of energy and motivation that manifest in ideas, images, urges, and strivings. From this it may be deduced that *psyche* is located in the space between instinct and *archetype*, matter and spirit, the body and the transcendent mind. "Psychologically, however, the archetype as an image of instinct is a spiritual goal toward which the whole nature of man strives" (Jung, 1960b, p. 212). He goes on to say that in reality humans cannot cut loose from their *archetypal* foundations without paying the price of a *neurosis*, any more than humans can rid themselves of their bodies and their organs without committing suicide. *Archetypes* are elements of *psychic* structure and, in that way, are vital and necessary components of that structure.

In his thinking about the problem of *archetype* and instinct, Jung turned to philosophy from antiquity as the following quotation indicates: "From Plato's high valuation of the archetypes in his theory of forms, which was maintained through to medieval philosophy, the archetypes had been reduced by Kant to a few categories" (Shamdasani, 2003, p. 242). Jung frequently links his theory of *archetypes* to Plato's "eternal, transcendent forms" (Jung, 1959, p. 33).

From the quotation in the above paragraph, it would appear that Jung was dismissive of Kant. This was far from the case as Jung turned to Kantian philosophy to distinguish between "the archetypic representations, and the *archetype* itself, similar to Kant's *das ding an sich* (the thing-in-itself) which is irrepresentable" (Shamdasani, 2003, p. 260). Kant's theory of knowledge divided human cognition into what it could grasp, namely, the *phenomenal* world, and what it could not. The latter Kant termed the *noumenal* world, that is, the *a priori*, timeless, space-less, and causeless entities both within and outside the mind. Jung linked Kant's thinking on the *a priori* entities to his notion of *archetypes*, thus locating this theory in the interface between the metaphysical thinking of Plato and the logical categories of Kant's philosophy.

Jung went on to claim that the *archetypic*, or *primordial image* as it was first called by him, is frequently met with in mythology and the great religions. The irruption of these *archetypic* images from *unconsciouness* into the *conscious* realm may be viewed as the basis of religious experience, and of the need for the mysterious and symbolic that underlies the quest for Jung's notion of *individuation*. As Jung states: "When … modern psychotherapy once more meets with the activated archetypes of the collective unconscious, it is merely the repetition of a phenomenon that has often been observed in moments of great religious crisis" (1953, p. 36).

According to the British analytical psychologist Anthony Stevens: "Jung took the term 'archetype' from the *Corpus Hermeticum* … where God is referred to as the archetypal light" (2006, p. 79). "With his theory of archetypes operating as components of the collective unconscious, Jung sought to define the living bedrock of human psychology" (p. 74). Murray Stein's (1998) definition of the term *archetype* is that *typos* means stamp, and *arche* means the original or master copy.

Bipolarity of the archetype

An important precursor of Jung's discovery of the bipolarity of the *archetype* was the pre-Socratic thinker, Heraclitus, whose theory of opposites is expressed in the term *enantiadromia*. This may be viewed as a natural law that denotes running contrariwise so that eventually everything turns into its opposite. Jung equated this with an *archetypal* way of behaving and states: "True opposites are never incommensurables; if they were they could never unite … God himself [is defined] as a *complexion oppositorum*" (1960b, p. 207).

Jung further conceived of *archetype* and instinct as opposites in the following manner:

> Archetype and instinct are the most polar opposites imaginable, as can easily be seen when one compares a man who is ruled by his instinctual drives with a man who is seized by the spirit ... They belong together as correspondences ... they subsist side by side as reflections in our own minds of the opposition that underlies all psychic energy. (Ibid., p. 206)

To underline his thinking of *archetype* as spirit, Jung goes on to state that: "The essential content of all mythologies and all religions and all isms is archetypal" (p. 206). From this, it may be deduced that both *archetype* and instinct are deeply implicated in religious and ethical questions, which Jung affirms as follows: "Confrontation with an archetype or instinct is an *ethical* problem of the first magnitude" (p. 208; original italics).

In Jung's approach, spirit and instinct are united symbolically in the *archetypal* form of the *alchemical hieros gamos* or higher marriage of opposites.

> ... the symbolic has the great advantage of being able to unite ... incommensurable factors in a *single* image. With the decline of alchemy the symbolical unity of spirit and matter fell apart, with the result that modern man finds himself uprooted and alienated in a de-souled world. (1959a, p. 109)

Another pair of *archetypal* opposites, *anima/animus*, is relevant here, as follows:

> The archetypal images that link the self and ego-consciousness form a middle realm, which Jung calls *anima* and *animus*, the realm of soul. In Jung's view, polytheistic religions stem from and represent the realms of the anima and animus, while monotheistic religions base themselves on and point to the self archetype. (Stein, 1998, pp. 102–103; original italics)

Jung warns of the danger of *ego-consciousness* identifying with the archetype of the *self*, which can lead to grandiosity and subsequent dissolution of *consciousness*.

The phenomenological approach to archetype and religion

A group of scholars gathered together under the leadership of Jung called *Eranos*, an annual gathering organised by Olga Fröbe-Kapteyn, included the Romanian-French historian of religion, Mercea Eliade. He was a *phenomenologist*, who was interested in uncovering the *archetypal* structures and patterns of religious life. In his writings on religion (*Patterns of Comparative Religion*, 1958; *The Myth of the Eternal Return*, 1954; *Shamanism: Archaic Techniques of Ecstasy*, 1964), Eliade recognised a basic division between traditional religions such as the archaic cults of Asia, Europe, and America, and the historical religions of Judaism, Christianity, and Islam. The chief element in the former is the depreciation of history and the rejection of the profane, mundane world, combined with an emphasis on actions and things that repeat and restore transcendental models. Only those things that participate in and reflect the eternal *archetypes*, through which cosmos came out of chaos, are real in this way of thinking. The mode of expression in this model is in consequence *recursive*.

Post-archaic or historical religions such as Judaism, Christianity, and Islam tend to see a discontinuity between God and the world and to locate the sacred not in the cosmos but beyond it. These hold to linear views of history in the belief that the meaning for humankind is worked out in historical processes, which are seen to have a purposeful plan. For this reason, the historical religions have been monotheistic and exclusivist in their theologies.

The following *statements* from Jung demonstrate his *archetypal* approach in relation to Eliade's writings on religion:

> The life of Christ is understood by the Church on the one hand as an historical, and on the other hand as an eternally existing, mystery … From the psychological standpoint this view can be translated as follows: Christ lived a concrete, personal, and

unique life which, in all essential features, had at the same time
an archetypal character. (Jung, 1958a, p. 88)

He says Catholicism "gives the archetypal symbolisms the necessary freedom and space in which to develop over the centuries while at the same
time insisting on their original form" (p. 465). And again, "… archetypal
situations only return when specifically called for. The real reason for
God's becoming man is to be sought in his encounter with Job" (Jung,
1958b, p. 397).

Criticisms and revisions of the theory of archetypes

Jung's theory of *archetypes* has been the object of criticism from many
sources, including the French structural anthropologist, Lévi-Strauss,
summarised in his view that it is possible to "dispose of theories making use of the concept of 'archetypes' or a 'collective unconscious'"
(1996, p. 65). He accuses Jung of attempting to find universal *contents*
in his concept of *archetypes* but, as the analytical psychologist, Wolfgang
Giegerich, says of Jung's later thinking:

> He (Jung) is no longer concerned with any substance, any
> entity … he simply expresses the abstract notion of the oppo-
> sitional *structure* or *form* of the psychic … *What* the opposites
> are is here not said, and it cannot, should not be said in the con-
> text of this late work (*Mysterium Coniunctionis: An Inquiry into
> the Separation and Synthesis of Psychic Opposites in Alchemy*),
> because this would be a relapse into "the substantiating style of
> thought that this title has long left behind." (Giegerich, 2007)

Brief summaries of the views of two analytical psychologists, George
Hogenson and Jean Knox, whose work represents major revisions of
archetypal theory, will be reproduced here. In addition to these two writers, there is the important work of other thinkers in this area such as the
prescient analytical psychologist, Joe Cambray, who views *archetypes*, as
well as various other key aspects of Jung's approach, as *emergent* properties from the complex interaction of the *psychic* system with the world;
and Patricia Skar, who takes a similar line and goes on to suggest that

archetypes are the early products of developmental self-organisation and should be considered to be a special category of *complexes*.

George Hogenson asks the key question: what architecture of mind is best suited to underwrite the theory of *archetypes*? His conclusion is that viewing cultural patterns as innate is "what most Jungians would recognize as archetypes" (2003, p. 108). Hogenson disagrees with this and proposes, instead, a less *a priori* structure of the mind. This is based on his study of robotics and dynamic systems theory whose "research paradigms conflict with the notion that strongly innate or *a priori* internal representations of the world are necessary to explain complex behaviour" (p. 109). Hogenson's interest in Baldwinian evolution (named after the psychologist James Baldwin) is succinctly expressed by Terence Deacon, professor of biological anthropology and linguistics at the University of California at Berkeley, referenced by Hogenson as follows:

> Baldwin proposed that by temporarily adjusting behaviors or physiological responses during its lifespan in response to novel conditions, an animal could produce irreversible changes in the adaptive context of future generations. Though no new genetic change is immediately produced in the process, the change in conditions will alter which of the existing or subsequently modified genetic predispositions will be favored in the future. (p. 110)

Jean Knox points to the convergence in recent times of cognitive science, neuroscience, and psychodynamic theory in recognising the self-organisation of the human brain, whereby genes do not encode complex mental imagery and processes but "… instead act as initial catalysts for developmental processes out of which early psychic structures reliably emerge" (2004, p. 4). Furthermore: "Archetypes are not 'hard-wired' collections of universal imagery waiting to be released by the right environmental trigger" (p. 4). Instead, she posits that *archetypes* as emergent structures play a key role in *psychic* functioning and symbolic imagery. The way *archetypes* have often been portrayed is that there is information stored in a genetic code waiting "like a biological Sleeping Beauty, to be awakened by the kiss of an environmental Prince. This … is frequently implicit in discussion about archetypes, in Jung's own writings and in that of many former and contemporary analytical psychologists" (p. 5).

The gradual emergence of *archetypal* material in analysis may enable the coming into being of the capacity for symbolisation.

The writers included in this last section are critical of any notion of *archetypes* as innate or encoded in the genome in their rethinking of Jung's theory of *archetypes*.

Dream material illustrating personal unconscious

My father is driving away from the house in his new car. He drives very clumsily, and I get very annoyed over his apparent stupidity. He goes this way and that, forward and backwards, and manoeuvres the car into a dangerous position. Finally, he runs into a wall and damages the car badly. I shout at him in a perfect fury that he ought to behave himself. My father only laughs, and then I see that he is dead drunk.

The above exemplifies Jung's theory of the *compensatory* nature of dreams as it is that of a young man in the early stages of analysis, who consciously harbours only positive feelings for his father, an unusually successful man. The young man's relation to his father is too good to be true, while the dream portrays a different view of father of which the son was completely unaware. It presages the beginning of a much-needed separation from identification with the idealised father so the young man may start to develop as an autonomous being instead of remaining a *puer*. This was related to me by a colleague who had previously presented this material on the patient.

Dream material illustrating collective unconscious

I was in a house I did not know, which had two storeys. It was "my house". I found myself in the upper storey, where there was a kind of salon furnished with fine old pieces in rococo style. On the walls hung a number of precious old paintings. I wondered that this should be my house, and thought, "Not bad." But then it occurred to me that I did not know what the lower floor looked like. Descending the stairs, I reached the ground floor. There everything was much older, and I realized that this part of the house must date from about the fifteenth or sixteenth century.

The furnishings were medieval; the floors were of red brick. Everywhere it was rather dark. I went from one room to another, thinking, "Now I really must explore the whole house." I came upon a heavy door, and opened it. Beyond it, I discovered a stone stairway that led down into the cellar. Descending again, I found myself in a beautifully vaulted room which looked exceedingly ancient. Examining the walls, I discovered layers of brick among the ordinary stone blocks, and chips of brick in the mortar. As soon as I saw this I knew that the walls dated from Roman times. My interest by now was intense. I looked more closely at the floor. It was of stone slabs, and in one of these I discovered a ring. When I pulled it, the stone slab lifted, and again I saw a stairway of narrow stone steps leading down into the depths. These, too, I descended, and entered a low cave cut into the rock. Thick dust lay on the floor, and in the dust were scattered bones and broken pottery, like remains of a primitive culture. I discovered two human skulls, obviously very old and half disintegrated. (Jung, 1963, p. 155)

Jung had this dream in 1909 during the course of a visit to the United States with Freud. Jung thought the dream depicted his discovery of the different layers in *psyche* culminating in the lowest level, that is the *collective unconscious*, the realm of the animal soul and of *archetypes*.

Conclusion of chapter on archetypes

This chapter has attempted to convey some sense of Jung's two signature concepts of *archetypes* and the *collective unconscious*, followed by critical comments from Jungian psychoanalysts. I will end with one of my favourite long quotations from Jung, purportedly about the *psychic* condition known as *inflation*, followed by a brief critical comment on it.

This phenomenon [i.e., inflation], which results from the extension of consciousness, is in no sense specific to analytical treatment. It occurs whenever people are overpowered by knowledge or by some new realization. "Knowledge puffeth up", St Paul writes to the Corinthians, for the new knowledge had turned the heads of many, as indeed constantly happens. This inflation has nothing to do with the *kind* of knowledge, but simply and solely with the fact that any new knowledge can so seize hold of a weak head that he no longer sees and hears anything else. He is hypnotized by it, and instantly believes he has solved the riddle of the universe. But that is equivalent to almighty self-conceit. This process is such a general reaction that, in Genesis 2:17, eating of the tree of knowledge is represented as a deadly sin. It may not be immediately apparent why greater consciousness followed by self-conceit should be such a dangerous thing. Genesis represents the act of becoming conscious as a taboo infringement, as though knowledge means that a sacrosanct barrier had been impiously overstepped. I think that Genesis is right in so far as every step towards greater consciousness is a kind of Promethean guilt: through knowledge the gods are as it were robbed of their fire, that is something that was the property of the unconscious powers is torn out of its natural context and subordinated to the whims of the conscious mind. The man who has usurped the new knowledge suffers, however, a transformation or enlargement of consciousness, which no longer resembles that of his fellow men. He has raised himself above the human level of his age ("ye shall become like unto God"), but in so doing has alienated himself from humanity. The pain of this loneliness is the vengeance of the gods, for never again can he return to mankind. He is, as the myth says, chained to the lonely cliffs of the Caucasus, forsaken of God and man. (Jung, 1966, p. 156)

From this quotation, the paradoxical dangers of following the *individuating* path are set out by Jung, namely, of uniting *unconsciousness* with *consciousness* leading to the synthesis of the *self* and to feelings of wholeness, as has been set out in this presentation. If it is one's destiny to *individuate*, then there is no choice in the matter but by gaining superior *consciousness* there is a danger of feeling isolated from other humans. I would suggest that what Jung is addressing is not *inflation* as such which, in the above context, points to an enlargement of *consciousness* as it assimilates the contents of the *unconscious*, but *grandiosity* that is its negative component, which is the result of the pathological condition diagnosed as *narcissism*, which does give rise to feelings of isolation as described in the quotation.

CHAPTER 5

Shadow and persona

"If the encounter with the *shadow* is the 'apprentice-piece' in the individual's development, then that with the *anima* is the 'master-piece'" (Jung, 1959a, p. 29). It will be noted that this quotation refers only to the *anima* and not its twinned *other*, the *animus*, which underlines the importance of the former for him versus his lack of real liking for or interest in the latter. Both phenomena come under the rubric of *archetypes* as do all the topics under discussion in these chapters on concepts.

According to Jung, the *shadow* is that part of ourselves we have no wish to be and the face that is never shown to the outer world. Instead, it is lived through projection of all the negative sides of the personality into the environment. This is where the paradox lies in the following quotation: "The whole world wants peace and the whole world prepares for war" (ibid., p. 23). For Jung, morality is innate and therefore central to human nature, and allows for the natural curbing of instinct required by society. This is a pragmatic attitude quite different from Freud's theory of *repression*, which is imposed by culture; on the contrary, Jung claims "The psyche has an inborn need for self-control, and societal institutions that facilitate this goal, such as religion and the legal system," so *psyche* has above all the need to behave oppositely to the *shadow* driven by "the desire to be good" (Segal, 2018, p. 151). *Acting-out shadow* on a collective level leads to war, which explains why the fundamental necessity of dealing with *shadow* is such a key component of Jung's approach.

Akin to Freud's *parapraxis*, Jung is pointing to slips and gaffes that are an everyday experience of those attributes associated with the *numinous* figure of the *trickster*: "The trickster is a primitive 'cosmic' being of *divine-animal* nature, on the one hand superior to man because of his superhuman qualities, and on the other hand inferior to him because of his unreason and unconsciousness" (1959a, p. 264; original italics). The dynamism associated with the *trickster* is related to the fact that it is unacceptable to *ego-consciousness* and has to be *repressed* into *unconsciousness* so that the dark aspects apparently disappear and it may be thought they are no longer there. On the contrary, one can see it most clearly at work when the individual is submerged in the masses as it was in 1930s Europe in the twinned phenomena of *fascism* and *communism*, extreme forms of mass takeover that are showing signs of a comeback in the form of "strong men" with revanchist and nationalistic policies: "… anything that has an '-ism' attached to it … is only a modern variant of the denominational religions" (ibid., p. 62). This sheds light on the intensity and religious fervour with which the "-isms" grip susceptible people either through identification or projection.

> A man may be convinced in all good faith that he has no religious ideas … His very materialism, atheism, communism, socialism, liberalism, intellectualism, existentialism … testifies against his innocence … Somewhere or other, overtly or covertly, he is possessed by a supraordinate idea. (Ibid., p. 62)

Jung's concept of *shadow* runs along a spectrum from *personal shadow* to *collective* and *archetypal shadow*, the latter lending itself to being associated with evil. Above all, denial of one's own *shadow* is in itself evil. Dreams of being invaded or one's house being broken into by a thief are about *shadow* contents of the *unconscious* invading *ego-consciousness*. These kinds of dreams may be experienced by one who has been through a sudden conversion from being a sociopath to becoming a respectable member of society. The sociopathic elements are still there repressed into the *unconscious* of such a person and will express themselves in sudden aggressive outbursts, somatic symptoms, and nightmarish dreams.

Jung's early experience of *shadow* has already been touched on in the childhood dream of God dropping the turd on the cathedral, often interpreted as Jung's awakening awareness of the *shadow* of Christianity. Jung gives a telling illustration of a theologian thirsting for the shining heights who had first to descend into the dark depths as the indispensable conditions for climbing any higher. The following dream illustrates the theologian's predicament.

> He saw on a mountain a kind of Castle of the Grail. He went along a road that seemed to lead straight to the foot of the mountain and up it. But as he drew nearer he discovered to his great disappointment that a chasm separated him from the mountain, a deep, darksome gorge with underworldly water rushing along the bottom. A steep path led downwards and toilsomely climbed up again on the other side. But the prospect looked uninviting. (Ibid., p. 19)

The somatic *unconscious*, unlike the cerebrospinal system, reaches down from the light of mentally and morally lucid *consciousness* into the sympathetic nervous system, which is where Jung locates the *shadow*. It is this realm that Jung refers to as the *collective unconscious* wherein dwell "the helpful powers slumbering in the deeper strata of man's nature"—the *other* in oneself.

Persona

A definition of the *persona* is neatly encapsulated in the following quotation from Jung:

> The persona is a complicated system of relations between the individual consciousness and society, fittingly enough a kind of mask, designed on the one hand to make a definite impression upon others, and, on the other, to conceal the true nature of the individual. (1966, p. 192)

The rest of this section on *persona* will be represented by selected extracts from an article written by a close friend and colleague from Texas, Alane Sauder MacGuire, who had been fascinated by Jung's notion of *persona* for a long time. She had often mentioned she would like to produce a book about it and started work on it in 2011, which she continued while, at the same time, struggling with bladder cancer, a battle she finally lost in March 2015. With the help of friends, her work was condensed into an article, "Embodying the Soul: Toward a Rescuing and Retaining of Persona", that was published by the San Francisco *Jung Journal: Culture & Psyche* in its 2017 Fall issue. Although the author's focus is on *Western* culture, much of what she wrote will have cross-cultural relevance.

> Within our souls dwell the aspects of personality that compose the authentic being we are meant to manifest in our lifetime. We are each given a unique combination and proportion of archetypal propensities to express during our life. They come together in a singularity that gives each of us our particular essence. Together and in synergy they make up the soul—what we are meant to be—the quintessence that makes each of us ourselves. Our charge, the work of personality development, is to live as soulfully as possible during the time we are given. To the extent we are able to do this, our lives will feel meaningful. If we lose connection to the spirit of our personae, life will lack meaning and be untrue to the innate potential we are born with. In turn the face we show to the world, our persona, will likewise be false.
>
> The persona, if it is to be a tool of soul embodiment, must portray our essence in a manner that facilitates the soul's manifestation in our lifetime. Without a fully psychological persona, aware of the soul, others will identify who we are through the image they have of us. Our lives are a stage for the various personae that make up our personality, and the world is our audience. The play the world sees, our persona, is either performed with awareness of our personae or it is a jumble of parts acted out with no director. To the extent that the play we present is true to our innate being and aware of our image, it will have elegance and flow, enlivened by the imaginal energy that stems from the eternal archetypes. If our performance of life is not true to our soul, it will be deadened by falseness or cursed by ambivalence,

or just a series of random happenings and encounters with others and probably very boring.

In terms of persona, Jung was most concerned with the malady he labeled "identification with the persona", an affliction rife in European society at the beginning of his career (Jung, 1953, p. 193). For instance, Jung described his own father acting the part of clergyman as expected by his milieu without the creativity that an embodiment of a unique soul would engender. Jung thought that the persona was adapted to be accepted by the world, then the adaptation became what we believed we were, and the reality of the soul was lost.

He described those so afflicted as living but a partial life. For him, they displayed only those qualities that fit a certain social role or a narrowly specific adaptation, a false trapping that worked against the authentic development of an individual. These people seemed unaware of the reality of the soul or of their own uniqueness and complexity. Dostoevsky described them in his novel *The Idiot* as having "a decorous lack of originality" (1868, p. 298), and Jung would have agreed because for him persona was more of an impersonation of roles that would satisfy social norms and customs than a way of portraying the soul's image. Because Jung wrote about this in the early twentieth century when the malady of identification with the persona was almost an epidemic psychic affliction, he felt that the rigidity of the typical persona needed to dissolve in order for the authentic personality to come forth. Jung's writing about persona has a marked lack of emphasis on persona's potential to present the soul's truth in its image. (Sauder MacGuire, 2017, pp. 45–80)

The article is of far greater length than the brief extract reproduced here but what has been quoted from it in these pages offers sufficient information on the *persona* to convey a reasonable idea of what Jung meant by this notion. What can be seen from the above is that Jung himself had a somewhat negative view of *persona* for reasons that are set out in the extract, which continues to be present in the Jungian community. Sauder MacGuire has done a service to psychoanalysis in rectifying this by demonstrating that *persona* does indeed have a creative role in both the inner and outer worlds of the individual.

Another fine mess ...

Every Laurel and Hardy fan will instantly recognise the truncated quotation in the above heading that is always associated with those two comic geniuses, whose names are conjoined as they were/are as inseparable as *shadow/persona*. As he is on the receiving end of the quotation, one would have to equate Laurel with *shadow*, who brilliantly personifies that unwittingly troublesome side of each of us which, over and over again, gets us into a *fine mess*. As is the case with many well-known quotations, this one went into public circulation incorrectly and should, instead, be: *Here's another nice mess you've gotten me into*, which is what Hardy says to Laurel in several of their films, including the hilarious *Sons of the Desert*. This twosome is one of the greatest duos of all time due to its *archetypal* nature that renders it timeless and universal. The situations they get into are equally *archetypal*, namely, the dragon wife/mother from whom they constantly, though unsuccessfully, try to hide their childish misdemeanors, as well as their recurrent struggle against negative authority figures and life's exigencies.

Churchill

Winston Churchill was the greatest Englishman of all time and the greatest man, along with President Franklin D. Roosevelt, of the twentieth century. They represented a benign duo in that one was not the *shadow* of the other as neither was at pains to hide his own *shadow*, Churchill even more than Roosevelt. I have chosen one quotation from the myriad quotable sayings of Churchill to show his awareness of *shadow*—his own as well as of the greatest evil the world has known:

> Man ... has it in his power to solve quite easily the problems of material existence ... There lies before him, as he wishes, a golden age of peace and progress. All is in his hand. He has only to conquer his last and worst enemy—himself. (Roberts, 2018, p. 916)

In 1946, when Churchill paid a "highly symbolic visit to Switzerland" (Bair, 2004, p. 520), he was asked whom he would like to meet, he put Jung's name first on the list. This, combined with the quotation about *shadow*, leads one to conjecture about the possibility that he had actually read Jung.

CHAPTER 6

Anima/animus

The *psychic* contra-sexual images of the "feminine" and "masculine" *intrapsychic* notions postulated by Jung are called *anima/animus*, *archetypal* structures that he thought of as yoked to each other—though it is the *anima* that held particular fascination for him. It is no exaggeration to say the notion of the *anima* is one of his most impassioned contributions to psychology, which Jung sometimes described as a personification of the *unconscious*. He postulated the *anima* is first constellated for the male child by his mother—the protecting, nourishing, charmed circle of the mother in which psychological stage a male may remain as a child "seeking his childhood and his mother, fleeing from a cold cruel world which denies him understanding" (Jung, 1959b, p. 11). Psychologically, the end result of this is the mythological marriage of mother and son. The *animus* of a female would be constellated by a similar relationship to the father.

In a *classical* Jungian analysis, the *shadow* is the first thing that has to be worked through, thus opening the way to *anima/animus* which, according to Jung, are further away from *consciousness* than is *shadow*. "Whereas the shadow is accompanied by more or less definite and describable feeling-tones, the anima and animus exhibit feeling qualities that are harder to define. Mostly they are felt to be fascinating or numinous" (ibid., p. 28). The *individuation process* is the key concept in Jung's psychology, namely, becoming who we really are as distinct from others and, at the same time, in relationship to others. An essential part of this process, according to Jung, is for a male to become *conscious* of his *anima*, and a female of her *animus*, in order to be differentiated from them so that one is not dominated by them as in the example of the incestuous mother/son relationship just described.

Jung has been criticised for reproducing the gender stereotypes of his time in his depiction of *anima/animus* due to the fact that an inner and outer heterosexual couple was portrayed as the ideal, thus conflating *anima/animus* with those gender stereotypes. On the other hand, the concepts of *anima/animus* are helpful in explaining the phenomena of falling in love and of developing a fascination about another onto whom *anima* or *animus* projections are made. They also explain *impossible* love and why people behave sometimes in a relationship in ways they do not intend and do not understand, for example, a female taking on an *anima* role that is being projected into her by a male. Alternatively, a male may find himself trying to be a knight in shining armour to his girlfriend because of her *animus* hero projections into him.

Jung came to discover these inner figures through his own experience of exploring his fantasies in *The Red Book* following the break with Freud in 1913. The female figure of the seductive young girl, Salome, that appears in some of these fantasies was a prominent feminine appearance that led to the development of the notion of *anima*. He later proposed that females must also have a similar contra-sexual internal male figure, which he called the *animus*. This was represented for Jung by the Philemon character in *The Red Book*, who turned into an inner guide that Jung claimed taught him *psychic* objectivity and the reality of the *psyche*—vital contributions by Jung to psychology. Philemon is an *archetypal* figure who personifies the *wise old man*, of great assistance to both females and males at troubling times in their lives. The feminine equivalent would be the *wise old woman*. From this, we observe that Jung is suggesting that *anima/animus* dwell in both females and males as yoked entities though Jung himself states that the *anima* is the male's inner feminine equivalent, and the *animus* is the female's. These yoked terms are Latinised as the word for soul in Latin is *anima*, as *animus* is for spirit.

Further developments

Jung makes an interesting link between *anima/animus* as *psychic* structures that are complementary to the *persona*, which has been explored already. For instance, the *anima* is seen as a compromise formation between the primordial images of the *collective unconscious* so that a male with a strongly masculine *persona* would have an equally strong *anima* in his *unconscious*. One might think here of Donald Trump as an example of this with his aggressively male *persona* behind which lie his irrational, unpredictable outbursts, which according to Jung's model, would exemplify negative *anima*.

Jung elaborates this connection further in the following way: "The animus and the anima should function as a bridge, or a door, leading to the images of the collective unconscious, as the persona should be a sort of bridge to the world" (1963, p. 350). As may be deduced from this quotation, the function of *anima/animus* is to make a connection with the depths of the *psyche*.

Complications with Jung's concepts of *anima/animus* are inherent in the way he writes about them, complications which one comes across quite often in Jung's written work. As he is not a rigorous thinker nor a particularly clear writer, it is often difficult to know when and where he is situating his concepts, as exemplified by the following quotation:

> If I were to put in a nutshell ... what it is that characterizes the animus as opposed to the anima, I could only say this: as the anima produces *moods*, the animus produces *opinions* ... But in reality the opinions are not thought out at all; they exist ready-made, and they are held so positively and with so much conviction that the woman never had the shadow of a doubt about them. (1966, p. 207)

It is unclear whether he is describing *anima/animus* at a specific stage of development, that is, when *ego* has not separated from the mother *complex* (moods) or from the father *complex* (opinions). Further in the same section is the following:

> The animus is the deposit, as it were, of all woman's ancestral experiences of man—and not only that, he is also a creative and procreative being ... He brings forth something we might call the ... spermatic word. Just as a man brings forth his work as a complete creation out of his inner feminine nature, so the inner masculine side of a woman brings forth creative seeds which have the power to fertilize the feminine side of man. (p. 209)

As Jung in most of his writing on *anima/animus* states, men have *anima* and women *animus;* the quotation implies a man has an even more inspiring feminine nature as a *femme inspiratrice*, whereas actual woman is denied any creativity. But, in Jung's fantasies about Philemon as an inner positive *animus* figure, it is implicit in his thinking that women and men both share the yoked *anima/animus* equally, which has been made explicit in post-Jungian revisions of his theory. In this way, Jung comes close to the ancient Greek idea that the spirit inspires the soul and through this interplay things are brought into being. This goes some way to ameliorating Jung's devaluation of actual woman in contrast to his idealisation of the *anima*.

Anima/animus share with *shadow* the fact that they become apparent when they are projected onto another, as follows:

> The animus likes to project itself upon "intellectuals" and all kinds of heroes (including tenors, artists, and sporting celebrities). The anima has a predilection for everything that is unconscious, dark, equivocal and unrelated in woman, and also for her vanity, frigidity, helplessness, and so forth. (Jung, 1954, pp. 303–304)

The "dark, equivocal" projection onto woman gives rise to the phenomenon of the *femme fatale* of which the mythological Circe in Homer's *Odyssey* is an example. There is a male equivalent known as an *homme fatale* for the sort of man who is deadly attractive to women, personified by the English Romantic poet, Lord Byron. One of his paramours famously referred to him as mad, bad, and dangerous to know. To return to the *individuation process* mentioned earlier in this section, it is necessary to understand one's *anima/animus* in order to free the *conscious* personality from these *archetypal* influences. If they remain unintegrated, *anima/animus* can behave as autonomous *complexes*, with negative effects, for instance, feeling fated to be drawn into destructive relationships with males or females. If *anima/animus* are brought into *consciousness*, they can enhance creativity, and this differentiation between *ego* and *anima/animus* is what Jung called the "masterpiece" of analysis (1959a, p. 29). As has already been mentioned, he compared this with the work on the *shadow* as the "apprentice-piece" (ibid.). For Jung, anything to do with the *anima* is touched by the gods and becomes *numinous*.

The idea of the *syzygy* that is, the yoked *anima/animus*, is related to the divine couple united in marriage found in many mythologies, which Jung thought was a universal motif. It is in the *syzygy* that the *archetypal* union of the parents is located, the mother corresponding to the *anima*. This has implications for analysis and, in particular, for *psychological alchemy*, wherein this *archetypal* union is played out in the *transference–countertransference*. The term *transference* used in psychoanalysis applies to unresolved *Oedipal* issues and other unresolved *complexes* from childhood that are projected onto the analyst by the *analysand*/patient; *countertransference* is related to the feelings evoked in the analyst by the *analysand*/patient, which is a valuable source of information as to what is happening in the internal world of the *analysand* when projected into the analyst. This may be called the *transference work*.

Jung writes about the *anima* with great ardour as evidenced by the following quotations: "the deepest reality in a man" (1959b, p. 13), "this perilous image of Woman" (ibid.), "she is the solace for all the bitterness of life" (ibid.). He also points to the *anima* as the illusionist and the seductress that can lure a man into the "greatest danger" where good and evil, success and ruin, hope and despair counterbalance one another. We shall be looking at his own experience of these highly emotive depictions when we explore *psychological alchemy* later in the book. For him, the projection-making factor is the *anima* "or rather the unconscious as represented by the anima" (ibid.).

Jung has been criticised for some of his writings about gender issues, as in the following quotation in which he says that *anima* and *animus* can be realised "only through relations to a partner of the opposite sex, because only in such a relation do their projections become operative"

(1959b, p. 22). Though he also states that not all the contents of *anima* and *animus* are projected as many of them appear in dreams and fantasies, which can be elucidated in analysis. It goes without saying that his statement about a partner of the opposite sex would, of course, not be acceptable in today's world as people of the same sex equally carry images of *anima* or *animus*.

Jung certainly contributed to the gendering of *anima/animus* as can be seen in the difficulty that arises from depicting *anima/animus* as female/male or feminine/masculine unless it is made clear that one is dealing with *archetypal* forces which are not gendered. For instance, the usage of these terms is simplified by practitioners when the *anima* is referred to as female aspects of a male and the *animus* as male aspects of a female. To express them in these ways as gender stereotypes indicates a lack of awareness that they are *archetypal* concepts as, for instance, when destructively aggressive behaviour in a female is diagnosed as negative *animus* and moody irrational behaviour in a male as negative *anima*. Nevertheless, when the latter is personified by a male figure in a woman's dream there is no satisfactory alternative to interpreting it as negative *animus*.

A contemporary way of conceptualising *anima/animus* is to see the *animus* as the *archetypal* active principle and the *anima* as the *archetypal* receptive principle. In Jung's "classical" theory, the *animus* was situated in the woman's *unconscious* and the *anima* in the man's. Contemporary thinking has revised this to incorporate the yoked *syzygy* equally into the *unconscious* of female and male. Jung's thinking on this also evolved in his own lifetime from his earlier model of *Logos* belonging to *animus* and *Eros* to *anima*, as may be seen in the following:

> Just as the anima becomes through integration the Eros of consciousness, so the animus becomes, through integration a Logos; and in the same way that the anima gives relationship and relatedness to a man's consciousness, the animus gives to woman's consciousness a capacity for reflection, deliberation, and self-knowledge. (1959b, p. 16)

This developed when he was over sixty years old, leading to the transformation of a rather naive image of *anima* as full of potential to one where it has now gone through the suffering of tears and bitterness and is capable of ruthlessness. One sees this in his *psychological alchemical* rendering of *Luna*, namely, the moon as an initiated *unconscious* that is ready to interact with the initiated heroic *consciousness* that is *Sol*, namely, the sun, to produce the integration of personality that Jung calls *individuation*.

Syzygy

The Swiss analytical psychologist, Verena Kast, has explored the idea of the *syzygy*, the *anima/animus* seen as a couple, and has utilised this in working with people in mourning. She discovered that the acceptance of death was easier for those who were aware of the fantasies underlying their relationships. They come to an understanding of which fantasies bound them to their partner when the relationship was at its most vital and which aspects of their own personality their partner enlivened. The crucial work in mourning is often the laying bare of the fantasies contained in the relationship. These fantasies, which change in the course of a lifetime, can reveal the meaning of the relationship in terms of an individual's development and life. Underlying these fantasies are mythological images of the sacred marriage such as the one between Shiva and Shakti and Zeus and Hera, and how myths of the sacred marriage are mirrored in human relationships, as both women and men possess *anima* and *animus*, which can often be experienced in *unconscious* material as a couple. The clinical implication of this is that if there is an imbalance in the *anima/animus* internal relationship, it can be *worked through* in the *transference–countertransference* of the analytic couple.

This is why it is vital that mother and father *complexes* are *worked through* psychoanalytically as the development of *anima/animus* involves moving away from fusion with these *complexes*. Kast goes on to say that *individuation* requires not only separation from the actual parents but *psychologically* from the parental *complexes*. In the early stages of an analysis, *anima/animus* figures are conflated with mother and father *complexes*, thus obscuring their *archetypal* identity and function. This is where *archetypal* parental images are helpful in aiding individuals to differentiate themselves from actual parents. It is important to bear in mind that *anima/animus* as *archetypes* cannot be assimilated into *consciousness*—only their contents may be. As *archetypes* "they are the foundation stones of the psychic structure, which in its totality exceeds the limits of consciousness and therefore can never become the object of direct cognition" (Jung, 1959b, p. 20).

Research

Kast conducted a research project looking at around 600 dreams, in the course of which she found various categories of *anima/animus* showing the relation to the mother and father *complexes*, that also indicate the possibilities of development into independent *anima/animus* figures. These categories were as follows:

- Authority figures: teachers, politicians, priests and priestesses, kings and queens. Such figures closely resembled images of father and mother.
- Brother/sister figures (with an *archetypal* quality).
- Mysterious strangers: nixies, gypsies, travellers from outer space, gods and goddesses.
- Wise old woman/man.
- Unknown girl/boy. These figures, often connected with the *archetype* of the *divine child*, seem to represent developmental stages of the *anima/animus*; new configurations of *anima/animus* are often first symbolised as an unknown child.

If these images in dreams are identified only with mothers, fathers, sisters, and brothers, the *unconscious* is reduced to the status of a family graveyard. The *archetypal* dimension to these images, on the other hand, means the *ego* can be opened up to the influx of the *collective unconscious* so that *analysands*/patients can begin to discover new realms in their *psyche* that are not determined by actual familial relations.

The figure of the *anima* differs from other female figures in dreams in a number of ways: the characteristics of the figure can be categorised as evincing fascination, strangeness, radical fervour, wisdom, bringing about transformation, and helping in dangerous situations. These categories can be subdivided into *anima* as guide, *anima* as guide to transformation, and *anima* as stranger.

A Critical Dictionary of Jungian Analysis

In the entry on *anima/animus* in their *A Critical Dictionary of Jungian Analysis*, Andrew Samuels, Bani Shorter, and Fred Plaut (1986) state that possession by either *anima* or *animus* transforms the personality so as to give prominence to those traits which are seen as *psychologically* characteristic of the opposite sex. In that way, a person loses individuality and, for a male, domination by the *anima* leads to restlessness, promiscuity, moodiness, sentimentality—what may be described as unconstrained emotionality. For a female, domination by the *animus* can lead to being obstinate, ruthless, and domineering.

An interesting point Jung made was when he said males accepted the *anima* readily enough when she appeared in a novel or as a film star—one need only think of the enduring fascination with Marilyn Monroe. But it was a different matter when it came to understanding the role she played in their personal lives, namely, in the form of *anima* projections onto mother, wife, sister, daughter. Similarly, the other way around for a female who secretly hoped, in former times, to be rescued by a knight in shining armour or, more likely today, when males are often seen as adversaries to be overcome. Either way, female discourse still appears to focus on males. The only way to be released from this kind of obsessional behaviour is for females and males to become aware of the *unconscious* influence of the *archetypal anima/animus* on the way they conduct their lives.

Dreams

The following are dreams that incorporate *anima/animus* contents. These are not taken from my own analytic practice as I never reveal any material from that but are reproduced here from an online site on which they have already been published. I chose them as they are telling examples of the different personalities *anima/animus* can assume.

A dream illustrating positive anima/animus

There is this girl. The only way to describe her is simply perfect, literally the girl of my dreams. We hang out, carefree. It is summer and life is amazing. Near the end of the dream we have to go to separate places. We leave each other notes saying where we'll be. The weird thing is, by the end I feel like I've known her forever. What does it mean?

This is the dream of a male in his forties who has always been identified with his active side, that is, decisive, aggressive, independent. The dream is introducing him to his receptive side, portrayed in the dream by the "perfect girl", which is intuitive, nurturing, cooperative. Integrating these two aspects of his personality will help make him a strong, sensitive man. The dream occurred when he was in the summer of his life, that is, in his forties. The feeling of having known the girl forever underlines the fact that *she* has been there forever but he has only just discovered her. The notes indicate that they can go separate ways but also keep in touch.

This dream exemplifies what Jung called the *compensatory* function of dreams, an important principle in his theory of dreams, which differs from Freud's theory of the *dreamwork* that explores the *manifest* and *latent* content in dreams.

A dream illustrating negative and positive animus/anima figures

I'm with a drunken man. We'd been drinking the night before but he's still drunk. We enter a restaurant and the host is a man that recognises me. He says he catered a party I had a year or so ago. My friend is embarrassing me. As we leave the host holds my hand and says it was nice to see me again. My drunk friend gets jealous. We leave there and get in the car. The road is icy and we skid all over. I take over driving. A police officer stops me and tells me that my mother is in the hospital. She had a heart attack. I go to the hospital and comfort a girlfriend who is sobbing uncontrollably.

This is the dream of a woman in her fifties and contains both positive and negative *animus* figures. Bearing in mind what has already been said about being vigilant with regard to the possible dangers of rendering *animus* as a gendered entity, this particular dream fits well with being interpreted as portraying negative and positive *animus* figures. For instance, the restaurant host represents a positive *animus* figure, who behaves in a caring and supportive way towards her as a source of emotional nourishment. The drunken friend, on the other hand, personifies a negative *animus* figure. In outer life, the woman has a drink problem and the negative *animus* symbolises this destructive tendency. The negative *spirit* represented by alcohol in the dream is jealous of the positive *animus* personified by the (receptive) host as the negative *animus* does not want to relinquish control of the woman's life. The negative *animus* figure is at the controls of the car in the beginning, which indicates the woman has been going through life under the dominance of the negative *animus*. The road is icy and they skid all over the place which indicates that the woman is under the influence of alcohol, namely, too much negative *spirit* that can spin her out of control. The ice suggests frozen feelings but at this point the woman (dream *ego*) takes over the controls of the car. She is then stopped by an authority figure, personifying the *self*, who informs her about mother, that is, the feeling and nurturing dimension of her personality. The heart attack suggests an injury to her capacity for feeling as the heart is the centre of one's emotional life. As the dream shows, she has been living under the domination of the belittling attitude of her negative *animus* so that her femininity, represented by the sick mother and sobbing friend, is suffering.

This interpretation covers every occurrence and figure in the dream, which is a vital way of proceeding in dream interpretation. Nothing is too small or insignificant to be overlooked when working with dreams in analysis.

CHAPTER 7

Puer/puella vs narcissism

Jung's *archetypal* concept of the *puer/puella* is linked to its equally *archetypal* opposite of *senex*. The latter denotes the *wise old man/ woman* or, in its negative form, the embittered aspects of each of them. A brief description of the twinned term, *puer/puella*, is that it applies to a psychological and emotional *eternal youth* of either sex, which in its positive form is the creative force in an individual; whereas in its negative form it is unable to mature into adulthood. Jung's notion of the *puer/puella* has a degree of overlap with Freud's concept of *narcissism* though is by no means identical with it.

Narcissism

A brief description (largely based on Laplanche and Pontalis's excellent *Language of Psychoanalysis*) follows of Freud's negative view of *narcissism*, both in relation to his *topographical* model and later as it appeared in the *structural* model. Freud first used the term—borrowed from the psychiatrist Havelock Ellis—in 1910 in his work on the *Schreber Case*. This usage of the term located it as a stage in the infant's sexual development between *auto-eroticism* and *object* love from which he claimed the *ego* develops. Freud's lack of clarity on just how the latter comes about was addressed by Lacan in his notion of the *mirror stage*, which offered a new formulation of *ego* development as *objectivation* of the *ego*, that leads the infant to refer to him- or herself in the third person thus demonstrating an obliviousness of the "I" or *subject*. This reformulation is a major reason Lacan was negative about the *ego psychology* that was developed in the USA by Heinz Hartmann and by Anna Freud in the UK.

In 1914, Freud produced "On Narcissism: An Introduction", one of the metapsychology papers wherein he set out the following schema on *narcissistic object-choice*. The latter is based on the following: what a person is; what he/she was; what he/she would like to be; or on someone who was once part of him or herself. In this way, Freud was asserting that the withdrawal of *libidinal cathexis* from the *object* and *re-cathecting* the *ego* indicated that the more the *libido* was invested in the *ego* inevitably resulted in the depletion of the *libido* available for *object* relating. In his metapsychology paper, *narcissism* is now viewed not as a developmental stage but as a damming up of the *libido* which no *object-cathexis* can completely overcome as it leads to a *narcissistic* identification with the *object*. Accordingly, Freud thought patients suffering from *narcissistic disorder* have difficulty forming *transferences* onto other *objects*, hence his view that this disorder was unsuited to psychoanalytic treatment.

Following the split from Freud, Jung did not use the term *narcissism* though there is mention of "*a Narcissus state*" which he goes on to describe as follows: "He is buried in the depths of *self, as if in the earth*; really a dead man who has turned back to mother earth" (1916, pp. 290–291; original italics). Instead, Jung explored the *archetypal child* as a *symbol* that represents the *divine child* whose advent is the end product of the *psychological alchemical* process, to be explored at length later in this book. The appearance of the *divine child* signals a future change of personality. In actual living, the child stage, like every *archetypal* stage of development, has to be lived fully and then sublated (a term to be found in Hegelian dialectics to denote the overcoming of a previous stage while at the same time preserving—not losing it) in order to move to the next stage of development. Remaining *only* a child means being stuck in childish ways of thinking and behaving; such a person is suffering from arrested development, an unattractive way of being and one that is deeply frustrating for the person him- or herself and anyone unfortunate enough to be in their vicinity. As every parent will testify, dealing with an adolescent child is the most challenging stage in the parent–child relationship but dealing with a (chronological) adult *puer/puella* is worse as it is *pathological*.

Puer/puella

In Jung's thinking, the positive side of the *puer* lies in the fact that it is the source of an individual's creativity; the negative side is represented by the fact that the *puer* remains psychologically infantile and thus always in the service of the *Great Mother*. The related *archetype* of the *hero* is differentiated from the *puer* by the fact that the *hero* sets out to achieve something and consequently matures into adulthood; the *puer* is terrified of failure and therefore never risks trying to achieve anything, in that way remaining psychologically unborn.

Dealing with a *puer/puella* patient presents difficulties in analysis as she or he is unable to tolerate any hint of criticism, and the *transference* can easily turn pathological with the analyst being experienced as a *persecutory superego* figure. This is *acted-in* by the patient turning the analyst into a protagonist trying to drag him unwillingly down to earth as opposed to remaining ungrounded through living six feet up in the air. If the patient experiences the analyst in this negative light, he is likely to fly away like *Peter Pan* as the *puer/puella* refuses to be grounded in reality, most of all, in the passing of time. Remaining stuck in the psychological state of the *eternal youth* has its dangers as one sees with actual adolescents who have an abiding fantasy of immortality—the reason why so many have fatal accidents with drink, drugs, and dangerous driving.

The above highlights the reason why adolescence is both a fantastic experience and also a time of terrible suffering for the young person trying to negotiate it, as life will never again present such extremes of joy and despair—the latter reasserting itself at times of grieving. Interestingly, Freud first begins his exploration of *narcissism* in his metapsychological paper "Mourning and Melancholia". These extremes of emotion are what the permanent adolescent is trying desperately to hold onto but the sad outcome of this impossible endeavour with the passage of time is a flipping over into the cynicism of the negative *senex*. This unattractive fate applies to ordinary mortals but there are gifted individuals who retain the creativity of the *puer* into older age. Further on in this section, there will be an example of a positive *puer* figure; that is followed by an example of a negative one illustrating Jung's concept of a negative *puer/ senex* and Freud's concept of *narcissism*.

Ovid's myth of *Narcissus*

Ovid's myth of *Narcissus* is relevant to both Freud's and Jung's concepts and is reproduced in full here. The main character is depicted as male though the myth applies equally to both males and females, and it begins by praising Tiresias, the blind seer, as *wise old man*, who, of course, also features prominently in the *Oedipus* myth.

> He, famed far and near through all the Boeotian towns, gave answers that none could censure to those who sought his aid. The first to make trial of his truth and assured utterances was the nymph, Liriope, who once the river-god, Cephisus, embraced in his winding stream and ravished, while imprisoned in his waters. When her time came the beauteous nymph brought forth a child, whom a nymph might love even as a child, and named him Narcissus. When asked whether this child would live to reach a well-ripened age, the seer replied: "If he ne'er knows himself." Long did the saying of the prophet seem but empty words. But what befell proved its truth—the event, the manner of his death, the strangeness of his infatuation. For Narcissus had reached his sixteenth year and might seem either boy or man. Many youths and many maidens sought his love; but in that slender form was pride so cold that no youth, no maiden touched his heart. Once as speech beheld him, resounding Echo, who could neither hold her peace when others spoke, nor yet begin to speak till others had addressed her.
>
> Up to this time Echo had form and was not a voice alone; and yet, though talkative, she had no other use of speech than now—only the power out of many words to repeat the last she heard. Juno had made her thus; for often when she might have surprised the nymphs in company with her lord upon the mountain sides, Echo would cunningly hold the goddess in long talk until the nymphs were fled. When Saturnia realized this, she said to her: "That tongue of thine, by which I have been tricked, shall have its power curtailed and enjoy the briefest use of speech."

The event confirmed her threat. Nevertheless she does repeat the last phrases of a speech and returns the words she hears.

Now when she saw Narcissus wandering through the fields, she was enflamed with love and followed him by stealth, and the more she followed, the more she burned by a nearer flame; as when quick-burning sulphur, smeared around the tops of torches, catches fire from another fire brought near. Oh, how often does she long to approach him with alluring words and make soft prayers to him! But her nature forbids this, nor does it permit her to begin: but as it allows, she is ready to await the sounds to which she may give back her own words.

By chance the boy, separated from his faithful companions, had cried: "Is anyone here?" and "Here!" cried Echo back. Amazed, he looks around in all directions and with loud voice cries: "Come!"; and "Come!" she calls him calling. He looks behind him and, seeing no one coming, calls again: "Why do you run from me?" and hears in answer his own words again. He stands still, deceived by the answering voice, and "Here let us meet," he cries. Echo, never to answer another more gladly, cries: "Let us meet"; and to help her own words she comes forth from the woods that she may throw her arms around the neck she longs to clasp. But he flees at her approach and, fleeing, says: "Hands off! Embrace me not! May I die before I give you power o'er me!" "I give you power o'er me" she says, and nothing more.

Thus spurned, she lurks in the woods, hides her shamed face among the foliage, and lives from that time on in lonely caves. But still, though spurned, her love remains and grows on grief; her sleepless cares waste away her wretched form; she becomes gaunt and wrinkled and all moisture fades from her body into the air. Only her voice and her bones remain: then, only voice; for they say that her bones turned to stone. She hides in woods and is seen no more upon the mountainsides; but all may hear her, for voice and voice alone, still lives in her.

Thus has Narcissus mocked her, thus has he mocked other nymphs of the waves or mountains; thus has he mocked the companies of men. At least one of these scorned youth, lifting up his hands to heaven, prayed: "So may he himself love, and not gain the thing he loves!" The goddess, Nemesis, heard his righteous prayer. There was a clear pool with silvery bright water, to which no shepherds ever came, or she-goats feeding on the mountain side or any other cattle; whose smooth surface neither bird nor beast nor falling bough ever ruffled. Grass grew all around its edge, fed by the water near, and a coppice that would never suffer the sun to warm the spot. Here the youth, worn by the chase and the heat, lies down, attracted thither by the appearance of the place and by the spring.

While he seeks to slake his thirst another thirst springs up, and while he drinks he is smitten by the sight of the beautiful form he sees. He loves an unsubstantial hope and thinks that substance which is only shadow. He looks in speechless wonder at himself and hangs there motionless in the same expression, like a statue carved from Parian marble. Prone on the ground, he gazes at his eyes, twin stars, and his locks, worthy of Bacchus, worthy of Apollo; on his smooth cheeks, his ivory neck, the glorious beauty of his face, the blush mingled with snowy white: all things, in short, he admires for which he is himself admired.

Unwittingly he desires himself; he praises, and is himself what he praises; and while he seeks, is sought; equally he kindles love and burns with love. How often did he offer vain kisses on the elusive pool? How often did he plunge his arms into the water seeking to clasp the neck he sees there, but did not clasp himself in them? What he sees he knows not; but that which he sees he burns for, and the same delusion mocks and allures his eyes. O fondly foolish boy, why vainly seek to clasp a fleeing image? What you seek is nowhere; but turn yourself away, and the object of your love will be no more. That which you behold is but the shadow of a reflected image and has no substance of its own. With you it comes, with you it stays, and it will go with you—if you can go.

No thought of food or rest can draw him from the spot; but stretched on the shaded grass, he gazes on that false image with eyes that cannot look their fill and through his own eyes perishes. Raising himself a little, and stretching his arms to the trees, he cries: "Did anyone, O ye woods, ever love more cruelly than I? You know, for you have been the convenient haunts of many lovers. Do you in the ages past, for your life is one of centuries, remember anyone who has pined away like this? I am charmed and I see; but what I see and what charms me I cannot find—so great a delusion holds my love. And, to make me grieve the more, no mighty ocean separates us, no long road, no mountain ranges, no city walls with close-shut gates; by a thin barrier of water we are kept apart.

"He himself is eager to be embraced. For, often as I stretch my lips towards the lucent wave, so often with upturned face he strives to lift his lips to mine. You would think he could be touched—so small a thing it is that separates our loving hearts. Whoever you are, come forth thither! Why, O peerless youth, do you elude me? Or whither do you go when I strive to reach you? Surely my form and age are not such that you should shun them, and me too the nymphs have loved. Some ground for hope you offer with your friendly looks, and when I have stretched out my arms to you, you stretch yours too. When I have smiled, you smile back; and I have often seen tears, when I weep, on your cheeks. My becks you answer with your nod; and I suspect from the movement of your sweet lips, you answer my words as well, but words which do not reach my ears—Oh, I am he! I have felt it, I know now my own image. I burn with love of my own self; I both kindle the flames and suffer them. What shall I do? Shall I be wooed or woo? Why woo at all? What I desire, I have; the very abundance of my riches beggars me. Oh, that I might be parted from my own body! And, strange prayer for a lover, I would that what I love were absent from me! And now grief is sapping my strength, but a brief space of life remains to me, and I am cut off in my life's prime. Death is nothing to me, for in death I shall leave my troubles; I would he that is loved might live longer; but as it is, we two shall die together in one breath."

He spoke and, half distraught, turned again to the same image. His tears ruffled the water, and dimly the image came back from the troubled pool. As he saw it thus depart, he cried: "Oh, whither do you flee? Stay here, and desert not him who loves thee, cruel one! Still may it be mine to gaze on what I may not touch, and by that gaze feel my unhappy passion."

While he thus grieves, he plucks away his tunic its upper fold and beats his bare breast with pallid hands. His breast when it is struck takes on a delicate glow; just as apples sometimes, though white in part, flush red in the other part, or as grapes hanging in clusters take on a purple hue when not yet ripe. As soon as he sees this, when the water has come clear again, he can bear no more; but, as the yellow wax melts before a gentle heat, as hoar frost melts before the warm morning sun, so does he, wasted with love, pine away, and is slowly consumed by its hidden fire. No longer has he that ruddy colour mingling with the white, no longer that strength and vigour and all that lately was so pleasing to behold; scarce does his form remain which once Echo had loved so well.

But when she saw it, though still angry and unforgetful, she felt pity; and as so often as the poor boy says "Alas!" and his hands beat his shoulders she gives back the same sounds of woe. His last words as he gazed into the familiar spring were these: "Alas, dear boy, vainly beloved!" and the place gave back his words. And when he said "Farewell!" "Farewell!" said Echo too.

He dropped his weary head on the green grass and death sealed the eyes that marveled at their master's beauty. And even when he had been received into the infernal abodes, he kept on gazing at his image in the Stygian pool. His naiad-sisters beat their breasts and shore their locks in sign of grief for their dead brother; the dyads, too, lamented, and Echo gave back their sounds of woe. And now they were preparing the funeral pyre, the brandished torches and the bier; but his body was nowhere to be found. In place of his body they find a flower, its yellow centre girt with white petals.

When this story was noised abroad it spread the well-deserved fame of the seer throughout the cities of Greece, and great was the name of Tiresias. (Schwartz-Salant, 1982, pp. 7–11)

This account encapsulates great psychological truth as the Narcissus/Echo dyad is often encountered in couples. It was present in Jung's relations with his many female acolytes though not in the marriage to his wife, Emma, about whom more will appear towards the later stages of this book. It is possible to view Jung's insensitivity in importing his mistress, Toni Wolff, into the family home where she was a constant presence as a *narcissistic* punishment of Emma for not being his "echo". Like Sabina Spielrein, who will feature in another section of the book, Wolff also started off as a patient of Jung's, indicating an *acting-out* of the erotic *transference–countertransference* and an imbalance of power right from the start. As the possibility of a child, actual or fantasised, was a key issue in the relationship with Spielrein, it makes one wonder how that might have played itself out in the interaction with Wolff. Jung's *Black Books* were published in 2020, in which the Jung scholar Sonu Shamdasani has the following to say about this triangular relationship:

At the inception of their relationship, Toni Wolff was not interested in marriage and having children. She was critical of what she had observed of marriage: it seemed to make men less active and less enterprising—merely content with being fathers. It made both men and women less interested in culture. After having children, women often didn't need their husbands, and their own problems tended to return. Her mother hadn't learned to work and had consequently plagued her children with unused libido. Toni Wolff was also critical of the bondage of marriage. (Shamdasani, 2020, Volume 1, Page 31)

Shamdasani goes on to say, the two women in Jung's life found a respectful modus vivendi for this triangular relationship.

Nevertheless, both episodes raise questions about Jung's attitude to women in general—I am hardly the first writer to do that—as well as to those who were closest to him in his life. This point would seem to be confirmed by the fact that Emma is only mentioned briefly in relation to her work on the *Grail* legend, in *Memories, Dreams, Reflections* (*MDR*), and Toni Wolff not at all. According to Sonu Shamdasani, who is working on the *Protocols*, the interviews Aniela Jaffé conducted with Jung in their work on *MDR*, there are several references to Emma in those.

David Bowie/David Jones

An outstanding example of a world-renowned figure who kept the creativity of the *puer* alive and brilliantly integrated it into adulthood, was David Bowie. This extraordinarily charismatic, creative artist, composer, and performer died of cancer of the liver in January 2016 only two days after the release of his final album *Blackstar*. He retained his creativity (a vital part of the *archetypal puer/puella* personaltiy) whilst, at the same time, he managed to mature into an admirably intelligent adult who inspired people of all ages whilst alive and whose death was marked by a worldwide outpouring of collective grief.

Bowie's long-term fascination with Jung's work is described in a chapter entitled " '*Crashing Out with Sylvian*': David Bowie, Carl Jung and the Unconscious" (Stark, 2015) in a recent book on the artist. Bowie visited *The Red Book* exhibit curated by Sonu Shamdasani at the Rubin Museum in New York in 2009, although Shamdasani has confirmed he did not meet Bowie on that occasion nor did he know about Bowie's visit to the exhibit. A close friend of Bowie states the following: "David Bowie inhabits Carl Jung's world of archetypes, reading and speaking of the psychoanalyst with passion" (Devereux, Dillane, & Power, 2015, p. 83).

All of Jung's central concepts feature prominently in Bowie's personality and work such as the *integration of opposites, spirituality, numinous, shadow, persona, anima/animus, dreams, complexes, visions, mythology, cabiri (gnomes and dwarves)*, and so on. Stark suggests the reference to *Sylvian* "could plausibly refer to the Sylvian fissure in the brain" which, when stimulated, produces hallucinogenic visions and "an illusory shadow person" (2015, p. 88). She goes on to point out that in Michelangelo's Sistine Chapel painting "… the American Medical Journal reported that the portrait of God appears to conform deliberately to the neuro-anatomical shape of the brain" with God's arm protruding from the Sylvian fissure (p. 89). Bowie's interest in Jungian theory and in Michelangelo's work testifies to his high intelligence—readily confirmed by watching online interviews he gave while alive.

Above all, Bowie is a living exemplar of Jung's alchemical *hermaphrodite*, and the title of his best-known persona, *Ziggy Stardust*, is most probably a deliberate play on the Gnostic term, *syzygy*, a central concept in Jung's *psychological alchemy*. Bowie's fascination with *alchemy* is expressed in his own words: "As with alchemy, the end result isn't as important as the long process whereby all the inessential aspects of 'you' have been stripped away" (ibid., p. 95).

Another central character is *Major Tom* who "has become conscious of the powers of the unconscious and the horrors of the shadow within him and society, strung out between opposing polarities … desperately seeking psychological reconciliation" (p. 101). A lot of images were drug-fuelled visions on Bowie's part though he eventually managed to lift himself out of that nightmare world inhabited by self-destructive *puer* and *puella* figures of the rock music world. His last years were spent in Manhattan in a stable marriage with his wife, Iman, where *Ziggy (Syzygy) Stardust* became grounded in the ordinary man, David Jones.

Shadow Man

The words from Bowie's 1971 song, *Shadow Man*, show his indebtedness to Jung's concept of *shadow*, in particular verses five, six, and eight. The lyrics can be found online.

Julian Assange

Bowie exemplified the creative aspect of the *puer* who is able to mature into manhood. This next account is of a *very* different kind of person who represents another aspect of the *puer*, namely one that never matures but, instead, flips over into the negative *senex* of embittered old age without reaching adulthood. That sad state is personified by a character called Julian Assange, who took up temporary residence in the block of flats in which I live in central London.

A brief account of his sojourn is as follows. In June 2012, Julian Assange, the founder of Wikileaks, an online media outfit that publishes news leaks and classified information, sought refuge at the Ecuadorian embassy, which is housed in a spacious apartment in Knightsbridge, a central London borough. Assange was wanted in Sweden on allegations of rape, and by the United States for allegedly publishing secret US government files. The London Metropolitan Police issued a warrant for his arrest, which he breached by jumping bail set by a British court.

The then president of Ecuador, a left-winger antagonistic to the United States, delighted in offering Assange refuge in the country's London embassy. For his part, Assange claimed he was seeking refuge for fear of being extradited to the United States because of his long-standing relations with the Russians. The whole affair, which is ongoing, is complicated, involving as it does several global jurisdictions, including the United Kingdom, the latter having to pay for 24-hour police presence within the block of flats and its surrounding vicinity over several years. These were no ordinary police but the elite diplomatic police who are licensed to bear arms, which is unusual among the UK constabulary.

The previously peaceful lives of the residents of the block of flats was overnight turned upside down with the arrival in their midst of Assange. These inhabitants include the personnel of the Ecuadorian and Colombian embassies, several distinguished people from the United Arab Emirates, including their royal family, the Grimaldis, a smattering of residents from Saudi Arabia, and the author of this book. In addition, the world's media were in constant attendance on the pavement outside the block; these arrived in full force at the beginning and their vigilance would ebb and flow depending on the latest twists and turns, including the making of a commercial film, of this long-running saga that played out for more than seven years.

Following a regime change in Ecuador, the new president, who appears to want more cordial relations with the United States, dubbed Wikileaks a hostile intelligence service that allegedly subverted the 2016 US presidential election. As a result, refuge for Assange at the Ecuadorian embassy was subsequently withdrawn and he was carried out of the block by police in April 2019. At that time, it was startling to see the emergence of a bearded ageing man with receding hair in place of the fresh-faced youth of 2012.

The above is an expurgated account of this bizarre affair which, at the time of writing, is going through various legal processes. In the meanwhile, Assange languishes in a London prison, where life is presumably of a different order from his seven years of self-imprisonment at the Ecuadorian embassy, where he received frequent visits from well-heeled individuals, such as the *puella* daughter of the billionaire, James "Jimmy" Goldsmith.

CHAPTER 8

Self

S ome of the contents of this chapter first appeared in *The Encyclopedia of Psychology and Religion* (2010), edited by David Leeming, Kathryn Madden, and Stanton Marlan, which is now into its third edition.

The notion of the *self* lies at the heart of Jung's conceptualising on the structure and dynamics of the *psyche*. He first encountered what he later termed the *self* in mid-life during the turbulent years starting in 1913 whilst undergoing his *creative illness* (Ellenberger, 1970, p. 672) following the breakdown of his relationship with Freud. As a result, Jung took mid-life to be universal for experiences of the *self* to come into being, a view that has been contested by later analytical psychologists. Jung's definition of the *self* is that it is the totality of the *psyche* as well as being the prime *archetype* that keeps the *psyche* from disintegrating at times of stress. Furthermore, he claimed it transcends and goes beyond *psyche*.

If it is conceptualised as the prime *archetype*, the *self* would be the *container* of opposites, above all perhaps those of good and evil. In this regard, Jung refers to it as a "complexio oppositorum [which] proves to be not only a possibility but an ethical duty" (1954, p. 320). This is to be found at the very centre of what it is to be human, which is also an analogy of God:

> Man is God, but not in an absolute sense, since he is man. He is therefore God in a human way … every endeavour of our human intelligence should be bent to the achieving of that simplicity where contradictories are reconciled. (p. 320)

Here Jung is quoting Nicholas of Cusa of whom he says: "The alchemists are as it were the empiricists of the great problem of opposites, whereas Nicholas of Cusa is its philosopher" (p. 320). Furthermore: "The self is a union of opposites *par excellence*, and this is where it differs essentially from the Christ-symbol. The androgyny of Christ is the utmost concession the Church has made to the problem of opposites" (Jung, 1953, p. 19).

On the other hand, Jung's writings contain many references to the synonymous nature of the *self* with the God-image. For instance: "*Christ exemplifies the archetype of the self*" (1959b, p. 37; original italics). "The Christ-symbol is of the greatest importance for psychology in so far as it is perhaps the most highly developed and differentiated symbol of the self, apart from the figure of the Buddha" (1953, p. 19). In so doing, Jung claims he was not trying to take on the mantle of a religious thinker but, instead, always saw himself as an empirical psychologist. "Strictly speaking, the God-image does not coincide with the unconscious as such, but with a special content of it, namely the archetype of the self. It is this archetype from which we can no longer distinguish the God-image empirically" (1958a, p. 757). This image of wholeness rises independently in the *conscious* mind from the depths of humankind's *psychic* nature. In the same work he says: "… the self is not a philosophical concept like Kant's 'thing-in-itself', but an empirical concept of psychology, and can therefore be hypostatized" (p. 262).

Self and individuation

In Jung's thinking, the *self* is all important not only in what he refers to as the *individuation* process of individuals but also in that of collective groups though the symbols of the *self* are different at different historical epochs. Jung elaborated this in his work *Aion*, the name of which is taken from the Mithraic god that rules over time, as follows:

> … 'wholeness' … is nevertheless empirical in so far as it is antici-
> pated by the psyche in the form of spontaneous or autonomous
> symbols. These are the quaternity or mandala symbols, which
> occur not only in the dreams of modern people … but are widely
> disseminated in the historical records of many peoples and many
> epochs. Their significance as *symbols of unity and totality* is amply
> confirmed by history as well as by empirical psychology. (1959b,
> p. 31; original italics)

Jung goes so far as to say the *self* represents *psychic* totality and is both *conscious* and *unconscious*. From the latter realm, it may manifest in dreams, myths, and fairy tales in the figure of the "supra-ordinate per-sonality" (1971, p. 460). In this way, it takes on the form of king, hero, prophet, saviour, or a symbol of wholeness such as a circle or cross.

> I have called this wholeness that transcends consciousness the
> 'self'. The goal of the individuation process is the synthesis of the
> self … symbols of wholeness frequently occur at the beginning of
> the individuation process, indeed they can often be observed in
> the first dreams of early infancy. (1959b, p. 164)

This tantalising glimpse into Jung's interest in infancy was developed by the analytical psychologist, Michael Fordham, whose ideas will be expanded further in this work.

Encounter with the self

In exploring the connection between the *self* and *ego*, Jung turned to the biblical story of the *Book of Job*. Likewise, the analytical psycholo-gist Edward Edinger compares the relationship between the story of Job with its relevance for the *psyche* of modern-day humans, and consid-ers William Blake's *Illustrations of the Book of Job*. As Edinger states: "… the Job story is an archetypal image which pictures a certain typical encounter between the ego and the Self. This typical encounter may be called the Job archetype" (1986, p. 11). Edinger further states:

> The term 'Self' is used by Jung to designate the transpersonal centre and totality of the psyche. It constitutes the greater, objective personality, whereas the ego is the lesser, subjective personality. Empirically the Self cannot be distinguished from the God-image. Encounter with it is a *mysterium tremendum*. (p. 7)

An encounter between *self* and *ego* always results in a defeat for the latter. If it can sustain the ordeal, however, and at the same time become aware of its meaning, *ego* may experience an insight into the *transpersonal psyche*. In the Blake drawings, Job is first depicted as living in a state of *unconscious* innocent contentment. In the second picture, Satan manifests in a stream of fire between Yahweh and Job and represents the urge to *individuation*, which is a challenge to complacence and living *unconsciously*. "Dionysian energy of excess has erupted into the Apollonian order" (Edinger, 1986, p. 19).

The later pictures illustrate the growing dynamism of Dionysian energy and its impact on *ego* by destroying its containing structures, depicted in the Job story as the loss of his children and their families. *Psychologically* this corresponds to the onset of bad dreams and neurotic symptoms such as *depression* and *psychosomatic* symptoms. *Ego* may try to deal with these by splitting them off and dissociating them from *consciousness*, which results in an impoverishment of the *conscious* personality.

The book goes on to illustrate the complete breakdown of Job (*ego*) when confronted with the dark side of the *self* (Yahweh), which a later picture depicts as God on high pointing down to the chthonic aspects of the *numinosum*, Behemoth and Leviathan. "This is the other side of the *numinosum*, which we must always remember is a union of opposites" (Edinger, 1986, p. 55). As Edinger goes on to say:

> Job is being shown the abysmal aspect of God and the depths of his own psyche, which contains devouring monsters remote from human values ... God reveals his own shadow side, and since man participates in God as the ground of his being he must likewise share his darkness. (p. 55)

Blake's pictures and the *Book of Job* end with Job's fortunes being restored and with an enlargement of his personality through an encounter with the *self*. As Jung says: "… the widening of consciousness is at first upheaval and darkness, then a broadening out of man to the whole man" (1971, p. 171).

Primal self

The analytical psychologist James Astor views Michael Fordham as the last of the founders of a movement in analysis who tapped into something essential in the discipline. Fordham's pioneering work led to a developmental model of Jung's ideas of the *self*. "His most radical departure from Jung was to describe the actions of the self in infancy and childhood such that the infant, far from being uncentred at birth, as Jung originally thought, is a person with an individual identity even in utero" (Astor, 2007, pp. 75–92). There is a longer piece dedicated to Fordham's work later in this book but, as his revision of Jung's original theory is of such importance and for his rethinking of the concept of the *self*, it is relevant to include some of his thinking about it in this section.

The way Fordham revised Jung's thinking on the *self* was in demonstrating how, through interacting with the environment, the *self* helped to mould and create it. In this way:

> The self, as Fordham conceived it, was the instigator as much as the receptor of infant experience. This conception gave rise to the particularly Jungian theory of ego development in which the interaction between mother and baby ensured the uniqueness of the situation, a uniqueness created as much by the infant as by the mother. (Ibid.)

The prospective nature and self-regulating function of the *psyche* through the *self's* unifying characteristics "could transcend what seemed to be opposite forces" though in the course of that it could be "exceedingly disruptive" both "destructively and creatively" (ibid.).

Astor sums up Fordham's revisionist thinking on Jung's theory of the *self* to include a primary *self* or original state of integration as follows:

> This primal self, he thought, gave rise to structures from inter-action with the environment which it in part created. It existed outside of time and space, and was similar to a mystical (or con-temporary scientific concept such as emergence), whose mani-festations had archetypal form. This primary self was integrated, and in Jung's sense it was an agency of the psyche which tran-scended opposites. (Ibid.)

Astor links this to Fordham's innovative thinking about the *dynamic structure* of the *self*, which infant research is arriving at quite separately from analytic thinking. "Fordham took the innateness of Jung's arche-typal psychology and demonstrated the way in which the environment affected it" (ibid.). Furthermore,

> By having a theory of deintegration we are able to think about the observed behaviour of the infant as being continuous with the self. What this means is that the development of the individual baby is in effect an early form of individuation. (Ibid.)

Fordham also challenged Jung's thinking about the *self* as both the total-ity of the *psyche* and as an *archetype*.

> As for the archetype definition, Fordham notes that it accounts for a range of phenomena related to wholeness (archetypal images) and, in fact, is closer to the data than the totality defini-tion. This data, however, '… cannot also be the totality' because it excludes the ego, which Jung differentiated from the archetypes. (Urban, 2005, p. 574)

In conclusion, it is worth noting that the term *self* is spelt with a capital "S" in some instances and a small "s" in others. The former tends to be used by *classical* Jungians, which term denotes those analytical psychol-ogists who remain close to what Jung originally said viewing the *Self* as synonymous with the God-image. When *self* is used by analytical psy-chologists of the *developmental* school of thought founded by Michael

Fordham, it is spelt with a small "s". While he was not an atheist: "Much of Fordham's work has countered this religious aspect of Jungianism" (ibid.). At the same time: "His respect for Jung and his understanding of the value of his studies of the manifestations of the collective unconscious led him to try to take a balanced position with respect to both the psychological and religious perspective" (ibid.).

Dream addressing the reality of the self

I found myself in a dirty, sooty city. It was night, and winter, and dark, and raining. I was in Liverpool. With a number of Swiss— say, half a dozen—I walked through the dark streets. I had the feeling that there we were coming from the harbor, and that the real city was actually up above, on the cliffs. We climbed up there. It reminded me of Basel, where the market is down below and then you go up through the Totengäggschen ("Alley of the Dead"), which leads to a plateau above and so to the Petersplatz and the Peterkirsche. When we reached the plateau, we found a broad square dimly illuminated by street lights, into which many streets converged. The various quarters of the city were arranged radially round the square. In the center was a round pool, and in the middle of it a round island. While everything round about was obscured by rain, fog, smoke, and dimly lit darkness, the little island blazed with sunlight. On it stood a single tree, a magnolia, in a shower of reddish blossoms. It was as though the tree stood in the sunlight and was at the same time the source of light. My companions commented on the abominable weather, and obviously did not see the tree. They spoke of another Swiss who was living in Liverpool, and expressed surprise that he should have settled here. I was carried away by the beauty of the flowering tree and the sunlit island, and thought, "I know very well why he has settled here." (Jung, 1963, p. 189)

Jung felt the dream confirmed his ideas about the *self* being the principle and *archetype* of orientation and meaning. The flowering tree represents the *self*, the prime *archetype* that is, as has already been noted, individual to the person unlike the other *archetypes* that are universal. The name of the city of Liverpool represents in the dream the pool of life.

CHAPTER 9

Numinous

Apart of the material in this section is based on the "numinous" entry about the *numinosum* written for *The Encyclopedia of Psychology and Religion* (2010), edited by David Leeming, Kathryn Madden, and Stanton Marlon. That entry was based on chapters by different authors who contributed to *The Idea of the Numinous*, a book I edited with the academic, David Tacey, in 2006 for Routledge.

The term *numinous* is an all important one for Jung as he makes clear in the quotation that appears as a paragraph on its own at the front of *The Red Book*, published in 2009. This states as follows:

> The years of which I have spoken to you, when I pursued the inner images, were the most important time of my life. Everything else is to be derived from this. It began at that time, and the later details hardly matter anymore. My entire life consisted in elaborating what had burst forth from the unconscious and flooded me like an enigmatic stream and threatened to break me. That was the stuff and material for more than only one life. Everything later was merely the outer classification, the scientific elaboration, and the integration into life. But the numinous beginning, which contained everything, was then.

Jung appropriated the term, *numinous*, from Rudolf Otto's *The Idea of the Holy: An Inquiry into the Non-rational Factor in the Idea of the Divine and Its Relation to the Rational*, written during the First World War. This is a philosophical work that incorporates thinking from Husserl and neo-Kantianism, amongst others, although it is the central notion of the *numinous* that attracted Jung's attention. Otto coined the word from the Latin *numen* meaning "nod", "hint", or "will", the last owing much to Schopenhauer's usage of the term. The intellectual depths of the latter's thinking, aligned to the clarity of expression in his writing, made Schopenhauer an inspiration for Jung and, previous to that, to the greatest composer of music drama, Richard Wagner, who will be revisited later in this book. Wagner, Freud, and Jung owe an enormous debt to Schopenhauer—for Wagner it was Schopenhauer's emphasis on the pre-eminence of music among the arts and of redemption through compassion; for Freud it was the emphasis on sexual love and the *will*, the latter a precursor for his theory of the *unconscious*. Jung, likewise, thought of the *will* in the same way, and took Schopenhauer's depiction of outer life as illusory or *Maya*, a term he borrowed from the Hindu Upanishads. For both Schopenhauer and Jung, looking *East* to the study of Hinduism and Mahayana Buddhism represented vital turning points in their lives wherein lay the discovery of the *will*, the ultimate expression, as Jung saw it, of the blind way the *collective unconscious* and *archetypes* dictate an individual's unwitting path through life, exemplified by the following: "Thus the bird builds a nest for the young it does not yet know" (Schopenhauer, 1819: para. 191).

As to Otto himself—he was a theologian who travelled widely in Europe, the United States, India, China, and Japan. As the subtitle of his book suggests, Otto pointed to the need to keep the rational and non-rational in some kind of balance when dealing with religious matters. This balance applied also to his notion of the *numinous*, depicting it as both attractive and repellent in giving rise to feelings of supreme fascination and tremendous mystery, of nameless dread and fear, of submergence and personal nothingness before the awe-inspiring directly experienced object—the *numinous* raw material for the feeling of religious humility. As he puts it: "... the numinous ... is at once daunting, and yet again singularly attracting, in its impress upon the mind" (Otto, 1917, p. 42).

Otto's prevailing importance for Jung is to be found in frequent reference to the *numinous* in the latter's work starting in the mid-1930s, though Jung adapted this notion to fit with what he referred to as his empirical *psychological* approach to religious issues. For instance, he states it would be a regrettable mistake to assume from *archetypal* God-images that they prove the existence of God. Instead, they are "... the most we can assert about God psychologically" (Jung, 1958a, p. 59). Both Otto and Jung draw on the *Book of Job* from the *Old Testament*, though here again, Jung's focus is on the "psychic nature and effects of 'the extraordinary numinosity' of the God-images" (1958a, p. 363).

The following are a few extracts from the various chapters by contributors to *The Idea of the Numinous* (Casement & Tacey, 2006), interrupted by a pertinent reference to the work of the neuropsychoanalyst Mark Solms on his theory of the origin of *consciousness*.

The Bionian psychoanalyst James Grotstein's Foreword shows the close connection between Jung and the psychoanalyst Bion's later work, in their approach to *numinosity*. Grotstein makes it clear that this is in sharp contrast to Freud in the following: "The concept of the numinous offers a dimension to our unconscious lives that is utterly missing in Freud" (p. xiv). David Tacey writes: "Jung does not challenge us with sexuality, but with something equally primary and perhaps more terrifying; the reality of the *numinous*" (p. 219). Similarly, Grotstein points to the psychoanalytic realisation of the primacy of affects rather than the primacy of the instinctual drives arising from the modernist trend towards subjectivity and intersubjectivity where they "begin to approximate the numinous because they are, originally, infinite in nature—and numinosity does seem to constitute an expression of affect, all be it, an affect of a very particular and ineffably distinctive nature" (p. xii). Furthermore, "Jung's allusions to the numinous are many, and most often concern the emotional, affective experience of the unconscious" (Huskinson, ibid., p. 202).

* * *

A brief digression seems relevant here to the work Jaak Panksepp and Mark Solms have done in this area, which led to their discovery that *consciousness* originates in the *affects* arising in the upper brain stem, not in the *cortical* region of the brain as previously postulated in psychoanalysis. This suggests that the fundamental form of *consciousness* is quintessentially *interoceptive* not, as formerly thought, *exteroceptive*. Since Jaak's recent death, when the discipline of *neuropsychoanalysis* founded by him and Mark lost one of the most brilliant affective neuroscientists of our time, Mark has continued with their joint work which led to his formulation of the theory of the *Conscious Id*. I have been to several presentations since the first conference of this new discipline in 2000 in London, when I became a founding member, and recommend the interested reader to Mark's and the brilliant neuroscientist and psychiatrist (and cleverest man in England according to Regius Professor of Psychiatry Sir Simon Wessely, past President of the Royal Society of Medicine) Karl Friston's paper on the *hard problem*, titled "How and Why Consciousness Arises: Preliminary Communication" (Solms & Friston, 2018) in the *Journal of Consciousness Studies*.

Mark's latest book is titled *The Hidden Spring: A Journey to the Source of Consciousness* (2021), in which he sets out his solution to the hard problem of consciousness. The vital work he is doing compensates for the fact that Freud's prescient *Project for a Scientific Psychology* has been criminally overlooked, with the exception of MIT's Marvin Minsky, in the literature on mind and brain. Readers interested in the latter topic are recommended to review work from the pioneering founders of the metascience of cybernetics. As a far-sighted analysis of control and communications, cybernetic principles such as feedback continue to underpin theories on mind and brain in the social and computational sciences. I have the good fortune to be tutored in cybernetics by a close associate doing research into AI and machine learning, and warmly urge interested readers to acquaint themselves with innovative thinkers like Mark or analytical psychologist members of the IAAP working on the mind–brain nexus.

I would like now to turn to the greatest literary author, Proust, for an exquisitely insightful depiction of varying states of *consciousness*:

> For me it was enough if, in my own bed, my sleep was so heavy as completely to relax my consciousness; for then I lost all sense of

the place in which I had gone to sleep, and when I awoke in the middle of the night, not knowing where I was, I could not even be sure at first who I was; I had only the most rudimentary sense of existence, such as may lurk and flicker in the depths of an animal's consciousness; I was more destitute than the cave-dweller; but then the memory—not yet of the place in which I was, but of various other places where I had lived and might now very possibly be— would come like a rope let down from heaven to draw me up out of the abyss of not-being, from which I could never have escaped by myself: in a flash I would traverse centuries of civilization, and out of a blurred glimpse of oil-lamps, then of shirts with turned-down collars, would gradually piece together the original components of my ego. (1913, p. 4)

* * *

Further references from other contributors to *The Idea of the Numinous* underline Grotstein's statements as follows:

> Jung ... personally engaged the 'God within' in a wholly psychological manner, and while he related to the *imago Dei* with the same passion and feeling for its mystery and awesome emotional power as did Otto, he related to it psychologically. (Stein, in Casement & Tacey, 2006, p. 120)

"For Jung, God seemed to be both divine and, in a terrible way, anything but divine ... 'on the one hand a bloody struggle, on the other supreme ecstasy'" (Bishop, ibid., p. 120). "... archetypal representations referring to Apollo and Dionysus ... show how they seem to be pointing at underlying psychic structures which are involved in the experience of that emotionally charged and consciousness-transforming *mysterium tremendum* which Otto named 'numinous'" (Giaccardi, ibid., p. 138). "What Jung called 'the numinous' and Derrida the 'sublime' ... engages the passions of ... the struggle between the logos god and eros goddess ... wrestling for the soul of modernity" (Rowland, ibid., p. 116). "The numinous affects what is uncontrolled in people and so can let loose dangerous psychic reactions in the public" (Main, ibid., p. 159).

Numinosity and the *alchemy* of individuating

Jung's writings often point the way in which his *psychological* approach to the analytical process is centred on the *numinous*, as the following quotation demonstrates: "… the main interest of my work is not concerned with the treatment of neuroses but rather with the approach to the numinous" (1973, p. 377). The following writers acknowledge this as exemplified by Murray Stein's statement: "The individuation process … typically includes experiences of a numinous nature" (Stein, in Casement & Tacey, 2006, p. 34). The late John Dourley stated: "Jung's equation of therapy with the experience of the numinous and with religious conversion has little or nothing to do with religion as commonly understood" (Dourley, ibid., p. 172). And Dourley again: "The psychological reality of Christ is the numinous experience of the self becoming incarnate in consciousness" (p. 181). And, Lucy Huskinson: "The numinous object cannot be forced or summoned into consciousness; it is not subject to the ego's control. Rather, the numinous object is discovered in its autonomous manifestation where it calls the ego into response" (Huskinson, ibid., p. 200).

As Edward Edinger said about the biblical *Job*, in his inspiring "little" book *Encounter with the Self*:

> If he were to decide that his misfortunes were all his own fault he would preclude the possibility of a manifestation of the *numinosum*. The ego-vessel would be broken, would lose its integrity, and could have no divine manifestation poured into it. By holding fast to its own experience as an authentic center of being, the Job-ego brings about the visible manifestation of the "other" the "transpersonal center". (1986, p. 43)

Jung states that *archetypes* possess a certain *numinosity* so that "… it is a psychological rule that when an archetype … becomes identified with the conscious mind of the individual … [it] produces an inflation of the subject" (1958a, p. 315). He is not referring to *narcissism* but to the enlargement of *consciousness*.

> I think that Genesis is right in so far as every step towards greater consciousness is a kind of Promethean guilt: through knowledge

the gods are as it were robbed of their fire, that is, something that was the property of the unconscious powers is torn out of its natural context and subordinated to the whims of the conscious mind. (1953, p. 156)

The knowledge meant here is that of greater *consciousness* which leads to an enlargement or inflation of the *ego*. This is an inevitable part of the *individuating* process though not without its dangers as the *ego* that remains identified with "unconscious powers" is in danger of becoming grandiose. It is this grandiosity that is a prime feature of *narcissism* that can be punctured and bring a person crashing down to earth.

The concept of dread

At the time of the Enlightenment, the contents of the Bible, in particular the myth of the fall of Adam and Eve, came under fresh scrutiny, depicting as it does the *numinous* conflict between good and evil. "Our angst-ridden age was heralded by Kierkegaard's *The Concept of Dread*, which postulates that dread is a *prelude* to sin not its *sequel* and may precede a shift from a state of ignorance to attainment of new awareness" (Casement, 1998, p. 70). Thus, if dread is a prelude to sin which precedes the attainment of new awareness, it follows on logically that dread is prospective.

This prospective component of *numinous* dread is akin to Jung's thinking on the prospective or purposive nature of *unconscious psychic* contents. Lucy Huskinson contrasts Otto's non-purposive interpretation of Job's *numinous* encounter with God with the purposive orientation of the "Jungian psyche", stating that the latter is grounded in the *holy* "as that which instils meaning and content in the *tremendum* … (as the wrath of God) … Without such mediation, we are unable to make sense of, and thus utilise, the creative energies unleashed in the numinous experience" (Huskinson, in Casement & Tacey, 2006, p. 208).

Paul Bishop, in his turn, points to Goethe's "… the Numinous, in the sense of the Monstrous" which links to 'analogous experiences in the case of C. G. Jung' and back to the Goethe quotation in Otto's work: 'When our eyes have glimpsed a monstrous act' " (Bishop, ibid., p. 118). It is this monstrous core of the *numinous* that "shows"—from the Latin *monstrare* meaning to show—*ego consciousness* the way towards what Jung terms *individuation* and the fateful transformations that are encountered by anyone travelling that path. It is in this way that Jung's psychology may be thought of as being embedded in the notion of the *numinous*.

Dream illustrating numinosity

> A terrible noise broke out in the night. I get up and discover that a frightened horse is tearing through the rooms. At last it finds the door into the hall, and jumps through the hall window from the fourth floor into the street below. I was terrified when I saw it lying there, all mangled. (Jung, 2001, p. 23)

The dreamer was a young woman who had been referred to Jung by another specialist, who suspected that she was suffering from an illness—possibly muscular atrophy. Jung's first thought was that the patient had a potentially fatal organic illness and his diagnosis was confirmed by the dream. The horse represents the animal life of the body and the dream shows the animal life destroying itself. Dreams may often portray the death of the dreamer though those usually point to a symbolic death. As can be seen from this particular dream, the death of the patient is not specified but the dream's *numinous* content is pointing to that.

CHAPTER 10

Individuation

A study in the process of individuation

The subtitle of this chapter replicates one by Jung in *Volume 9(i)*, and is a critical response to the study of an analysis he conducted in 1928 of an unmarried fifty-five-year-old American woman, referred to as Miss X, presumably to conceal her personal details. It is, in fact, easy to identify her as Kristine Mann from the information Jung included on her in the piece dated 1950. The series of paintings used for the study were done by her between 1928 and 1938.

Mann was one of a triumvirate of eminent women physicians in New York that included Eleanor Bertine and Esther Harding (there is a separate section on them later in this volume) who promoted Jungian psychology in the United States and who formed the nucleus of the group that developed into the New York C. G. Jung Society. This still houses the Kristine Mann Library, both of which I have visited from time to time. Mann also hosted Jung on his trip to New York in 1924. According to the ethos of the time, although Jung was well acquainted with her, he was, nevertheless able to see her for analysis. Needless to say, it would not be considered ethical practice in today's psychoanalytical world in the

UK and other parts of the world—though not all—to conduct analysis with an individual with whom one has such a close professional relationship. At that time, things were quite different with psychoanalysts of every persuasion taking it for granted it was acceptable to socialise with patients and even take them on holiday.

At the beginning of the study, Jung states that though unmarried, Mann "lived with the equivalent of a human partner, namely the animus (the personification of everything masculine in a woman) ..." which he goes on to elaborate perceptively as follows: "Her animus was not of the kind to give her cranky ideas. She was protected from this by her natural intelligence and by a remarkable readiness to tolerate the opinions of other people" (1959a, p. 291). In other words, she was a woman who had achieved an admirable maturity. Prior to arriving in Zürich to continue her studies and to have analysis with Jung, she visited Denmark, the homeland of her mother, where she was most affected by the landscape, which induced in her a desire to paint. As a result, she began to create watercolour landscapes that gave her "a strange feeling of contentment" (ibid.). She brought one of these to Jung, in which she is depicted with her lower half imprisoned in one of the rocks in the painting, which Jung interpreted as her *unconsciously* imprisoned in the mother. Some of the other rocks have a distinctively *phallic* shape, about which Jung states the following: "The sexual symbolism, which for many naïve minds is of such capital importance, was no discovery for her" and which, according to Jung, had no significance for the patient (ibid., p. 292). The quotation is an obvious criticism aimed at Freud; these appear frequently in Jung's writings, and indicate the fact that Jung, himself, was stuck in negative feelings towards Freud. This was to prove disastrous for Jung personally, as witnessed by the subsequent stain of anti-Semitism still associated with his name, as well as for Jung the psychoanalyst, as it led him to completely dismiss any *erotic transference*, glaringly apparent in some of the material Mann produced. Instead, he claims that, in view of the patient's age, it was not relevant in her case.

Simultaneously with eschewing this much-needed work in the *transference–countertransference*, Jung states as follows: "I could already see what solution the unconscious had in mind, namely individuation" (1959a, p. 293). This extraordinary assertion may be an unfortunate mistranslation of what he *actually* wrote, as this statement, as it stands, makes the claim that the "the *unconscious*" has a *conscious* mind. As that goes against the law of non-contradiction, the reader is left to draw the obvious conclusion *that* is what the analyst had in mind, of which there is ample evidence throughout this account. In any case, does Jung's notion of the *individuation* process at any life stage not include developing oneself as a fully embodied being? Did Jung not learn from his own erotic encounters how essential that was? On the contrary, the impression one gains from this account is that he was stuck in his head and had little experience of the erotic side of life, which is contradicted by what is known about his biographical details. Furthermore, how does one reconcile his dismissal of sexuality with his statement about the necessity of linking *consciousness* with "the instinctual foundation. Anyone who overlooks the instincts will be ambuscaded by them" (1959a, p. 350)? Though he states: "Sex in this case is … no problem at all" (p. 318).

There are other certainties running through this account, for instance, the following: "There can be no doubt that the dark stone means the blackness, i.e. the unconscious" (ibid., p. 301). And, again: "It would be idle to talk of 'repression' here, since *we know* that the unconscious goes straight for its goal" (ibid., p. 303; my italics). Who are "we" and to what does "know" refer? These kinds of dogmatic assertions on Jung's part are among the unsettling features of this study, along with the lack of any consistent analytical, as opposed to academic, approach to the work with the patient accompanied by yet another dig at Freud. The above are only some instances of the language in this study that need to be deconstructed.

Another point that needs closer investigation is where Mann was encouraged to continue with her paintings, many of which are reproduced in the book and which are, unsurprisingly, *mandalas*, mirroring Jung's own obsession with them. This *acting-in* of the *transference* was not interpreted to the patient but was, instead, used by Jung to illustrate his own thinking on *alchemy*, *archetypes*, *psychological types*, and mythology. At the same time, he states: "… there could be no question of my having unintentionally infected her … These pictures are, in all essentials, genuine creations of the unconscious" (ibid., p. 304). The latter statement is not based on any supporting evidence. It is the case that Jung's knowledge about *alchemy* did not exist at that time but he certainly knew about *archetypes*, *mandalas*, mythology, and *psychological types*, rendering his disclaimer hollow. As a result, for much of the study, the individual patient is buried under a welter of esoteric speculation. It is unsurprising that Emma Jung is reported to have said to her husband: "You know very well that you are not interested in anybody unless they exhibit archetypes!" (Fordham, 1993, p. 117). As already noted, this is an instance of the analyst letting his own obsession get in the way of analysing the patient, instead using her as an object on which to project his ideas. In the few instances in this material when Jung focuses on the actual patient as an *individual*, he makes perceptive comments about Mann's *psychology* as reported at the beginning of this critique.

The interaction between the two protagonists remained on a safe intellectual, "spiritual" level most of the time, recapitulating the *actual* relationship with her father. The patient had brought her presenting problem to the analysis in her first picture where the lower half of the body remained imprisoned in a rock. That would point to her lack of access to her own erotic side confirmed by the fact there is no mention of her sexual orientation, sexual experience, or anything to do with her sexuality throughout this long account. She tells Jung at the beginning that she experiences him as a medieval sorcerer with a magic wand, which could usefully have been interpreted in the *transference* as a *phallic* magic wand that could help release her *Eros* from imprisonment.

The whole analysis should have been grounded in the here-and-now of the *transference–countertransference*. It is, in fact, the patient who comes to the realisation that her *transference* onto the analyst was that of father's daughter, and that she was behaving in the sessions like "an intelligent, understanding pupil". As a result of this insight, she finally became more aware of herself as an earthy being which, according to Jung, "is more characteristic of women", thus keeping himself above any reciprocal *countertransference* earthy feelings (1959a, p. 334). This breakthrough on the patient's part enabled her to mourn her regret at never having had children, in relation to which Jung states: "Real liberation comes not from glossing over or *repressing* painful states of feeling but only from experiencing them to the full" (p. 335), a much-needed *regression* he appears to have done nothing to foster. This kind of necessary *regression* in an analysis is greatly facilitated through the use of the couch by a patient, a practice that was/is eschewed by Jung and by *classical* Jungians as a vital part of analytical practice because it is (negatively) associated with *mainstream* psychoanalysis. I have seen the consulting rooms of some of these practitioners and have noted there is no couch to be utilised when needed.

Over the course of decades of practising as a *psychoanalyst*, I came, a long time ago, to the realisation that each patient is an individual needing a bespoke treatment geared to her or his own needs. In order to do this, I set about familiarising myself with other psychoanalytic and psychotherapeutic approaches, including *classical Freudian, contemporary Freudian, neuropsychoanalysis, Kleinian, Bionian, neo-Kleinian, Lacanian,* and *cognitive behavioural therapy* (particularly helpful in treating *obsessive compulsive disorder*), either through attending seminars and conferences on them or having supervision or co-supervision with an analyst/therapist from those orientations or, in the case of neuropsychoanalysis, by being a part of its inception. For a number of years, I chaired one of the profession's regulatory bodies in the UK that has on its register practitioners from all those disciplines, during which time I informed myself about them as best I could, which has broadened my own psychoanalytic approach—theoretical as well as practical. This is what is meant by *continuing professional development* as it is known in the UK, and is also the best way psychoanalysts and psychotherapists can be of service to their patients/*analysands*, the prime purpose of being in the profession.

Another aspect of this study that needs a critical eye cast on it is that it was written up some years after the analysis ended, but it is not specified what parts of it belong to the time it was taking place or what parts are esoteric speculation added later and at which times. Towards the end, Jung states: "… sixteen years later, Miss X became fatally ill with cancer of the breast" (ibid., p. 344). Again, it is unclear when exactly that was. As the work was not grounded in any *transference–countertransference*, the study has the air of an academic speculative work, which is interesting enough as an insight into the development of Jung's thinking but not of a psychoanalysis.

The presentation of psychoanalytic material needs to convey a sense of being *real* without becoming *actual*, a difficult task which is why so many presentations given at conferences, whatever the presenting problem or whether it is based on insecure attachment, trauma, borderline personality disorder, or any other current pathologies, are mostly worthy but dull. One only has to think of the current obsession with the *here-and-now* that is interpreted solely *in* the *transference–countertransference* practised by many psychoanalysts at the British Psychoanalytical Society, where every allusion to another person by the patient is reflected back as *You Mean Me!* This was prominently on display at the July 2019 centenary conference of *The International Journal of Psychoanalysis* in London, where world-renowned (at least in the psychoanalytic arena) speakers happily trotted out this kind of tedium without being challenged by any of the participants. A glaringly obvious *slip* on the part of one of the aforementioned "world-renowned" practitioners was passed over without comment, the whole tone of the proceedings being one of sycophancy mirrored by self-congratulatory showboating. One of *the* pioneering discoveries of the twentieth century has not been well served by many of its practitioners, nor has the creative genius who founded that great discipline in the late nineteenth century.

Genius or not, even Freud needs to be subjected to retrospective criticism of some of his actions, though criticising the ancestors of the psychoanalytic profession is fraught with difficulty, none more so than the founding father himself. But remaining stuck in unresolved idealisations is worse and does not facilitate what Jung refers to as *individuation*. A few years ago, the neo-Kleinian, Ron Britton, launched a critique of Freud's two analyses of his daughter, Anna. I agree with his claim, "… it is absolutely necessary we return to these historical events armed with … current psychoanalytic concepts" (Britton, 2003, p. 60), and also with his caveat that "… it is not a comfortable thing to do, as nowadays we live in a culture of disparagement that is hungry for any information that might be used to discredit rather than inform" (ibid.).

As the greater part of this chapter has focused on a critical review of Jung's 1950 study, it is something of a relief to end on a positive note in his direction with the following quotation that is as relevant today as it was when it first appeared.

> The political and social *isms* of our day preach every conceivable ideal, but, under this mask, they pursue the goal of lowering the level of our culture by restricting or altogether inhibiting the possibilities of individual development. They do this partly by creating a chaos controlled by terrorism … and surpasses in horror

the worst times of the so-called "Dark" Ages ... This problem cannot be solved collectively, because the masses are not changed unless the individual changes. (1958a, p. 349)

Jung was referring to the "horror" of his times in the form of the twinned *isms* of fascism and communism, but what he says has a disturbing reso-nance with the present epoch situated in the first quarter of the twenty-first century where myriad *isms* are constantly projected outwards by those who lack any capacity for self-reflection on their own *shadow*. Today's world is filled with the shrill cacophony of these screechers.

CHAPTER 11

A critical appraisal of C. G. Jung's *Psychological Alchemy*

Preface

An earlier version of this chapter was given as part of a lecture at Gakushuin University in Tokyo, in August 2016. Its focus will be on two models of *psychological alchemy* separated by a brief interlude on the ten well-known *Zen* ox-herding pictures. Following the Preamble, the first account is a lengthy description of Jung's thinking on the subject of *psychological alchemy*. The second part is devoted to Wolfgang Giegerich's critique of this.

Preamble

Psychological alchemy as theorised and practised by Jung and some of his followers was, as this chapter claims, one of the most important contributions to twentieth-century psychology, which has its roots in the ancient practice of *alchemy*. The latter is a cross-cultural phenomenon dating back to antiquity in various parts of the world, including Arabia, China, Egypt, England, France, Germany, Greece, India, Japan, Persia, and Spain. The founding father of *Eastern alchemy* appears to have been

Wei Po-yang, who produced the earliest known Chinese treatise on *alchemy* in 142 CE, although it had been practised in China for some centuries before that time.

In the *West*, *alchemy* appears to have originated in Hellenistic Egypt in approximately 300 BCE; its purported originator being named Hermes Trismegistus (Thrice Great) by the Greeks, who is associated with the Egyptian scribe god, Thoth, the personification of wisdom, and with the Greek god of communication, Hermes. *Hermetics*, the body of knowledge that grew out of *alchemy*, incorporates the physical, astral, and spiritual disciplines over which Hermes (or *Mercurius*—see below) rules, is the highest knowledge one can attain. The term *Hermetic* also means tightly sealed, which is relevant to the alchemical *container*, a metaphor for the secure *analytical container*. "As above, so below" (Jung, 1967, p. 140) is the saying from the Emerald Tablet of Hermes Trismegistus associated with this body of knowledge that Jung often quotes in his writings. From 1300 to 1600 CE, *Hermetics* was an important source of knowledge for scientists as it incorporated a way of influencing and controlling nature.

An analysis of the insightful saying "As above, so below", the key axiom from *alchemy*, is the following: "As above" indicates the macrocosm, namely, the universe or God. "So below" points to the microcosm, namely, the physical world of human beings. This has been linked theoretically to the *global* and *local* inextricably mixed in *chaos theory*, a branch of mathematics that studies the behaviour of dynamical systems that are highly sensitive to initial conditions, for instance, a butterfly flapping its wings in New Mexico at the right point in space–time can cause a hurricane in China—referred to as the *Butterfly Effect*.

Alchemy's heyday in Europe was during medieval and early modern times, the latter period spanning the late fifteenth century, when printing was invented, and the eighteenth century. One of its best-known practitioners, Paracelsus, the sixteenth-century Swiss physician and alchemist, is often referenced by Jung. There were three main aims in the practice of *alchemy*: turning base metals into gold; trying to find a panacea (the *elixir* or *philosopher's stone*) that would prolong life; and the attempt to produce various substances that would increase the production of vegetation. In early modern Europe, alchemists were mostly concerned with creating pharmacological concoctions though most attached some religious significance to their work as they were dealing with God's creation—nature.

The pre-eminent seventeenth- to eighteenth-century scientist, Isaac Newton, spent between thirty and forty years experimenting on *alchemy* in his laboratory; apart from any other outcome, this helped inform his treatise on light called *Opticks*. Newton produced an enormous volume of writing in his quest for the *philosopher's stone*; some parts of these writings were later purchased by the twentieth-century economist, John Maynard Keynes, who contributed them in 1946 to Cambridge University. Newton had to keep secret his alchemical experiments (called "chymistry" at that time) as they would have been considered heretical by the Christian Church. Newton was well aware that science advances through effort accumulated over centuries when he acknowledged that if he had seen further it was by standing on the shoulders of giants. I dare speculate that although this well-known sentiment is usually attributed to his forerunners in science such as the polymath, Descartes, he was also alluding to the mysteries unravelled in the course of his alchemical quest.

Following this brief preamble, the purpose of which was to illustrate the universality of the practice of *alchemy*, let us now turn to Jung's interest in the discipline. Almost everything that was important in his life was presaged by dreams, as was the case with his discovery of *alchemy*. That particular dream series culminated in the following crucial one in 1926:

> I was in the South Tyrol. It was wartime. I was on the Italian front line with a little man, a peasant, in his horse-drawn wagon. All around us shells were exploding, and I knew that we had to push on as quickly as possible, for it was very dangerous.
>
> We had to cross a bridge and then go on through a tunnel whose vaulting had been partially destroyed by the shells. Arriving at the end of the tunnel, we saw before us a sunny landscape, and I recognized it as the region around Verona. Below me lay the city, radiant in full sunlight. I felt relieved, and we drove out into the green, thriving Lombard plain. The road led through lovely springtime countryside; we saw the rice fields, the olive trees, and the vineyards. Then, diagonally across the road, I caught sight of a large building, a manor house of grand proportions, rather

like the palace of a North Italian duke. It was a typical manor house with many annexes and outbuildings. Just as at the Louvre, the road led through a large courtyard and past the palace. The little coachman and myself drove in through a gate, and from here we could see, through a second gate at the far end, the sunlit landscape again. I looked round: to my right was the façade of the manor house, to my left the servants' quarters and the stables, barns, and other outbuildings, which stretched on for a long way.

Just as we reached the middle of the courtyard, in front of the main entrance, something unexpected happened: with a dull clang, both gates flew shut. The peasant leaped down from his seat and exclaimed, "Now we are caught in the seventeenth century." Resignedly I thought, "Well, that's that! But what is there to do about it? Now we shall be caught for years." Then the consoling thought came to me: "Someday, years from now, I shall get out again." (1963, p. 194)

The Secret of the Golden Flower

Another relevant dream that preceded this one depicted him being in a large house, or wing of a house, where he discovered a wonderful library dating from the sixteenth and seventeenth centuries. It contained a number of books full of copper engravings of a strange character and symbols he had never seen before, which he realised many years later were alchemical symbols. At the time of these dreams, Jung was mystified as to what these could relate to until, in 1928, the Sinologist, Richard Wilhelm, sent him an exposition on Chinese *alchemy* called *The Secret of the Golden Flower*. I have been informed by the Chinese scholar, Dangwei Zhou, that the original Chinese title of this text was *The Mystery of the Golden Light of the Supreme Unity*. Jung and Wilhelm published this text in the November 1929 *Europäische Revue, Volume 2/8*, though, following Jung's suggestion, the title was changed to *The Secret of the Golden Flower*.

In this text, Jung claimed he had discovered a parallel with the analytical process, namely, the alchemical *opus* of extracting gold from base metals. For Jung, this was the equivalent, in *psychological* terms, of the extraction of the gold of *consciousness* from its source deep in the base metal/matter of *unconsciousness* ultimately leading to the higher union of the two *psychic* realms.

Jung's commentary on *The Secret of the Golden Flower* contains some of his memorable sayings, for example, his warning to anyone who believes they have outgrown gods and demons, as follows:

> What we have left behind are ... not the psychic facts that were responsible for the birth of the gods. We are still as much possessed by autonomous psychic contents as if they were Olympians. Today they are called phobias, obsessions, and so forth; in a word neurotic symptoms. The gods have become diseases. (1967, p. 37)

In the same commentary, he also states that the fundamental problems of life cannot be solved but simply outgrown. This is inherently so, according to Jung, as they express the necessary polarity in the *psyche*'s self-regulating system. It is remaining stuck in a problem that is pathological.

Why *alchemy?*

In order to address the question embedded in the title above, we shall return to some of the salient points in the foregoing dream which are relevant to our topic. First, although World War I had ended eight years before this dream, Jung deduces from it that the conflict continues to be fought *intrapsychically*. As a result, he had to turn his vision "inwards" to find the solution to the problems represented by the dangerous shells exploding around him and the peasant. In doing so, Jung arrived at the conclusion that they were missiles from the realm of the *collective unconscious*, the primordial inherited structure of the brain from where everything irrational proceeds, already defined earlier in this book. It is relevant to repeat here that the *self* refers to the totality of the personality and is the essence of individuality as against the *archetypes*, which are universal and belong to the generality. When *archetypal* contents erupt into *consciousness*, they have a highly charged emotional impact and bring with them an experience of *psychic reality*. It is these deeply structured phenomena introduced by Jung that we shall be dealing with in this section.

The second point to note from the dream is the coachman's realisation expressed as follows: "Now we are caught in the seventeenth century." That century was the heyday of alchemical experimentation in trying to *transmute* lead, or base matter, into gold, which Jung knew nothing about at the time of the dream. Furthermore, the *little* peasant coachman puts one in mind of the *homunculus* or "Little Man", who is an important figure in *Faust*, Part 2. He is created by Faust, the alchemist, in the *alembic* or glass jar used by alchemists in their experiments, and acts as a *psychopomp*, that is, a guide to the inner world. It is the *homunculus* that realises Faust needs to develop his feminine side, who thus leads him to the land of Greek mythology and an encounter with Helen. The Italian landscape in the dream may stand for an idyllic pastoral vision, a Garden of Eden, wherein lives the *noble savage* uncorrupted by civilisation, namely, the trappings of *ego*.

In the sixteenth-century alchemical text we shall be studying in this chapter, Jung registered the fact that certain words or phrases reappeared throughout, for example, *Mercurius, vas, lapis, prima materia, philosopher's stone*. Following a prolonged study of alchemical texts, Jung came to realise that the alchemists were expressing themselves in *symbols*, through their oft-repeated saying that their gold was *not* the common gold. As symbols are key components of Jung's *psychological* approach, this led to his conclusion that analytical psychology and *alchemy* overlap in many ways. He goes on to speculate—a key stance in *psychological alchemy*—that the alchemists preferred to be thought of as gold-makers rather than be accused of heresy, a serious charge at that time.

Proceeding from this discovery, Jung began to make an all-important historical link between *alchemy* and intellectual *Gnosticism* though the former was closer in time to his *psychological* work. Finding this historical link gave credence to the *archetypal psychic* contents he had discovered in his work with patients. Furthermore, the earthy erotic images of *alchemy* were compensatory to the sexless imagery of Christianity. Jung remained a lifelong, albeit critical, Protestant despite his interest in other religions and esoteric phenomena, so that his *psychological* work may be seen as a kind of religious quest. Above all, what he claimed to be the true *opus* of the more serious-minded alchemists was equated with his own quest of *individuation*. "My life has been permeated and held together by one idea and one goal: namely to penetrate into the secrets of the personality" (Jung, 1963, p. 197). These latter points underline the fact that Jung, the psychologist, was a *religious* thinker. Furthermore, the *archetypal* transmutation at work in *alchemy* gave Jung insight into his inner relationship to Goethe, and in particular to the latter's *magnum opus, Faust*. We have already touched on the *homunculus*, though the figure of Mephistopheles from that work bears a striking resemblance to *Mercurius*, the *trickster* ruler of *alchemy* who stands for the spirit buried in matter. For Jung, *alchemy* was above all a *metaphor* for his way of working with *unconscious* material in analysis.

Before proceeding further, it is vital to have Jung's definition of *Mercurius*, the central figure in *alchemy*. As is suitable for such an elusive substance, Jung associates *Mercurius* with mercury, slippery, difficult to get hold of, which appears to be all things to all people. For instance, *Mercurius* consists of all conceivable opposites, namely, feminine and masculine; matter and spirit; it is the alchemical process itself that transmutes the lower into the higher and vice versa; is the devil as well as God's reflection in physical nature; and stands for all the Jungian notions that have already been elaborated above, namely, the *self, collective unconscious*, and the *individuation* process. It is the dialectical work of *psychological alchemy* to release this *mercurial* spirit from the base matter of the *unconscious*, namely, nature, through a *recursive* process of *fermentation, corruption, putrefaction, mortification, refinement, distillation*—alchemical terms—in the laboratory of the mind.

As we can see from the foregoing, there were many cogent reasons for Jung's fascination with and dedication to the alchemical *opus* from 1929 (he also sometimes gives the date as 1930) until the end of his life in 1961. The approach favoured in this chapter, however, is based on a hypothesis of another deeply personal reason as to why Jung had to undertake this work, namely, that of *incest*.

Transference–countertransference

The twinned term *transference–countertransference* is central to the *psychological alchemical* process we shall be exploring in this work so I shall start with a definition of what that means. In psychoanalytic terminology, the *transference* applies to the *projections* from the *analysand* onto, or, more precisely, *into* the analyst. On one level, these *projections* are made up of *shadow* contents along with those of *complexes*, feeling-toned autonomous sub-personalities that exist in all of us. The latter phenomena generally link back to the patient's past life. A simple example to illustrate this would be if the patient had a negative relationship with the personal father leading to a *negative father complex* being constellated, as a result of which, the analyst might be experienced as a negative paternalistic authority figure. *Transferences* are loaded with *affect* and can have a powerful impact on both *analysand* and analyst. This kind of *transference* is related to unresolved childhood deprivations and desires still alive in the adult *analysand* that need to be *worked through* by way of *regression* to infantile states. In this way, the patient is helped along the path of the maturational process.

The term *countertransference* applies to the feelings that are *introjected* by the analyst as a result of the analysand's *transference projections*. This may be termed the *personal transference–countertransference* where the analyst is largely in control and the *analysand* is being analysed *by* the analyst with a view to enabling the *analysand* to come to terms with outer reality, known as the *transference work*.

The emphasis in this presentation will be on another kind of *transference–countertransference* which is not aimed at helping the *analysand* to "grow up". This may occur in the course of an in-depth analysis and is referred to by Jung as *archetypal transference–countertransference*. This will be elucidated as we explore the structure of the process, to be seen in the way Jung frames in-depth analysis along alchemical lines. This is a dialectical process that involves both *analysand* and analyst in an immersion in *unconscious* contents that can result in the *mutual* transformation of both. This *transference process* arises from an *incestuous* relationship between analyst and *analysand* as both are linked through kinship and psychologically share the same familial goal of bringing *unconsciousness* back to *consciousness*.

A point to note here is that the alchemical process is not a once-and-for-all experience but may recur in the course of in-depth analysis. This results in analyst and *analysand* becoming increasingly aware that alchemical processes are not to be found only in analysis but are recurring experiences, usually initiated by problems and difficulties, throughout life. In *working through* these, analyst and *analysand* discover their own path in life or what Jung called *individuation*. Incestuous relations underlie all early familial experiences, which become manifest in the psychoanalytical relationship. At those points, it is vital they are not concretised and *acted-in* but recognised and valued for what they are and then worked on through the *psychological alchemical* process of *corruption* and *distillation* until they can be symbolised.

The symbolic cannot be reduced to something else, which is what is depicted in the sixteenth-century alchemical text we will be studying here.

> This does not mean that the adept ceased to work in the laboratory, only that he kept an eye on the symbolic aspects of his transmutations. This corresponds exactly to the situation in the modern psychology of the unconscious: while personal problems are not overlooked (the patient himself takes very good care of that!), the analyst keeps an eye on their symbolic aspects, for healing comes only from what leads the patient beyond himself and beyond his entanglements in the ego. (Jung, 1967, p. 302)

Sabina Spielrein

Following on from what has been said in the preceding section, one begins to get an insight into Jung's intense preoccupation with *alchemy*, which led to his insistence that the first English translation of the *Collected Works* should be *Psychology and Alchemy* (personal communication, Gerhard Adler). Jung was particularly interested in the affinity between the ideas expressed in *alchemy* and his thoughts about *archetypal transference–countertransference*, which he went on to explore in his 1946 work "The Psychology of the Transference". In order to do this, he undertook a lengthy analysis of what he saw as *symbolic* transformation in ten woodcuts from a 1550 alchemical text called *The Rosarium Philosophorum*, rendered in English as *The Rosary of the Philosophers* or, alternatively, as *The Rose Garden*.

Jung claimed there was an analogy between these ten woodcuts and the analytic situation, wherein an *incestuous* attraction may arise between analyst and *analysand* when *archetypal* processes are activated in the course of an in-depth analysis. The energy or *libido* that is released as a result of this may flow simultaneously in a variety of directions leading to states of great confusion. At these times, the analytic relationship is tested to the full and may, indeed, break down if the powerful energies are not contained but, instead, are *acted-in*. These ten woodcuts are reproduced on pp. 120–130.

"The Psychology of the Transference" may be viewed as a final working through of the powerfully erotic encounter Jung had, as a young psychiatrist working at Burghölzli Hospital in Zürich, with Sabina Spielrein. The latter was a nineteen-year-old Russian Jewish patient who had been admitted in 1904 diagnosed as suffering from *hysteria*. Jung had read Freud's *The Interpretation of Dreams* (1900a), and was so impressed by it that he adopted the new technique of psychoanalysis in his work with Spielrein, his first psychoanalytic patient. She was discharged from Burghölzli Hospital in 1905 still under Jung's care and, from that time, their joint erotic *transference–countertransference* feelings began to emerge as set forth in her diaries and letters. The intensity of their relationship peaked in the years 1908 to 1911, during which time both were in touch with Freud seeking his help. Jung was, by now, afraid of jeopardising his personal life (recently married with a child) and professional career, and they eventually went their separate ways, though as the Jungian psychoanalyst, Aldo Carotenuto, states:

> It is reasonable to suppose that whenever Jung touched on the subject of the analyst's relations with the patient, his thought, both conscious and unconsciously, was nourished by his former experience, and in *The Psychology of the Transference* the memory of one of the first intense relationships in his life may well have reappeared with renewed ardour. (1980, p. 207)

Let us look more closely at what was taking place in the *transference–countertransference* between Spielrein and Jung. The most easily observable of the patient's symptoms were tics, grimaces, and gestures of abhorrence, accompanied by severe headaches. The patient's premature sexuality, compulsive masturbation, and anal eroticism initially remained hidden but, once they manifested, were linked by Jung to the physical punishment the father inflicted on her, often hitting her on her bare buttocks in front of her brothers. She saw herself as a bad and corrupt person who should not be allowed to associate in the company of others. Jung was regularly reporting on the case to Freud so it seems extraordinary that neither psychoanalyst diagnosed her illness as having its origin in the *incestuous* relationship with father.

One may speculate that, for Freud, this oversight related to his abandonment in 1897 of his earlier hypothesis of *actual* incest between father and daughter. Instead, he substituted *incestuous* fantasies on the part of the daughter for the father and of the son for the mother. This represents a vital turning point in Freud's theorising that gave birth to psychoanalysis, with the situating of the universal *Oedipus complex* at the core of individual development as Freud substituted the *reality* of fantasy for the *actuality* of physical incest. The omission of a diagnosis of incest on Jung's part may well relate to the fact that he was always ambivalent about Freud's *libido* theory, though his notes contain the following about the beatings "... even though the peak of the experience was that her father was a *man*" (Graf-Nold, 2001, p. 87). It is the aim of this chapter to show that the abundant references to incest that appear on almost every page throughout "The Psychology of the Transference" may be Jung's way of making reparation for his previous oversight of the importance of dealing with the *incestuous transference–countertransference* in psychoanalytic work—both literal and symbolic. "... the fatal touch of incest and its 'perverse fascination' symbolizes union with one's own being as a psychic reality, i.e., *individuation* through the endlessly recurring *uroboric* process" (1954, p. 217). This *incestuous* relationship with oneself is fundamentally what Jung was exploring through *psychological alchemy*.

What Jung writes about Nietzsche's *Thus Spoke Zarathustra* may equally apply to the way he experienced working on the *transference–countertransference* in the *The Rosarium*: "... *Zarathustra* is one of the books that is written with blood, and anything written with blood contains the notion of that subtle body the equivalent of the somatic unconscious" (Jarrett, 1988, p. 443).

For Jung, this reached its culmination in "The Psychology of the Transference", in which *anima/animus*, twinned *archetypes*, are central to the *transference–countertransference process* of *working through affectively* laden *incestuous* longings that are present in *archetypal transference–countertransference*, the instigator of which is, inevitably, familial. Jung's emphasis on the fact that analysis is a relationship, albeit a special kind of relationship, which needs to be contained in the *analytic container* or the *alchemical retort*, is a hugely important discovery for psychoanalysis.

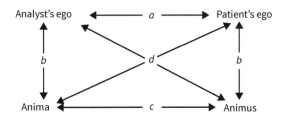

Diagram illustrating the transference–countertransference

The series of triangles in this economical diagram created by Jung that appears at the beginning of "The Psychology of the Transference", express the various directions that *transference–countertransference* can take in the course of in-depth analysis. The straight line (a) at the top is the relatively uncomplicated personal relationship which helps create the *treatment alliance*. The straight downward line (b) on the left side indicates the analyst drawing on her *unconscious* and being in touch with her inner *wounded healer* for an understanding of the patient's suffering. The straight downward line (b) on the right represents the patient's initial awareness of the problems but also *resistance* to that awareness. The two diagonal lines (d) indicate the impact of the analytical relationship on the *unconscious* of the two participants; while the bottom straight line (c) points to a direct *unconscious* communication between them which underpins the core of Jung's approach to *archetypal transference–countertransference*.

Particular attention should be paid to line (c) as it describes the phenomenon of *psychic contagion* or *projective identification*. Let us return to Jung and Spielrein to bring these notions to life. In the course of the erotic relationship that existed between them, she wrote to Freud in 1909 as follows: "Four and a half years ago Dr Jung was my doctor; then he became my friend and finally my 'poet', i.e., my beloved. Eventually he came to me and things went as they usually do with 'poetry'" (Carotenuto, 1984, p. 93). Freud thought that with a bit more analysis everything could be resolved, including Spielrein's fantasy that "poetry" would lead to the birth of an actual child, Siegfried. Jung, who was Christian, and Spielrein, who was Jewish, fantasised about having an Aryan-Semitic love child. In this regard, Jung eventually wrote to Spielrein in a letter dated 21st January 1918: "You are always trying to drag the Siegfried symbol back into reality, whereas in fact it is the bridge to your individual development ... That is, individuation" (Carotenuto, 1984, p. 54).

It is valid to hypothesise that Jung's working through of the turbulent emotions evoked in him by the affair eventually led to his 1946 paper "The Psychology of the Transference" in which appears the symbolic "*coniunctio*", namely, the union of *anima/animus* as depicted in line (c) of the diagram. This leads to the culmination of the alchemical process, namely, the birth of the symbolic "*divine child*", that is, *individuation*, which links to the longed-for *Siegfried*. Spielrein was also the inspiration for Jung's notion of *anima* and for deepening his experience of *countertransference*. This diagram succinctly illustrates Jung's view that *alchemy* was a metaphor for *archetypal transference–countertransference*, which results in an *incestuous* attraction not only between the two participants but, even more importantly, *within* the *analysand* and the analyst that Jung termed *kinship libido*. The latter stems from what Jung refers to as the "... numinous idea, the archetype of incest" (1967, p. 301). He claimed that it was through the *symbolisation* of this incestuous *libido* that the *psychological alchemical* work comes to its fruition. This is illustrated by way of the following ten woodcut images.

The Rosarium Philosophorum

Figure 1 contains much alchemical symbolism: the sun and moon as opposites; the four elements depicted by four stars; and the mercurial fountain and vessel (*vas*), namely, the *alchemical retort* as an analogy of the psychoanalytic *container* wherein transmutation takes place. The rise and flow of the water in the fountain characterises *Mercurius*, the ruler of *alchemy*, as the serpent endlessly fertilising and devouring itself until it gives birth to itself again, the *uroboros* that is the *recursive* work of *alchemy*. Here we see, even at this early stage, the *recursive* nature of the

Figure 1. The Mercurial Fountain

alchemical process. The aroused energy of transformation is depicted by the image of the water flowing from the fountain, underlining the fact that psychoanalysis is not an intellectual exercise but one that is driven by *affect* which, at the same time, must be *distilled* and *contained* in the analytic vessel or *vas*.

As previously mentioned, Jung saw *alchemy* as connecting him in a deep way to *Faust*, the scholar and alchemist of Goethe's well-known text already touched on, who projected his own unredeemed dark side into *alchemy* until Mephistopheles, the devil (*Mercurius/Trickster*) manifested in his life.

> I regard my work on alchemy as a sign of my inner relationship to Goethe. Goethe's secret was that he was in the grip of that process of archetypal transformation, which has gone on through the centuries. He regarded his *Faust* as an *opus magnum*. (1963, p. 197)

Let us look at how **Figure 1** may be applied to actual analysis between two people. To begin with, one has to take on board the fact that the alchemical process is not a once-and-for-all experience but is, as has already been stated, a dialectical *recursive* process. This means that in the course of a long in-depth analysis, there are likely to be repeated experiences of an alchemical nature, for instance, when a new or recurring problem presents itself in the patient/*analysand*'s life. This may be signalled by a dream about a family member from the *analysand*'s early life who continues to be particularly problematic for the *analysand*. This will usually be accompanied by an increase in *affect* with corresponding anxiety levels likely to go up as *consciousness* once more descends to its source in *unconsciousness*. In this way may be seen the dialectic of the alchemical process as a *spiral* whereby the analysis keeps coming back to the same place but each time with a slight increase of awareness into the problem. The pair are garbed in royal clothes to underline their *archetypal* nature. The quintessential star in the picture represents transcendent *wholeness*.

A word of caution is needed here, namely, that it is helpful to view Jung's essay on *alchemy* as providing a theoretical framework to the psychoanalytic process rather than as an exact depiction of what takes place in the consulting room.

Figure 2 brings out in the open the element of incest that is an essential component of *archetypal transference–countertransference*. The king and queen, bridegroom and bride, are depicted standing on the sun and moon, these latter pointing to the *incestuous* relationship of Apollo and Artemis, the Greek mythological brother and sister. This is further emphasised by the left-handed contact between the two—that is from the sinister or *unconscious* side. Further associations with the left side are to do with the heart, which is related to love but also to all the moral contradictions that are connected with *affective* states.

The couple are holding a device of two flowers in their right hands which represent the criss-crossing of the analytic relationship as set out in the preceding section. This represents the multiple relations that may be constellated between analyst and *analysand* in the course of in-depth analysis. The four sides of the cross each represent the four elements as fire and air, active and masculine; and on the other, as water and earth, passive and feminine. These are further crossed at their meeting point from above by a flower held in the beak of a dove descending from the quintessential star and representing the dove of the Christian Holy Ghost, or the point at which opposites are reconciled.

Figure 2. King and Queen

Imagination is the star in man, the celestial or supercelestial body. This astounding definition throws a quite special light on the fantasy processes connected with the *opus*. We have to conceive of these processes not as the immaterial phantoms we readily take fantasy-pictures to be, but as something corporeal, a "subtle-body", semi-spiritual in nature. (Jung, 1953, p. 277)

This is a vital message to take on board as what Jung is pointing to here is that, in an age before empirical psychology, this kind of concretisation was inevitable because everything *unconscious*, once it was activated, was projected into matter—a hybrid phenomenon, half spiritual/half physical. The act of imagining was a physical activity and the alchemist related himself not only to the *unconscious* but directly to the very substance which he hoped to transform through the power of imagination. In that way, there existed an intermediate realm between mind and matter, that is, a *psychic* realm of "*subtle bodies*", whose characteristic is to manifest itself in a mental as well as a material form.

It is important to bear in mind that, although Jung was critical of Christianity, he remained a lifelong Protestant (personal communication, Sonu Shamdasani) so that his writings were permeated with Christian symbolism. He did, of course, also cite references in his work to texts from other religious and esoteric sources, as evidenced by alchemical allusions.

According to Jung, the *incest* that is portrayed in **Figure 2** is a central characteristic of the alchemical approach to analytical work, though it should be noted he is not advocating *actual* incest between analyst and *analysand* but is, instead, pointing to the *kinship libido* that has been constellated between them being lived symbolically in the incestuous *transference–countertransference*. What this means analytically is that *individuating*, namely, becoming one's own person, entails a symbolic re-entry into the mother, that is, a *regression* back to an *incestuous* state in order to be reborn. Symbolic incest, therefore, represents a coming together with one's own being, a union of like with like, which is why it exerts an unholy fascination, as actual incest is seen as sinister and perverse but also fatally attractive—hence the taboo that exists against it in conventional society. The intervention of the dove (the Holy Ghost) depicts the hidden message of this *mystical union* of "brother" and "sister".

In Jung's own writing about *anima/animus*, the former stood for a man's inner femininity, while the latter represented a woman's inner masculinity. As has already been set out earlier in the book, this way of conceptualising has been rethought in more recent times, but we will stay with Jung's original configuration as it results in an interesting reversal of what is depicted; in other words, the king is the *animus* of the female analyst or *analysand*; the queen is the *anima* of the male *analysand*. This results in a counter-crossing of the sexes with the male *analysand* represented by the queen and the female analyst represented by the king thus representing the contra-sexual side of the *analysand* and analyst.

Figure 3 shows the king and queen in naked confrontation with the dove once again between them. The eroticism of the picture is mediated

Figure 3. The Naked Truth

by the dove as a symbol of the *soul* which provides the relational aspect between the king, who personifies spirit, and the queen, who personifies body. In this way, the spiritual and instinctual *archetypal* duality of the *psyche* is depicted. The nakedness of the king and queen at this stage points to the fact that the *persona* has dropped away and the naked truth or *shadow* material is becoming constellated, at which time, the *analysand* reveals his *shadow* in the course of analysis. The analyst, on the other hand, keeps her *shadow* concealed from the analysand though, at some point in the analysis, through an error of judgement or being late for an appointment, this will inevitably reveal itself. When that occurs, the analysis may break down if the *analysand* cannot cope with the shattering of his idealised *transference* onto the analyst. This would apply to the first kind of *transference* that was alluded to earlier when personal unresolved issues to do with childhood are being *worked through*. If the

Figure 4. Immersion in the Bath

analysand can accept the less-than-perfect analyst, namely, the idealised parental figure who was needed at the initial reparative stage of the work, then the analytic couple are able to enter fully into the incestuous *kinship libido*.

Figure 4 shows the two figures naked in the alchemical bath with the dove again between them. The psychology of this stage centres on a descent into the *unconscious*, the path taken in all heroic endeavours leading to symbolic rebirth. At this time, there is increased transparency on the part of the *analysand*, which facilitates a further descent into *shadow* realms in the *psyche*, which also involves the analyst. As a result, both **Figures 3** and **4** depict times in the analysis when it is in danger of breaking down as the *analysand* may not be able to accept that the analyst has weaknesses. Even if this happens, the *analysand* will leave the *analytic container* freer of his or her initial *complexes* (autonomous sub-personalities in the *personal unconscious*) and be able to relate to others more authentically.

"The unrelated human being lacks wholeness, for he can achieve wholeness only through the soul, and the soul cannot exist without its other side, which is always found in a 'You'" (Jung, 1954, p. 244). Jung is not talking about the synthesis of two individuals in saying this but

Figure 5. The Conjunction

of the union of the *ego* with everything that has been projected into the "You". That is the true meaning of the *coniunctio*, namely, that union on a biological level is symbolic of union on the highest level. The analytic relationship paves the way for *individuation* where wholeness is an *intrapsychic* process.

Figure 5 illustrates the *coniunctio*, or conjoining, wherein the passionately embracing pair are enclosed by the water, a "night sea journey", as they have returned to the chaotic beginning, which at first sight looks as if instinct has triumphed. The union depicted here, however, denotes the symbolic union of opposites and of instinctive energy being transformed into symbolic activity. The dove, as the uniting symbol, has disappeared as the pair, in coitus as natural process, has been transformed into symbolic union.

That is a summary of Jung's interpretation though it is necessary to add that this is the stage when the erotic *transference–countertransference* is heightened and may be enacted between analyst/analysand. This would amount to *actualising* the incestuous content of the analytic relationship where, instead, the alchemical *container* of analysis needs to be able to contain these powerful emotions and let them continue to work themselves through in *uroboric* fashion. It is salutary, at this stage, to remind oneself that the philosopher, William James, called psychoanalysis "a most dangerous method".

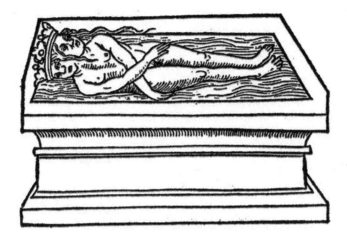

Figure 6. Death

Figure 6 shows the death or *nigredo* stage that follows from the con-joining of the pair which is the cease in the flow of energy once opposites unite. Death means the extinction of *consciousness* and the stagnation of *psychic* life at the stage when the two are united in one body with two heads. "The situation described in our picture is a kind of Ash Wednesday" (Jung, 1954, p. 260). This annual lamentation, which takes place in many cultures, corresponds to an *archetypal* event. This is linked to the *incestuous* theme which runs through *The Rosarium* and the resulting dilemma that confronts anyone undertaking a confronta-tion with the *unconscious*. Either way, nature will be mortified as to com-mit incest goes against nature, but so equally is not yielding to ardent desire. With the integration into the *ego* of the powerful contents in the *unconscious* there results an inevitable inflation that has a serious impact on the *ego*, which experiences it as a kind of death. This is the *putrefac-tion* stage as the conjunction was *incestuous* and therefore sinful and has to be punished but also no new life can come into being without the death of the old.

Figure 7 shows the *soul* mounting to heaven out of the decaying uni-fied body of the king and queen. This corresponds psychologically to a dark state of disorientation and the collapse of *ego-consciousness*. When the *ego* is overwhelmed by *unconscious* contents this is experienced as a loss of *soul*—the dark night of the *soul* that is depicted in the work of reli-gious thinkers such as St John of the Cross. Both **Figures 6** and **7** depict states of *depression* which are experienced as death-like, underlining

Figure 7.   The Ascent of the Soul

necessary states of *regression* for the *analysand*. These pictures show the *putrefaction* and *mortification* stages of the alchemical process when the soul leaves the conjoined analysand/analyst shown as an empty shell and re-enters heaven from where it originates. This stage depicts a difficult time for the *analysand* and the *analytic container* needs to be able to contain this despair and pain arising from the loss of the *soul*. It is necessary to withstand this dark night of the *soul* without intellectualising it so that it has to be felt deeply. Feeling is necessary to bind one to the reality and meaning of symbolic contents and to their ethical meaning. This is where the *analysand* needs sufficient *ego*-strength so as not to descend into *psychosis*.

Figure 8 shows the dead couple being sprinkled with falling dew from heaven. The previous stage of the darkness of death when the union of opposites reaches its nadir now begins to lighten. This is a psychological law whereby everything eventually transforms into its opposite, which underlies Jung's notion of the self-regulating propensity of the *psyche* and the related one of *compensation*. This brings renewed life to the analytic relationship with the dawning of new *consciousness* on the part of the *analysand* as well as the analyst. *Transformation* can take place only when feeling has been aroused and *worked through* bringing new *consciousness* to the analytic pair.

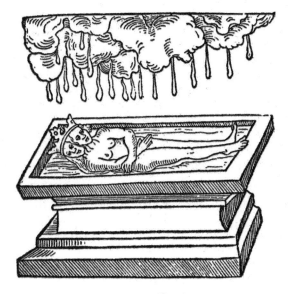

Figure 8. Purification

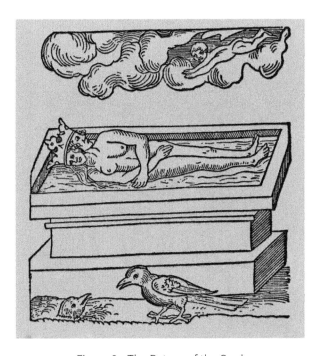

Figure 9. The Return of the Soul

Figure 9 shows the *soul* returning from heaven and unifying with the purified body. It is this unification which, according to Jung, is the goal of perceptive alchemists and depth-psychologists alike—in the latter case it is the freeing of *ego*-consciousness from contamination by contents of the *unconscious*. Just as relationship is at the centre of alchemical transformation so, too, in analysis it is the relationship between analyst and *analysand* that effects the transformation of both. In the alchemical process so also in the analytic one, the *ego* personality has to have been separated from the possibility of becoming grandiose due to its exposure to *unconscious* material. The *soul* that has been reunited with the body is the *One* born of the two, and the *anima*, as the result of a long analysis, has become a function of relationship between *consciousness* and *unconsciousness*.

The two birds at the bottom left of the picture represent the double nature of *Mercurius*, who is both a chthonic and a pneumatic being. The presence of these is a sign that, although the *hermaphrodite* in **Figure 9**

Figure 10. The New Birth

appears to be united, the conflict between the two realms has not yet disappeared but is relegated to the bottom left of the picture, that is, the sphere of the *unconscious*. This is further depicted in the theriomorphic appearance of the birds.

Figure 10 depicts the birth of the *hermaphrodite*, the symbol of wholeness, with the right side of the body being male and the left female. This signifies that the individual has reached the stage of *consciousness* where the opposites, represented by sun and moon, are held in balance. This is different to the earlier figure which represents the state of primordial (*unconscious*) union. In **Figure 10**, the *hermaphrodite* stands on the moon, the feminine principle, and holds a snake depicting the principle of evil which is connected with the work of redemption. Jung writes of the *hermaphrodite* that it is a "monstrous and horrific image" as *alchemy* was compensating for the cleaned-up images of Christianity which are "the product of spirit, light and good"; whereas the alchemical figures are "creatures of night, darkness, poison, and evil" that are to do with matter (Jung, 1946, p. 316).

At this point, it hardly needs stating that Jung's vision of the *psyche* was a highly eroticised, even *incestuous* one, though all this was with a view to the goal of achieving the *higher marriage*. To summarise, this is the relationship to the *syzygy*, the yoked *anima/animus* that has developed through the course of a lengthy analysis which results in a bisexual being who has integrated *consciousness* and *unconsciousness*.

Conclusion of section on Jung's alchemical approach

According to Jung, the union of opposites as personified by the *hermaphrodite* symbolises nothing less than the *philosopher's stone* or what he means by *individuation*. This, he claims, is the end product of a lengthy *alchemical process* during which the *libido* is slowly *distilled* from the alluring fascination of the eroticised *transference–countertransference*. As Jung states: "The symbol of the *hermaphrodite*, it must be remembered, is one of the many synonyms for the goal of the art" (1954, p. 316).

As stated at the beginning of this chapter, the *alchemical process* is a *recursive* dialectical one and is not a once-and-for-all event. Through the course of in-depth analysis, this *recursive* process brings increased awareness with each turn of the *spiral* of the dialectical process. These are everyday life experiences that can be lived only *unconsciously* but, on the other hand, when *worked through* in the alchemical process of analysis, allow for the *distillation* of problems and difficulties until a solution comes into being that brings with it increased awareness. Every reader of this chapter will have experienced dealing with problems and will know that immediate action, namely, reacting to situations, is seldom an effective way of resolving them. The capacity to contain the strong *affect* that accompanies problems in life is a hugely important step in travelling on the path to self-awareness. The latter is "a becoming of the self ... the total, timeless man ... who stands for the mutual integration of conscious and unconscious" (ibid., p. 313). A point worth reiterating is that the *alchemical process* is not a linear one as it is depicted in the ten woodcuts but is a *dialectic* process.

Summary of the colouring of the alchemical work

The *recursive alchemical process* passes through four stages conceptualised as follows: the *nigredo* that represents the blackening initial stage of chaos or *prima materia*. This signifies the decaying *ego* at the time of confrontation with *shadow* elements. The second stage is the *albedo* or whitening that represents *purification* in the form of freeing the *analysand* from identification with the social environment. This is marked by withdrawal from the outer world accompanied by the dawning of lunar enlightenment. *Citrinitas*, or the yellowing of the work, signals the death of lunar *consciousness* experienced as the dark night of the *soul*, the stage of *corruption* and *putrefaction*. This is followed by the dawning of solar consciousness, the ultimate goal of the *alchemical process*, entitled the *rubedo* or reddening of the work, which is the union of opposites, namely, heaven and earth, moon and sun, feminine and masculine.

Ox-herding pictures

At this stage, let us turn to the work of Hayao Kawai, the Japanese Jungian analyst. His comparison of the ten ox-herding pictures of Kuo-an from the twelfth-century Buddhist tradition to the ten medieval pictures of *The Rosarium* will be familiar to members of the Association of

Jungian Analysts, Japan (AJAJ). These are reproduced in his book titled *Buddhism and the Art of Psychotherapy*. I have included them in order to compare and contrast *Western* and *Japanese* psychological thinking. Buddhist scriptures compared the human mind with the wild ox, which had to be captured, tethered, and harnessed to make its sacred nature and the great power it symbolised available to humans. The early pictures depict the Zen initiate searching for the mislaid trace of her true nature with which she has lost touch in the mundane world of *ego consciousness*. Through following the pictures, the Zen initiate may experience her own mind and, through the process of meditation, anxiety and desire are subdued leading to an experience of oneness with all and ultimately *satori*, namely, enlightenment. The last picture depicts the Way of the Buddha going back to and mingling with the mundane world.

There are certain resemblances between the *Rosarium* and the ox-herding pictures, of which I would suggest the following are important: i) the initiate projects what Jung calls the *self* onto the Zen Master, which also happens in analysis *mutatis mutandi*; ii) both sets of pictures exemplify the process of self-realisation; iii) and taming the animal side through integrating it into human consciousness.

There are further similarities between the two ancient texts and pictures though several differences between them as well; for example, the themes of incest and the feminine that are emphasised in *The Rosarium* are not represented in the ox-herding pictures. The Zen Master is outside the work and there is a lack of erotic imagery, whereas in the *opus* of *psychological alchemy*, the analyst is very present in the work. In addition, the ox-herding pictures depict a circular rather than a *recursive* dialectical movement such as that seen in *alchemy*, and any one of the stages from *The Rosarium* can manifest in an analysis of long duration. The Zen circularity ends with the picture of an old man; the meaning inherent in this is that "Eastern consciousness proudly shows the old man's wisdom" (Kawai, 1996, p. 87). This is in contrast to what Kawai says about the *West*: "The modern Western ego feels pride in the strength of the young, mature man" (ibid., p. 87).

A major difference between the two sets of pictures is spelt out by Kawai as follows: "[It] seems to be significant for understanding the Japanese-Chinese type of psyche, in which the senex-puer archetype is of greater importance than the male female relationship" (ibid., p. 67). This would have been the norm in antiquity in the *West* at the height of the flourishing of the glorious eighty years of Ancient Greece when "bad" desire was seen to exist between male and female as it was deemed to be unmoderated by ethics and without the educative dimension that was at work in the "good" desire between older and younger men. Socrates's view was that the beautiful, noble, and gifted soul belonged to pederasty. Fluctuating perspectives on sexual mores from antiquity through Jung's time and into the twenty-first century manifest as diverse representations of the *archetype* of *Eros* and the *anima/animus syzygy*. In keeping with these shifting views, the ox-herding pictures may seem most appropriate at times; at others, the alchemical imagery will be deemed more applicable.

Figure 1. In Search of the Bull

In the pasture of the world,
I endlessly push aside the tall
grasses in search of the Ox.
Following unnamed rivers,
lost upon the interpenetrating
paths of distant mountains,
My strength failing and my vitality
exhausted, I cannot find the Ox.

Figure 2. Discovery of the Footprints

Along the riverbank under the trees,
I discover footprints.
Even under the fragrant grass,
I see his prints.
Deep in remote mountains they are
found.
These traces can no more be hidden
than one's nose, looking
heavenward.

Figure 3. Perceiving the Bull

I hear the song of the nightingale.
The sun is warm, the wind is mild,
willows are green along the shore—
Here no Ox can hide!
What artist can draw that massive head,
those majestic horns?

Figure 4. Catching the Bull

I seize him with a terrific struggle.
His great will and power
are inexhaustible.
He charges to the high plateau
far above the cloud-mists,
Or in an impenetrable ravine he stands.

Figure 5. Taming the Bull

The whip and rope are necessary,
Else he might stray off down
some dusty road.
Being well-trained, he becomes
naturally gentle.
Then, unfettered, he obeys his
master.

Figure 6. Riding the Bull Home

Mounting the Ox, slowly
I return homeward.
The voice of my flute intones
through the evening.
Measuring with hand-beats
the pulsating harmony,
I direct the endless rhythm.
Whoever hears this melody
will join me.

Figure 7. The Bull Transcended

Astride the Ox, I reach home.
I am serene. The Ox too can rest.
The dawn has come. In blissful
repose,
Within my thatched dwelling
I have abandoned the whip and
ropes.

Figure 8. Both Bull and Self Transcended

Whip, rope, person, and Ox—
all merge in No Thing.
This heaven is so vast,
no message can stain it.
How may a snowflake exist
in a raging fire.
Here are the footprints of
the Ancestors.

Figure 9. Reaching the Source

Too many steps have been
taken
returning to the root and the
source.
Better to have been blind and
deaf
from the beginning!
Dwelling in one's true abode,
unconcerned with and without—
The river flows tranquilly on
and the flowers are red.

Figure 10. Return to Society

Barefooted and naked of breast,
I mingle with the people of the
world.
My clothes are ragged and dust-
laden,
and I am ever blissful.
I use no magic to extend my life;
Now, before me, the dead trees
become alive.

Concluding remarks on Jung's psychological *alchemy*

In 1929 Jung became so animated by his discovery of the *psychological* potential of the *alchemical process* that the rest of his life was devoted to researching it in every way possible. The vital message at the heart of the *alchemical process* is that it (metamorphically) burns away the extraneous parts of anyone who can contain and endure its rigours. This applies to everyday living as much as it does to in-depth analysis. In other words, when caught on the horns of a dilemma, if one is able to endure the slow process of allowing it to distil within the metaphorical alchemical *container* and not *act-out* by reaching for hasty solutions, that inevitably leads to some kind of resolution of what can appear irresolvable. This is the great lesson of *psychological alchemy*, namely, it is the path along which one may lead one's life without seeking for easy solutions—there are none. Ultimately, a final resolution awaits every living being in what Heidegger calls *being-unto-death*, the path of *Dasein*—his philosophy taking on increasing vitality for the later stages of life.

As already claimed above, the discovery of Jung's realisation of the *psychological* potential in the *alchemical process* is his great contribution to his own discipline. As he himself put it: "... there is an eminently psychological reason for the existence of alchemy" (1959a, p. 344). As with most other Jungian concepts it is open to criticism, illustrated by what follows, but the essential discovery by Jung of the potential for individual development through alchemical processing leads this writer to conclude that *alchemy is good to think with*, a telling phrase from the twentieth-century discipline of *structuralism*. One can ask for nothing more in life than the stripping away of what is extraneous to existence until one is left with what is the ultimate attainment, namely, a Heideggerian ice-cold logic, the antidote to drowning in *affect*.

Wolfgang Giegerich's critique of Jung's approach to psychological *alchemy*

The material featured in this section is taken from articles written in collaboration with Wolfgang Giegerich himself, which I contributed to *The Journal of Analytical Psychology*. Giegerich is the Berlin Jungian psychoanalyst and foremost critic of Jung's psychology, who until 1984 was an uncritical admirer of Jung and an adherent of the *archetypal* school of analytical psychology, whose central tenets spring from imagery and myth. Before going into Giegerich's model of *psychological alchemy*, it is important to note some of his general criticisms of Jung. Giegerich will feature later in the book under the distinguished figures in analytical psychology section.

I am aware that many readers may well be familiar with Giegerich's thinking but I feel it is important to spell out some of his main concepts for those who are not. For the latter, I would like to add a word of encouragement as his ideas are not easy to grasp in one reading, which I found many years ago when I first started to grapple with his profound thinking.

To begin with, Giegerich is critical of Jung for reifying concepts such as *the unconscious* and *the collective unconscious*, the latter deemed to be full of content, namely, *archetypes*. Thus, in Jung's model, the mind is the product of a substrate of *archetypes*, myths, and *gods*. This is in contrast to the lack of ontic existence of the *objective psyche* that is a key feature of Giegerich's thinking. Furthermore, Jung's notion of *individuation* and his constant quest for *meaning* is dismissed as seeking wish-fulfilment rather than truth. In his emphasis on *meaning* and in the famous quote about God's existence: "I do not believe, I know," Jung reverts to pre-Kantian metaphysics as the statement runs contrary to the latter's categorical denial that anything could enter *consciousness* without being pre-organised by the mind. Instead, Kant asserted that he had to deny knowledge in order to make room for faith. He had already demonstrated that the human mind is inherent in outer reality which, prior to his *transcendental idealism*, had been seen as independent of humans. *Alchemy* has objectively reached a similar level of reflection as the *subject* is becoming *conscious* of itself as observer as well as active participant. With the advent of *alchemy*, humans have superseded the mythological stage as the whole of mythology and the imaginal is being worked on in the *alchemical retort* and the *adept* has risen to a new stage of *consciousness*.

> It is ('implicit'), i.e., structurally it *is* already thought, even if thought that is still deeply immersed and enveloped in the imaginal form of presentation … it provides the *real* bridge upon

which the soul could pass from its former status (mythologiz-
ing) to its new, modern status of (psycho-) logic, the status of the
Concept. (Giegerich, 2008, p. 138)

To summarise what has been said in the above: Giegerich's focus is on the
"logical" to be found in the *alchemical opus*, which may appear surprising at first sight as *alchemy* expresses itself through imagery, evidenced
in the early part of this chapter on *The Rosarium*. For Jung, medieval
alchemy was the historical link between *Gnosticism* and *Neoplatonism*
from the past to the present time wherein dealing with *soul* or *psyche*
happens through Jungian psychoanalysis, in particular, the psychology
of the *unconscious*. Giegerich, for his part, rejects this and sees *alchemy*
as the historical link between the imagination and dialectical logic.

To clarify this vital point further, the *alchemical opus* gives rise to
the *objective psyche* that is without concrete existence but is, instead, the
result of the alchemical process of *distillation, fermentation, sublimation,
corruption, mortification,* and *purification* of feelings, emotions, images,
dreams. Giegerich's further critique of Jung's psychology is that it largely
remains at the *semantic* level, that is, focusing on content, and has not
reached the *syntactical* level where the focus is on form and structure.

Furthermore, Jung's psychology is ahistorical rather than historical
as it takes no account of the developmental stages of the *Western* mind
from the Reformation, the Industrial and French Revolutions, and, perhaps above all, the Enlightenment. These were some of the foremost
ruptures of time in *Western* history that brought in their wake increasing secularisation, which led to the *objective psyche* emptying itself out
of mythical and religious ways of being. At the end of the nineteenth and
beginning of the twentieth centuries, these developmental stages have
resulted in a new *psychological consciousness*. "This *psychological* focus
is 'objective' to the personal standpoint of both patient and analyst and
is comprehended as 'other', because the standpoint comes from a shift in
perspective, it is not a literal or hypostasized other" (Hoedl, 2018, p. 126).

In this way, psychology evolved conceptually from a person-to-
person realm to a transpersonal *logic* of whatever is presenting itself,
for instance, a symptom, dream, or interpretation, which enabled the
move from a personalistic stance to the *objective psyche's* self-reflection.
In practice, this means that though Giegerich meets his patients in the
consulting room on a human personal level, giving them the emotional

support they need to be in touch with their repressed *affects*, his *psychological focus* is not on the person but on the concept.

In this way, Giegerich tries to penetrate *thinkingly* into psychological phenomena and thus bring out their internal dialectic. This may be thought of as the dynamic developmental process in which nothing is discarded or destroyed. Instead, it is *sublated* or overcome while, at the same time, being preserved not lost. *Negation* in the dialectic is the negation of a positive, tangible, demonstrable reality, a taking off deeper into the interiority of the phenomenon itself. *Absolute knowledge* is one freed (ab-solved) from the difference between the absolute and the empirical, the infinite and the finite; it is freed from the endless repetition of binary opposition culminating in a speculative stance that overcomes the alienation of subject and object.

A psychology informed by *alchemy* would have the task of freeing the spirit *Mercurius*, which is the thought that is imprisoned in matter, namely, image, emotion, bodily symptom. The true laboratory of the mind in the *alchemical opus* is the real historical process whereby the contradictory life of itself and its own other will have disappeared as something in their own right and been reduced to *sublated* moments of unity. Dialectical movement is structurally akin to that of the *alchemical opus* expressed in its language of *decomposition, fermentation, corruption*, and *solution*. In both instances, the *recursive* process of *negation* is expressed as the *sublimating, distilling*, and *refining* of the *prime matter* in the work.

According to Giegerich, *psychogenic* bodily symptoms and *affects* are essentially thoughts that are submerged into the natural, physical medium of body or emotion. "… body symptom is submerged emotion, emotion is submerged image, image is submerged thought, and conversely, thought is sublated image, image is sublated emotion, emotion is sublated body reaction" (Giegerich, 2007, p. 255). Giegerich emphasises that abstract thinking is what today's psychology needs in the shape of more intellect—not more feelings, emotions, body work. He dismisses the latter as "ego-stuff".

In Jung's exploration of *psychological alchemy*, he at times spells this out, as in the following quotation:

> This does not mean that the adept ceased to work in the labo-
> ratory, only that he kept an eye on the symbolic aspect of his

transmutations. This corresponds exactly to the situation in the
modern psychology of the unconscious; while personal problems
are not over looked [sic] (the patient himself takes very good care
of that!), the analyst keeps an eye on the symbolic aspects, for
healing comes from what leads the patient beyond himself and
beyond his entanglements in the ego. (1967, p. 302)

In the above, Jung is demonstrating that the more insightful alchemists
were moving away from working with concrete physical matter in their
laboratories—"our gold is *not* the vulgar gold—*aurum non vulgi*" (ibid.,
p. 166)—to symbolic ideas. Despite this, Jung often stays with ontic
images and outgrown myths. Giegerich, on the other hand, has moved
away from the imagery Jung depicts in his analysis of *The Rosarium* to
the logic of actually lived life at a given historical locus. *Psyche*'s main
alchemical laboratory is history, the history of culture and *consciousness*.

In Giegerich's view, Jung remaining in the mythological mode of conceptualising was stuck in a past of gods and super-heroes, where humans
are mere recipients of divine knowledge; whereas the *alchemical opus*
is an active work by *adepts* creating knowledge themselves. This is why
Mercurius cannot be a full-fledged *God* as it has the *adept*'s subjectivity
in itself; it is thus *objectivity* and *subjectivity* at the same time. "With the
advent of Alchemy, we could say, it begins to dawn on consciousness
that the life of the soul is *logical* life, is thought" (Giegerich, 2008, p. 137).

Today we live in a scientific and technological age, which is where
psyche is located and where psychology must also be. The latter should
be, as its name implies, a psychology of *logos*, that is, reflective thinking.
"We have to think from within our own historical situation and on our
own responsibility" (Giegerich, Miller, & Mogenson, 2005, p. 9). Instead,
Jung advocated the following: "… we are best advised to remain within
the framework of traditional mythology, which has already proved
comprehensive enough for all practical purposes" (1954, p. 270). This
represents a regression on Jung's part though, from time to time, he does
show awareness that *Psyche*'s work is noetic or reflective thought. For
instance, the following statement by Jung appears in "The Psychology of
the Transference": "… the Original Man (Nous) bent down from heaven
to earth and was wrapped in the embrace of physis—a primordial image
that runs through the whole of alchemy" (1946, p. 246). Further on in
the same piece this statement appears: "It restores the vanished 'man of

light' who is identical with the Logos in Gnostic and Christian symbolism" (p. 248).

The following quotation succinctly encapsulates Giegerich's approach to *psychological alchemy* as a dialectical process:

> The work of alchemy is *contra naturam* in displacing human existence from the biological sphere to the slow path to *mindedness*, the relation to or openness for the truth, i.e., the logic of actually lived life at a given historical locus, the freeing of the Mercurius imprisoned in the physicalness of the matter. What is at work here is *not* just the alchemical distillation of the *semantic* contents of ego, for instance, *images* into the logical form of *syntax* of soul; it is the *absolute negation* of the logical form of the content from within itself which arrives back at the starting point but at a transformed starting point. (Casement, 2011b, p. 716)

This may best be illustrated by the following simple progression: Starting position "A" from where the contradictions inherent in "A" lead to position "non-A" but the contradictions in position "non-A" lead to a new position "not-non-A". The contradictions in that position lead back to the starting point "A" but the latter is not exactly the same naive "A" that existed at the beginning of the dialectic as "A" has gone through several *negations* on the way and is enriched and refined by the history of all the *negations*. The superseded stages are not lost but are still there as *sublated* moments within the new position "A". This *spiralling* dialectical movement is structurally akin to the *alchemical opus* which also proceeds via *negations*. In both cases the *recursive* process of *negation* is in itself and simultaneously the process of *sublimating, distilling, refining* the *prime matter* here, and *consciousness* or the logic of the world there.

The simple equation above will resonate with anyone who has been in analysis and/or practised as an analyst. Let us turn to a common enough presenting problem for an individual seeking help in dealing with a problematic marriage. This would represent starting point "A". The *analysand* considers leaving or even divorcing the spouse as a way of resolving the contradictions as well as the tensions in the relationship, which then results in a shift to position "non-A". The contradictions in that position lead to "not-non-A", wherein contradictions continue unabated so there is a reversion back to position "A" but the *analysand* is not back at exactly where he started from as position "A" has been through various negations in its progression. If all this can be contained within the analysis and not *acted-out*, the *dialectical* process has a chance to do its work on the problem at hand.

The concept of the *container* is central to the alchemical process, indicated in the material already presented, as it is within the boundaries of the *container* that the alchemical work can take place without intrusion from the outside or leakage from within it. This has obvious applicability to the psychoanalytic *container*. Giegerich contributed a description of his way of practising analysis to an article I wrote up on his work in which he alludes to "going for a walk" with a patient during a session (Casement, 2011a, p. 540). This would be leaking from the *alchemical container* as opposed to keeping everything *hermetically* sealed within it as the *recursive* process continues with its refining of the *prima materia*. In psychoanalytic language, it would represent a form of "*acting-out*" of the *transference–countertransference*, which Giegerich also appears to misinterpret as in the following: "I do not systematically invite transference reactions. I do not offer myself as a kind of guru or so" (ibid., 2011a, p. 540).

This depiction of *transference* is alien to the understanding of *transference–countertransference* as practised by this writer, which is not to serve the analyst's self-aggrandisement but, rather, is in the service of the patient/*analysand*'s need to *work through* unresolved relationships with parents, siblings, and other figures from childhood, which also acts as a source of invaluable information for the analyst. The *recursive* action of *alchemy* that has been alluded to previously is what slowly though surely refines all the base matter, namely, raw sensations and emotions, that are distilled into thought. This central feature of analytic work helps the *analysand* even after the analysis has terminated as it becomes internalised as a way of containing and *working through* the problems and difficulties that are an inevitable part of life.

Final remarks

Jung stressed the *mutuality* of the alchemical process underlining his notion that the analyst/*analysand* are in an equal relationship. This is illustrated in the diagram already presented which emphasises symmetry in order to express the idea that the analyst is as much in analysis as the *analysand*, leading to the assumption that the analytic relationship is equal in every way. While fully supporting the notion of the essential *mutuality* of the two participants in the analytic *container*, the analytic relationship is, nevertheless, asymmetrical in the following respects: the analyst has been through analysis and training and has analysed previous patients/*analysands*. Furthermore, the analyst's relation to *anima/animus* is more firmly established and *ego* is stronger. As a result, the analyst's perception of the *analysand* is greater, leading to the capacity to use *projection* and *introjection* in a way that gives the analyst information about the *analysand's resistances* and helps the analyst not to *act-out*. Nevertheless, the potential for *mutual* transformation through the alchemical process is an important contribution of Jung's to psychology. In addition, Jung's emphasis on the importance of the relationship inherent in the analytic encounter is a further major contribution to the psychoanalytic community as is Giegerich's alternative mode of thinking. It has to be said that though Jung did not live up to his claim of *mutuality* between analyst/*analysand*, as I hope to have demonstrated in my critique of his analysis of Kristine Mann which appears earlier in the book, it does not undermine the notion of *mutuality* as one important difference between the Jungian psychoanalytic approach and that of mainstream psychoanalysis. One small but telling instance of this is the following: it is usual for a patient/*analysand* in Jungian psychoanalysis to talk of analysing *with* a particular analyst; in mainstream psychoanalysis, it is customary to talk of being analysed *by* a particular analyst.

Finally, I would like to add a few remarks in order to address the question of whether an experience of the *alchemical process* is possible through the use of technology in conducting analysis. From my long experience over many years of using Skype, Zoom, and/or the telephone for sessions, also known as *teleanalysis*, there has been no difficulty whatsoever in experiencing alchemical transformation by these means. In other words, *alchemy* and *teleanalysis* are completely compatible as technology is no hindrance to the production of *regression, incestuous longings*, and *transference–countertransference*.

CHAPTER 12

The notion of transformation in Jung and Bion

Preliminary remarks

The aim of this chapter is to explore the similarities to be found in the thinking of the psychoanalysts Jung and Bion. Its central focus, in particular, is on the primary importance in Jung's work that he gave to *transformation* through the *psychological alchemical* process already detailed in the preceding chapter. This is compared to Bion's notion of *transformation* in "*O*", with both approaches culminating in the birth of the *psychoanalytic child*. The chapter further examines the different perspectives these two psychoanalysts had in their writings on the *container* and the *contained*, inextricably linked concepts that were first formulated by Jung. The chapter's concluding hypothesis is that complementarity is to be found between Jung's thinking about *psychic infection* and Bion's reworking of Klein's original theory of *projective identification*. There is some necessary repetition of material relating to the *alchemical process* in order to link it to Bion's thinking and to incorporate Michael Fordham's clinical interpretation of Jung's succinct diagram summarising the analytical relationship.

At a seminar given at the Psychoanalytic Section of the British Association of Psychotherapy—as it then was—in London several years ago, the late James Fisher, formerly a member of the International Psychoanalytical Association (IPA), hypothesised that although Bion had acquired some useful tools from Melanie Klein with which to work, his real dialogue was with Freud. According to Fisher, Bion reworked Freud's apparatus of thinking that is related to the *reality principle* by adding "*linking*" to the latter's original formulation of *attention/memory/judgement*. Fisher's focus was on early Bion (1950–1962) before the latter's work on "*O*" and *Transformations* (1965); he critiqued that work as Bion's vague attempts to incorporate Kant's "*thing-in-itself*". Fisher was by no means alone in the mainstream psychoanalytic community to take a negative view of Bion's later work.

In the present chapter, it is this later work of Bion's that is of particular interest wherein it appears he may be regarded as a "closet Jungian" (Grotstein, 2006, p. xiii). So stated the Bionian psychoanalyst James Grotstein in the outstanding Foreword he contributed to *The Idea of the Numinous: Contemporary Jungian and Psychoanalytic Perspectives*, a book edited by Ann Casement and David Tacey. He goes on to say that the parallels between the ideas of Jung and Bion are "uncanny" (ibid., p. xiii). Grotstein attributes Bion's emphasis on the role of the mother in his concept of *maternal reverie*, and on the mother in her capacity as "*container*", to Klein's radical shift in emphasis from the prominence given to the father in Freud's writings. He compares that notion in Bion to the "image of the archaic Earth Mother archetype" from Jung's psychology (ibid., p. xii).

Grotstein goes on to say that, at the time he was in analysis with Bion, the latter often mentioned how surprised he was that Freud ignored "the religious passions [instincts] of man" (ibid., p. xiii). From this, it would appear that Bion believed these religious passions were as important, if not even more important, than the *libidinal* instincts of Freud's model. In view of what Grotstein says in the Foreword, it is a mystery as to why the review of *The Idea of the Numinous* in *The Journal of Analytical Psychology* failed to even mention the all-important statements linking Bion's thinking to Jung made by Grotstein—among the most important contents of that book. A crucial point to bear in mind in relation to both Jung and Bion is that they were psychoanalysts not mystics nor men of the cloth, and it may be no exaggeration to assert that Bion did as much as any avowed followers of Jung to carry forward the latter's ideas about the "religious passions" in psychoanalysis, albeit without acknowledging that that was what he was doing.

Some of what has been said in the above paragraphs will strike readers who are familiar with Jung's writings with a sense of *déjà vu*. This is hardly surprising, as it was Jung who first radically shifted the emphasis in psychoanalysis from the father to the mother in an early book called *Psychology of the Unconscious* by its American translator—reissued years later with its original title *Symbols of Transformation*. Jung was working on this book prior to his split with Freud in 1913, a work that has been cited as one of the precursors that led to that event, a claim which has been questioned earlier in this book. Some of the chapter titles bearing witness to this shift in emphasis to the mother are *Symbolism of the Mother and of Rebirth*, *The Battle for Deliverance from the Mother*, and *The Dual Mother Role*. From these, it would appear that he was influenced in his thinking by the Hindu concept of the *twice-born* as he quotes freely from Indian texts, including the Brihadâranyaka-Upanishad. In relation to this particular text, Jung states: "We previously saw that the 'mother libido' must be sacrificed in order to produce the world" (1916, p. 398). Jung's interest in Hindu texts was most probably sparked through his avid reading of Schopenhauer, whose philosophy is permeated with Hindu wisdom as testified by the following: "… the veil of Maya obscures the view of the uncultivated individual: to him, instead of the thing in itself, only the phenomenon is shown" (1819, para. 416).

An item of interest worth mentioning here is that Bion attended the lectures Jung gave at the Tavistock Clinic in London in 1935 (as did his patient, Samuel Beckett). In response to a point raised by Bion, Jung mentioned what he called "the controversial problem of psychophysical parallelisms" (Jung, 1968, p. 72), stating they are only separated by our minds but not in reality. (In passing it is worth noting that in the 1890s, Freud discarded the hypothesis of "psychophysical parallelisms" made by the English neurologist, John Hewlings Jackson, seeing it as useful only for the study of speech, not for developing a mind-based psychology.) Jung went on to state: "We see them as two on account of the utter incapacity of our mind to think them together" (ibid.). He went on to speak of the old civilisations of Asia where people have trained their minds in introspective psychology for thousands of years; whereas the *West's* study of psychology is a comparatively more recent phenomenon.

India

In point of fact, both Jung and Bion spent time in India, which was of vital importance to each of them. Like Bion, the author of this book had her origins in India, and the internal image she has carried since childhood is that of the imposing statue in the Elephanta Caves near Bombay (the city of her birth and childhood) of the *Trimurti*, the triad that is made up of the three great Hindu Gods, Brahma, Vishnu, and Shiva. These represent respectively the creator, preserver, and destroyer. The central one of Vishnu, the preserver, is a calm introspective representation of transcendence; whereas the ones on either side in their sensuous beauty and *numinous* terror reflect the creative and destructive aspects of the supreme divinity. In Brahminism, dialectical elements are to be found in the idea of the three phases of creation (Brahma), maintenance of order (Vishnu), and destruction (Shiva). This may be seen as the antagonism between good and evil, but, even more tellingly, as the dialectical relationship of harmony and discord, a theme that will be returned to further in this chapter in relation to Bion's thinking about these concepts. The German theologist, Rudolf Otto, who coined the term *numinous*, visited the Trimurti and recalled standing in front of it as one of *the* numinous experiences of his life (personal communication, Murray Stein). Jung did visit Bombay and it is likely he would have visited the Trimurti, which may also have been known to Bion given his Indian background though he came from a different part of the subcontinent.

Jung went to India in 1938 to deepen his grasp of Indian thinking:

> *Dharma*, law, truth, guidance, is said to be "nowhere save in the mind". Thus the unconscious is credited with all those faculties which the West attributes to God ... the transcendent function shows how right the East is in assuming the experience of *dharma* comes from within ... quite in accord with the formula "grace" or the "will of God". (Jung, 1958a, p. 506)

Bion had his (O)rigins in India which Grotstein writes about as follows:

> … Bion, though English by heritage, was Anglo-Indian cultur-
> ally, he undoubtedly brought with him many of the overt and
> hidden values of that mysterious land and integrated them with
> his … European left-brain respect for precision. His later venture
> into O is understandably thought by many to have issued from
> his Indian transcendental roots. (2007, p. 25)

An extract from the obituary I contributed on James Grotstein to *The
Journal of Analytical Psychology* is as follows:

> In the course of an early conversation with Jim Grotstein in
> Los Angeles I mentioned that from my limited reading of Bion
> it would appear the latter's notions of "maternal reverie", "con-
> tainer and contained", and, above all, "O", had their roots in the
> *Mataram.* He lit up at my use of this Hindi word for motherland,
> and became further animated to learn that I shared something
> of Bion's own background. For Jim, India was "that mysterious
> land" and he appeared to revere anyone who had their origins
> in its "transcendental roots". (quotations from *A Beam of Intense
> Darkness* (Grotstein, 2007)) (Casement, 2015, pp. 753–754)

Complementarity

As both Jung and Bion dared to address the deepest mysteries in their
common cause with Kant's *a priori* "ding an sich" or "thing-in-itself",
neither is easy to read nor can what they say be simplified or readily
digested. To this end, it is necessary to declare that I am mindful of the
pitfalls that await anyone trying to make comparisons between the thinking of two in-depth personalities, and realise I am in danger of falling
into what the Jungian psychoanalyst, Wolfgang Giegerich, has called "a
peace negotiation fantasy"(Giegerich, Miller, & Mogenson, 2005, p. 4).
This relates to the attempt by another writer to reconcile Hegel and Jung.

At the outset, I freely admit I have been a student of Jung's writings since the early 1960s, when I first became involved with the

psychoanalytic world, though I have far less familiarity with Bion's. I have attempted to make up this deficit over many years and have been greatly helped in recent times by James Grotstein's book *A Beam of Intense Darkness*. Rafael E. López-Corvo's *The Dictionary of the Work of W. R. Bion* has also been a useful reference work. Along with Grotstein, the Bionian psychoanalyst whose work I most admire is Rudi Vermote, who gave an inspiring paper at the *Wilfred Bion Today Conference* in London in 2005, which focused on Bion's later work. At that time, it became clear to me that what I had previously sensed, namely, a similarity between these later ideas and those of Jung's was indeed the case, and I have since been seeking ways of building bridges between the two thinkers. I have attended other events dedicated to Bion's work, in particular, the important conference "Bion-in-Boston: Growth and Turbulence in the Container↔Contained" in July 2009, at which this chapter had its first airing. In the course of that conference, the co-chair Howard Levine and I discussed the possibility of producing a book featuring Jungian and Bionian writers. To date, we have both been too busy to follow through on this idea.

Two key areas that may be identified in the work of both thinkers relate to the notions of the *numinous* and the *transcendent/transcendental*. A definition of the *numinous* is that it is an experience of fleeting intensity that derives from the Latin word *numen*, which may be translated in various ways, including "nod" or "divine will". *Numinous* experiences, though fleeting, have a lasting impact on the subject. A prime example of this is the well-known passage on the madeleine cakes in Proust's masterly *opus*, *In Search of Lost Time*, wherein he describes the experience that opened the door to his creativity:

> ... my mother, seeing that I was cold, offered me some tea, a thing I did not ordinarily take. I declined at first, and then, for no particular reason, changed my mind. She sent for one of the squat, plump little cakes called "petites madeleines", which look as though they had been moulded in the fluted valve of a scallop shell. And soon, mechanically, dispirited after a dreary day with the prospect of a depressing morrow, I raised to my lips a spoonful of the tea in which I had soaked a morsel

of the cake. No sooner had the warm liquid mixed with the crumbs touched my palate than a shiver ran through me and I stopped, intent upon the extraordinary thing that was happening to me. An exquisite pleasure had invaded my senses, something isolated, detached, with no suggestion of its origin. And at once the vicissitudes of life had become indifferent to me, its disasters innocuous, its brevity illusory—this new sensation having had the effect, which love has, of filling me with a precious essence, or rather this essence was not in me, it *was* me. I had ceased now to feel mediocre, contingent, mortal. (Proust, 1913, p. 51)

Anyone seeking the mysteries of life will find more satisfaction in reading Proust than in most psychoanalytic "literature", apart from Freud, who likewise was an evocative writer which he combined with acute psychological insight.

To return to Rudolf Otto, he first formulated the term *numinous* in his 1917 book *The Idea of the Holy: An Inquiry into the Non-rational Factor in the Idea of the Divine and Its Relations to the Rational*. Otto used it there to depict the tremendous, awesome, mysterious non-rational emotions that are generated by a recognition of something in the objective situation, and states that this experience cannot be transmitted, it can only be awakened "as everything that comes 'of the spirit' must be awakened" (p. 7). Furthermore, it passes from mind to mind through "a penetrative imaginative sympathy with what passes in the other person's mind" (ibid., p. xvii). The work of neuroscientists such as V. S. Ramachandran on mirror neurons has explored links between these and *empathic* communication.

For Jung, the *sublimation* and integration into *consciousness* of *numinous* experiences leads to the creation of what he called the *transcendent function* "in which thesis and antithesis both play their part ... in the shaping of which the opposites are united [in] the living symbol" (1971, p. 480). Likewise, for Bion, it can result in the evolved individual who has traversed beyond the *depressive position* in experiencing and intuiting "*O*" and thereby attained the transcendent position to be at one with "*O*".

Psychoid archetypes

In the seminars Jung gave on Nietzsche's *Thus Spake Zarathustra* between 1934 and 1939, he speaks of what he calls the *"subtle body"* derived from his studies of Gnostic writings, as follows:

> … the man Jesus who was hanging on the cross was only the material body, that during his struggle in the garden, hours before his crucifixion, the God had departed from him. So the God was never crucified. The body was hanging on the cross and not the God-man, the proof being that Christ himself said, "My God, my God, why hast thou forsaken me?" I mention this because all these ideas of the subtle body play a great role in the New Testament. The body, to St Paul is the gross, biological, physiological body, the corruptible body; but he speaks also of the incorruptible body which he put on with Christ, because Christ is in a way the soul or the *pneuma*, the incorruptible body that is beyond space and time … the subtle body [which is] the equivalent of the somatic unconscious.
>
> It is beyond our grasp *per definition*; the subtle body—assuming there is such a thing—is a transcendental concept which cannot be expressed in terms of our language or our philosophical views, because they are all inside the categories of time and space. (Jarrett, 1988, pp. 442–443)

With regard to the *subtle body*, Jung acknowledges his debt to Kant's notion of the *transcendental*, which is to do with the conditions for experience, for example, time and space as pure *a priori* forms of sensible intuition.

In the same *transcendental* vein, he went on to tackle this concept through his theory of *psychoid archetypes*, *psycho-physical* patterning structures that are irrepresentable in themselves, which may only be experienced through their manifestation in *psychic* or material reality. Jung worked on his theory of *psychoid archetypes* and *synchronicity*, an acausal connecting principle, with the Nobel Laureate quantum physicist Wolfgang Pauli. *Synchronicity* hypothesises that there is a meaningful connection between physical entities and *psychic* states that is *constellated* by an *archetype*. "With the concept of 'constellation' Jung moved away from the platonic notion of the archetypes being 'inborn'" (Gieser, 2005, p. 290). Instead, he appears closer to current thinking which posits the emergence out of chaos of complex adaptive systems (CAT). This model can be applied to the *psyche* as it displays the same self-organising features of a CAT exemplifying "the movement from low-level rules to higher-level sophistication [in] what we call emergence" (Johnson, 2001, p. 18). Jung is here also hypothesising that meaning is a function of *unconsciousness* located in matter as well as in *psyche*.

Grotstein suggests that Jung's concept of *synchronicity* may be at play in Bion's invocation of Kant's *noumen* or *thing-in-itself*, linking it in sound to the *numinous* (though, of course, they have different Latin roots). "Yet one wonders in the synchronicity of things whether or not they might be mystically related" (Grotstein, 2006, p. xiv). Bion certainly seems to come close to what Jung means by *synchronicity* in the following expression: "... it is durability in a domain where there is no time and space as those terms used in a world of sense" (Bion, 1970, p. 2).

Kant's term *transcendental* is employed by both Jung and Bion as synonymous with the *noumenon, thing-in-itself, psychoid, beta-elements, and "O"*, namely, the deepest mysteries of the *somatic unconscious*, also referred to as the *subtle body* by Jung.

Container↔contained

Jung and Bion had extensive experience of working with *psychosis*, which was of fundamental importance in developing their ideas. From 1900 to 1909, Jung was a psychiatrist at Burghölzli Mental Hospital in Zürich, the foremost psychiatric hospital in the world at that time. On the other hand, Bion's approach to *psychosis* "was close to his war experiences: attacks on linking, beta particles as projectiles, containment that is a military term, and nameless dread" (Vermote, 2005, p. 2). According to Grotstein, this gave rise to Bion's formulation of the concepts of *container↔contained, maternal reverie, alpha-function,* α- and β-*elements*, and, crucially, his de-pathologising of Klein's concept of *projective identification*, seeing it instead as *communicative projective identification*. In Bion's approach, *beta-elements* (β-*elements*) are equated with *raw sensations* which can be transformed through *maternal reverie* into *alpha-elements* (α-elements), namely, *proto-thoughts*.

In this chapter, these Bionian concepts will be examined more closely in relation to Jung's thinking. The first of these is his interlinked concept of α- and β-*elements*; the second of which is akin to Jung's focus on the *prima materia*. The latter is equated with incestuous contents of *transference* that Jung explores in his 1946 paper "The Psychology of the Transference". For Jung "incest symbolizes union with one's own being, it means individuation or becoming a self" (p. 218). By saying this, he is not advocating actual incest but is claiming, instead, that incestuous feelings, as a result of being *worked through* in the *alchemical container*, or *vas*, can be transformed into the gold of *consciousness*.

Bion first mentions the term "*contain*" in his 1967 paper "Attacks on Linking". He writes there of the fear "that the child could not contain" (p. 104), which the child strives to deal with through *projective identification* into a mother, who may turn out to be too anxious to tolerate the fear being projected into her. He has this to say about feelings that are too powerful for the infant: "Projective identification makes it possible to investigate his own feelings in a personality powerful enough to contain them" (p. 106). Further, in the Conclusion he states: "In this state of mind emotion is hated; it is felt to be too powerful to be contained by the immature psyche" (p. 108). In a further elaboration of his concept of *pre-conception*, Bion sounds almost identical with Jung's notion of *archetypal* as in the following: "Pre-conception would be … a state of expectation comparable with the supposition that the baby has an innate or a priori disposition towards the breast … and represents for Bion a kind of container–contained relationship" (López-Corvo, 2003, p. 217). In 1970, the *container* became the *container↔contained* represented by the feminine symbol ♀ and the masculine symbol ♂.

Several years prior to this, in 1925, Jung had written about the *container* and *contained* in an article entitled "Marriage as a Psychological Relationship". As the title makes clear, the article was aimed at the two protagonists in an actual marital union, as follows: "The one who is contained feels himself to be living entirely within the confines of his marriage; outside the marriage there exist no essential obligations and no binding interests" (1925, p. 195). On the other hand,

> The container … who in accordance with his tendency to dissociation has an especial need to unify himself in undivided love

for another, will be left far behind in this effort, which is naturally very difficult for him, by the simpler personality. (Ibid.)

Further in this article, he alludes to his concepts of the *anima* and *animus* denoting respectively the feminine and masculine principles, as follows:

> Anima and animus are both characterized by an extraordinary many-sidedness. In a marriage it is always the contained who projects this image upon the container, while the latter is only partially able to project his unconscious image upon his partner. (Ibid., p. 198)

Although what Jung and Bion designated by the terms *container* and *contained* is by no means identical, there is nonetheless an uncanny resemblance in the terms used and in their symbolic counterparts.

The psychology of the transference

As set out at length in the previous chapter, the woodcuts in the medieval alchemical text, *The Rosarium*, depicted in Jung's late article, "The Psychology of the Transference", provide the Ariadne thread of Jung's account of a particular type of *transference–countertransference* phenomenon. In order to link *psychological alchemy* to Bion's thinking, it will be useful to summarise in this chapter Jung's view of it as a metaphorical precursor to depth psychology's study of the *unconscious*, with its emphasis on emergence from below (instinct), or the presence of the divine in matter (*subtle body*). *Alchemy* itself was a critique of the sexless Christianity that abounded in the fifteenth and sixteenth centuries, which matched Jung's own critique of modern-day Christianity in the twentieth century and its influence on *Western* humankind. The alchemists' attempts to transform the base metal of lead into a pure substance, often depicted as gold, was viewed psychologically by Jung as seeking the release of spirit from base matter. The imagery used is depicted as oppositional, namely, masculine and feminine, while the transcending of these opposites resulted in a new entity, that is, a symbolic child. The dialectical process entailed in this procedure appeared to Jung to be a metaphor for the relationship of analyst and *analysand* whereby they are mutually transformed resulting in the production of a third.

This is comparable to Bion's approach "where the respective 'Os' of each participant can breed in relationship to the imaginatively conjectured infant of analysis held in mind by both …" (Grotstein, 2007, p. 24). This dialectical process is both an *intrapsychic* as well as an interpersonal interaction so that the latter, the analyst–patient relationship, can promote internal growth as well as vice versa. As Jung puts it: "The unrelated human being lacks wholeness … which is always found in a 'You'" (1954, p. 245).

Some of this material on "The Psychology of the Transference" has already been elaborated at length in Chapter 11 but is worth revisiting here to link it to Bion's conceptualising and to Michael Fordham's thinking on Jung's *alchemical process*. It is also to emphasise how hugely important Jung's contribution of *psychological alchemy* is for psychoanalysis. As has already been stated, Jung's writings in "The Psychology of the Transference" may be viewed, in part, as a final working through of the powerful encounter Jung had as a young psychiatrist practising at Burghölzli Hospital in Zürich in the course of his psychoanalytic relationship with Sabina Spielrein, the nineteen-year-old Russian Jewish girl who had been admitted as an inpatient in 1904 diagnosed as suffering from hysteria. Jung had read Freud's *Interpretation of Dreams* (1900a) and was so impressed by it that he adopted the new technique of psychoanalysis in his work with Spielrein, his first psychoanalytic patient. She was discharged from Burghölzli in 1905 still under Jung's care and, from this time, their joint *archetypal* erotic *transference–countertransference* feelings began to emerge, as testified in her diaries and letters. The intensity of their relationship peaked in the years 1908 to 1911, during which time both were in touch with Freud seeking his help. Jung was by now afraid of jeopardising his personal life (recently married to a wealthy wife and with a child) and professional career, and he and Spielrein eventually went their separate ways.

Psychic infection and projective identification

As has been intimated above, Jung and Bion's models of *containment* within the psychoanalytic relationship were based on their experience of working with *psychosis*. For Jung, this reached its culmination in "The Psychology of the Transference", which will be elaborated further in this chapter. *Anima* and *animus*, already described in Chapter 6, are central to this process and refer to twinned *archetypes*, patterning structures that make up the realm of what Jung called the *collective unconscious,* namely, the realm of the *"thing-in-itself".* He viewed these structures as "the *precondition* of each individual psyche, just as the sea is the carrier of the individual wave" (1954, p. 169; my italics). This is analogous to Bion's notion of *pre-conception,* which is in its turn similar to Kant's idea of "empty thoughts". Furthermore, lying behind both *archetype* and *preconception* is the concept of the *somatic unconscious.*

Michael Fordham's exploration of Jung's alchemical model starts with his own interpretation of the succinct diagram below which Jung used to illustrate its pertinent features.

Prior to enlarging on Fordham's views on Jung's alchemical model, it is necessary to give a short explanation of what the six lines denote, as follows:

(a) An uncomplicated personal relationship.
(b) A relationship of the analyst to the anima and of the patient to the animus.
(c) A relationship of anima to animus and vice versa.
(d) A relationship of the analyst to the animus and of the patient to the anima.

The two designations at the top of line (a) are Fordham's analytical substitutes for Jung's alchemical terms of *"Adept"* and *"Soror".* For the sake of clarity, these counter-crossing relationships are schematised by Jung in this economical diagram but, it goes without saying, that in an actual analysis they are not kept apart but are intermixed and occur simultaneously. To summarise, the straight line (a) at the top of the diagram denotes the relatively uncomplicated personal relationship which

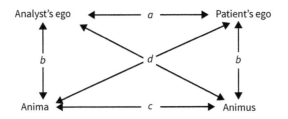

Diagram illustrating Fordham's revisions on transference–countertransference

contributes to the creation of the treatment alliance. The straight downward line (b) on the left side indicates the analyst drawing on her *unconscious* and being in touch with the *archetype* of the *wounded healer* for an *empathic* understanding of the patient's suffering. The straight downward line (b) on the right side represents the patient's initial awareness of problems but also *resistance* to that awareness. The two diagonal lines (d) indicate the impact of the analytical relationship on the *unconsciousness* of the two participants. At this point, I would like to draw particular attention to the bottom line (c) which indicates where the phenomenon of *psychic infection* or *projective identification* occurs. This may also be expressed as the *archetypal transference–countertransference* that takes place in the analytical *container*. As a point of interest, Klein published her first account of *projective identification* in her paper "Notes on Some Schizoid Mechanisms" in 1946, the same year Jung published "The Psychology of the Transference".

Fordham's interpretation of the above claims that what Jung was depicting as *archetypal* material in his analysis of *The Rosarium* was, in more analytical language, a *transference–countertransference psychosis*. The ten alchemical woodcuts are interpreted by Jung as a process into which both analyst and patient/*analysand* are *unconsciously* drawn and thereby transformed. As a result of being contained in the *vas*, the patient can experience the necessary *regression* and, at the stage of the *coniunctio*, an incestuous union finds a symbolic expression similar to that of the *unio mystica* in Christianity. The next stage is described by Fordham as follows: "According to the alchemists a deathly stillness reigns and Jung interprets the situation as psychic death of the ego, or the union of the animus and the anima ..." (Fordham, 1978, p. 87).

The sixth woodcut, *The ascent of the soul*, shows the fusion and death of the alchemical pair and the soul depicted as a child ascending to heaven. Fordham interprets this as the *transference psychosis* "analogous to the schizophrenic state" (ibid., p. 87) in which the patient's *ego* has been virtually destroyed. This results in states of disorientation akin to loss of *soul* at the alchemical stage of the *nigredo* which, in psychoanalytical language, would indicate a *schizoid depression*. The ultimate stage is the whitening (*albedo*) or purification of the dead "bodies" followed by the return of the *soul* and the birth of the *self*. This is depicted as a conjoined masculine/feminine figure or *hermaphrodite*.

Poetry

The diagram above illustrates Jung's contention that *alchemy* was a metaphor for *archetypal transference–countertransference* experienced in the course of an in-depth analysis. This emotional experience results in an incestuous attraction between the two participants that Jung termed *kinship libido*. It is through the spiritualisation of this incestuous libido that the psychological alchemical work comes to its fruition in the constellation of the *coniunctio*, or higher marriage, and the birth of the *divine child*, namely, *individuation*. The series of triangles in this diagram depict the dialectical nature of the *transference*, which is always in flux.

The emphasis here is on *psychic* processing itself, which was also of central importance to Bion. In this way, both he and Jung were able to work *in* the transference which, for Bion, was the way of experiencing and intuiting "*O*". Emotional experience is the key here: for Jung it was experiencing shifts in the *ego–self axis* that was mutative—the *self* being, for Jung, the *archetype* that is indistinguishable from the God-image. Similarly, for Bion it was experiencing transformation in "*O*" where his approach is

> … close to poetry and the opposite of the narrative. The narrative is an expression of logical articulation, which is the work of a thinking mind searching for unifying coherence. This is not the case with poetry, which does not add understanding and knowledge but which lets the unknowable Psychoanalytic Object be and evolve. (Vermote, 2005, p. 9)

There is an intriguing correspondence between what Vermote calls "poetry" and Sabina Spielrein's use of the term with reference to the erotic relationship that developed between her and Jung. In 1909 she wrote to Freud as follows: "Four and a half years ago Dr. Jung was my doctor; then he became my friend and finally my 'poet' namely, my beloved. Eventually he came to me and things went as they usually do with 'poetry'" (Carotenuto, 1984, p. 93). Freud's help had been sought by both parties, as a result of which he was drawn into this situation of "*transference love*" as he was later to call it. He thought that with a bit more analysis everything could be resolved, including Spielrein's fantasy that "poetry" would lead to the birth of an actual child, Siegfried. Jung, who was Christian, and Spielrein, who was Jewish, fantasised about having an Aryan-Semitic love child. It is not unreasonable to hypothesise from the extensive documentation that has been unearthed relating to the "poetry" between Spielrein and Jung, that the latter's future *working through* of the turbulent emotions evoked in him by the affair eventually led in his 1946 paper to what he came to call "*coniunctio*" and the birth of the "*divine child*". "You are always trying to drag the Siegfried symbol back into reality, whereas in fact it is the bridge to your individual development ... That is individuation" (Carotenuto, 1984, p. 54).

This was part of a letter dated 21st January 1918 that Jung wrote to Spielrein. By an ironic twist of fate, the Nazi firing squad that killed Spielrein in Russia in 1942 was called *Siegfried* (personal communication, Alain Gibeault, IPA psychoanalyst).

Alpha-function

When I presented a version of this paper at the "Bion-in-Boston" conference, I was fortunate in having the psychoanalyst Katina Kostoulas as the moderator of my session. What follows is the *coniunctio* that resulted from our interaction on Jung and Bion. It is the case that the mode in which Bion expresses transformation is, on the face of it, quite different to Jung's alchemical metaphor but, at a deeper level, their ideas in this regard can be seen to bear a marked similarity of approach.

Within the *analytic container*, the *alpha-function* of the analyst through *maternal reverie* is like that of the mother with her infant. This *reverie* has the potential for transforming the base metal or lead, that is, unmentalised β-*elements* or *nameless dread* into the gold of *alpha-elements* that leads to the growth of the patient's mind and to *containment*. In the course of this process, *splitting, taking apart,* or *deconstruction* is then followed by synthesis or integration of the two poles or opposites in the dialectic in such a way that the fundamental truth is found only in their unity. I am proposing here that this would represent the *coniunctio* in Bion's model. With regard to *truth*, Bion states: "... healthy mental growth seems to depend on truth as the living organism depends on food. If it is lacking or deficient the personality deteriorates" (1965, p. 38). Bion related truth to transformations in "*O*".

The opposition here is between *splitting* or division on the one hand, resulting in discord, and harmony on the other, the latter being conceptualised by Bion as "at-one-ment". It is possible to speculate here about *anti-alpha-function* in which the gold of α-*elements* is deformed into *anti-thought* or *beta-elements*. This would be at the negative pole of transformations in "*O*" which would be expressed as "-*K*". The former is a transcendence of the *ego* through union with the *Other* so that spiritual growth or development may be seen as coming about as a result of a process of *purification* leading to *illumination*. Bion uses the letter "*K*" meaning knowledge to depict the "capacity to know or to contain" (López-Corvo, 2003, p. 157).

> Knowledge has no meaning unless it means that someone knows something and this … is an assertion of relationship, or of some part of a relationship. The term, "knowledge" I propose provisionally to employ to describe a state of mind indissolubly associated with a relationship between communicable awareness on the one hand, and the object of which the person feels thus aware, on the other. (Bion, 1992, p. 271)

"*K*" is the understanding and experiencing of the energy of the Godhead; whereas the essence of the divine, namely, "*O*" is dark, formless, unknowable and may only be accessed through "*K*". As applied to the *analytic container*, "*K*" comes about through the analyst's *maternal reverie*. However, if the analytic couple's interaction is dominated by envy, the relationship becomes destructive, which can result in a lack of α-*function* where the *contained* is subdued by the *container*. The result of this is "-*K*" and a corresponding lack of transformation in "*O*".

Dark radiance

In their work, Jung and Bion confronted the dilemma that faces any who undertake a confrontation with *unconscious* material, which may be thought of in the following manner. The integration into *ego* of powerful *unconscious* contents results in an inevitable *inflation* that has a serious impact on the *ego* which experiences it as a kind of death. This may be expressed as the "dark night of the soul", echoing the writings of St John of the Cross, which Jung viewed as "a supremely positive state, in which the invisible—and therefore *dark—radiance* of God come to pierce and purify the soul" (1954, p. 271; my italics).

> There is a striking parallel here with what Bion said to Grotstein quoting from Freud: "When conducting an analysis, one must cast a *beam of intense darkness* so that something which has hitherto been obscured by the glare of the illumination can glitter all the more in the darkness." (Grotstein, 2007, p. 1; original italics)

As Grotstein goes on to say, this was the Ariadne thread that would run through Bion's later thinking, which is expressed in his exhortation to analysts to abandon memory and desire so as to have faith in the creative response of their own *unconscious*. "It was also the hallmark of his ultimate ontological epistemology, transformations in, from, and to "O", the Absolute Truth about an infinite, impersonal and ineffable Ultimate Reality" (ibid., p. 2).

For Jung, the alchemical figure of the *hermaphrodite* as the end result of the *coniunctio* symbolises nothing less than the *philosopher's stone* or what he calls *individuation*, and is the culmination of a long process of analysis during which the *libido* is extracted from the alluring fascination of the eroticised *transference–countertransference*. On a symbolic level, this is the birth of the *divine child*, analogous with Bion's approach where "… the analysand that experiences 'O' and awaits realization or incarnation with the analyst's interpretation is the ineffable subject of the unconscious, a numinous entity who may also be known as the 'once-and-forever-infant-of-the-unconscious'" (Grotstein, 2007, p. 127). For Bion, as for Jung, the systems $Cs\leftrightarrow Ucs$ are not in a state of conflict as Freud had it but of cooperative opposition in triangulating "O" (Bion) or *individuating* (Jung). A quote from Bion expresses this as follows:

> … that which is the ultimate reality represented by terms such as ultimate reality, absolute truth, the godhead, the infinite, the thing-in-itself … does not fall in the domain of knowledge or learning save incidentally … It is darkness and formlessness but it enters the domain "K" when it has evolved to a point where it can be known, through knowledge gained by experience, and formulated in terms derived from sensuous experience; its existence is conjectured phenomenologcally. (1970, p. 26)

Conclusion

Both Jung and Bion were interested in mathematical laws and their application to all life. Long before he discovered *alchemy*, Jung was interested in the dialectic between the systems $Cs{\leftrightarrow}Ucs$ and formulated his concept of the *transcendent function* which, he hypothesised, resulted from "the confrontation of the two positions [which] generates a tension charged with energy and creates a living, third thing ..." (Jung, 1916, p. 90). He borrowed the term *transcendent function* from mathematics, a function of the real and imaginary numbers, to extend his usage of the same term for the union of *conscious* and *unconscious* contents in the *individuating* process. "The secret of alchemy was in fact the transcendent function, the transformation of personality through the blending and fusion of the noble with the base components of the conscious with the unconscious" (Jung, 1953, p. 220).

Before passing on to Bion's mathematical thinking, it is worth digressing for a moment to take note of the critique of Jung's theory of the *transcendent function* to be found in the work of the Jungian psychoanalyst, Wolfgang Giegerich. He contends that the *transcendent function* conceived by Jung as a creative synthesis arising out of the tension of opposites "remains miraculous and what exactly it will be [is] unforeseeable—naturally so, because Jung operates with the idea of an *unconscious* as the mysterious 'author' or source *behind* the scene" (Giegerich, Miller, & Mogenson, 2005, p. 7). This is *positivistic* thinking on the part of Jung as he remains an external observer rather than getting into the process and viewing it "from within in its internal consistency" (ibid.). What is needed instead is the *recursive* processing inherent in *psychological alchemy* that entails the *corruption, sublimation,* and *distillation* of the *prima materia*.

At this point, we are in the realm of Heidegger's phenomenology that Giegerich readily admits is a profound influence on his thinking. Heidegger's analysis of *Being-in* means that one does not first experience oneself and then the world nor vice versa, rather "the two are simultaneously present in indissoluble union" (Safranski, 1999, p. 154). This experience is known as *intentionality*, the most important insight of phenomenology first put forth by the philosopher Franz Brentano, who was an influence on Freud amongst other original thinkers. *Being-in* leads away from the separation of subject and object or "a choice between subjective (internal) and objective (external) standpoints" (ibid.). This, in turn, underwrites the fact that there is nothing "behind" phenomena— one is in the world not outside observing it.

To turn now to Bion's model, he draws attention to some features of mathematical development which have their correlates in psychoanalysis and speaks of:

> ... the transition from the dark and formless Godhead of Meister Eckhart to the "knowable" Trinity. My suggestion is that an intrinsic feature of the transition from the "unknowability" of infinite Godhead to the "knowable" Trinity is the introduction of the number "three". The Godhead has become, or been, mathematized. (1965, p. 170)

Though he had also subtracted from the value of maths thus:

> Translation in "K" has, contrary to the common view, been less adequately expressed by mathematical formulation than by religious formulations. Both are defective when required to express growth, and therefore, transformation, in "O". Even so, religious formulations come nearer to meeting the requirements of transformations in "O" than mathematical formulations. (Ibid., p. 156)

As a result, both psychoanalysts have been called mystics because of their in-depth exploration of the mysteries inherent in the *psyche*. As Grotstein claims, Bion was transforming the *positivistic-mechanistic drive unconscious* into a *numinous*, mystical *unconscious*.

> ... Bion is telling us that the *deity, like the unconscious, is incomplete, not omnipotent, only infinite!* The deity needs man for it to become incarnated and realized—just as the unconscious needs consciousness to become known, to complete its mission. (Grotstein, 2007, p. 331; original italics)

This bears a striking resemblance to what Jung states in his late work *Answer to Job*:

> God acts out of the unconscious of man and forces him to harmonize and unite the opposing influences to which his mind is exposed from the unconscious ... God wants to become man. (1958b, p. 94)

For some time now, Jung and Bion's approaches are increasingly seen as subjective, relational, and intersubjective, for example where Jung states: "The unrelated human being lacks wholeness ... which is always found in a 'You'" (1954, p. 244). Though it is as well to bear in mind that he goes on to say: "I do not, of course, mean the synthesis or identification of two individuals, but the conscious union of the ego with everything that has been projected into the 'You'" (p. 245).

> The last is transformation in, of, and from "O". In psychoanalysis, the analyst becomes the container of the analysand's projections. He undergoes first a transformation in "O" to match the analysand's ... he then transforms his own sympathetic experience of "O" into "K"—knowledge *about* or *from* "O". (Grotstein, 2007, p. 231; original italics)

In the Bionian *container*, β-*elements* (*raw sensations*) are transformed into α-*elements* (*proto-thoughts*); in the alchemical *container* "the *opus* becomes an analogy of the natural process by means of which instinctive energy is transformed, in part at least, into symbolical activity" (Jung, 1954, p. 25; original italics).

Lastly, Jung's concept of the *coniunctio* is analogous with the *primal scene* in which Bion's female and male icons of ↓ ↗ symbolise the original act of creation. Sexual and erotic imagery has often been used to illustrate an intimate encounter with transcendence so it is unsurprising that Jung and Bion did likewise.

CHAPTER 13

Jung's transmutation: Siegried to Parsifal

Afirst version of this chapter was presented at the 2019 IAAP International Congress held in Vienna, the setting being an important reason for including a fair amount of material on Freud. The chapter is based largely on Jung's *Red Book* in its assertion that Jung's quest for his *soul*, as he expresses it in that work, is actually the *Quest for the Grail*. In the process of writing a chapter for Murray Stein and Thomas Arzt's *Jung's Red Book for Our Time: Searching for Soul under Postmodern Conditions*, I reread the entirety of Jung's *Red Book* and, in so doing, came across the myth of Parsifal embedded in the text. In *The Red Book* there are several allusions to that myth, which is the one associated with Jung's natal sign of Leo. "I took it upon myself to get to know 'my' myth" (Shamdasani, 2009, p. 15) is what he sets out knowingly to find though he appears to have come upon it unwittingly as, although there are frequent references to the Parsifal myth, I could find no acknowledgement that this was *his* myth.

As the present chapter is, to a large extent, based on the contents of *The Red Book*, I shall begin with my personal experience of the latter leading up to its publication in 2009. Prior to that date, I was already familiar with some of its contents from Aniela Jaffé's 1979 *C. G. Jung: Word and*

Image, which includes some text and images from it. I first recall hearing from my friend, Sonu Shamdasani, of his work on *The Red Book* in the early 2000s, though throughout that time he was bound by confidentiality agreements not to disclose any of its contents. Finally, in August 2009, Sonu and Maggie Barron hosted a private seminar lasting a few days for a small group of individuals at Cliveden, an elegant mid-nineteenth-century house in the English county of Berkshire. This private seminar preceded the formal launch of *The Red Book: Liber Novus* on 7th August 2009 at the Rubin Museum in New York, where the exhibition also included Jung's *Black Books,* the precursors of *The Red Book.* Before setting out for the New York launch in 2009, I managed to get hold of two copies of the first edition in order to write a review for *The Economist* that would coincide with the date of its publication. My editor on the paper was astonished by the high quality of Jung's artwork and queried whether he had done it all himself. These paintings show the influence of the indigenous civilisations of Ancient Egypt, India, Mexico, and Tibet, as well as the symbolist artist, Odilon Redon, and the Byzantine frescoes and mosaics in Ravenna.

That unforgettable time with Sonu and members of the Jung family as well as other luminaries such as James Hillman, George Makari, Frank McMillan, and Beverley Zabriskie, spent together in New York for the book's launch, consisted of eleven days of frenzied activity, particularly for Sonu, so much so that many of us were concerned for his well-being. This special event was followed in 2010 by an exhibit of the *Red* and *Black Books* at the Library of Congress in Washington, which was attended by the eminent Librarian of Congress, James Billington. Once again, some of the same people who came to the New York launch attended these proceedings in Washington, where the Swiss embassy put on a reception for all of us at the ambassador's residence in the US capital.

Immediately following the launch in New York, I conducted an interview with Sonu for *The Journal of Analytical Psychology,* in the course of which he discussed some of the main features of *The Red Book,* that Jung had worked on from 1914 to 1930. A key point about the work is that it is *not* a scientific study but a private cosmology forming the bedrock of Jung's public work in which he is exploring various questions. These consist of the impossibility of reconciling *Western* science with what science has forsaken; how psychology can differentiate religious experiences from psychosis; and what to do with irrational experiences that are so far from rationality. "What is prophetic in Jung's text is the rebirth of the God image and the image of God" (Casement, 2010, p. 36).

As Shamdasani goes on to say in the interview, there is a crisis of language in *The Red Book* that emerges from the tension between *directed* and *non-directed* thinking, with the text oscillating between the two poles. The literary content of the book was composed in such a way that it should be comparable to Dante's *Divine Comedy* and Nietzsche's *Zarathustra*, and the key figure of *Philemon* links to Ovid's *Metamorphoses* and Goethe's *Faust*.

Siegfried

I have given the above personal account as a prelude to homing in on the specific theme of this chapter, namely, Jung's claim that *The Red Book* depicts his own *transmuting process*, which may be seen in his shift from identifying with the Germanic hero, *Siegfried*, to the unwitting discovery of *Parsifal* as "his" own myth. This matches with Jung's theoretical construct of the first and second halves of life—according to which, the former is normally *extraverted* as it deals with *ego* development in the form of finding a partner, settling down to home and family, and developing a career, usually accomplished in Jung's time when an individual had reached their mid to late thirties. The second half of life, says Jung, is *introverted* whence the focus is on the inner life as a preparation for death, which brings to mind Heidegger's *being-unto-death*. The latter assertion is my own because Jung appears unread in Heidegger, testified to by the fact there are no references to the latter in the *General Index, Volume 20* of the *Collected Works*, only one to a J. H. Heidegger, a Swiss theologian. The following is a distillation of how I understand Heidegger's *being-unto-death*, his version of preparedness for death, which is expressed in the first person singular.

> When I take on board the possibility of my own not being, my own not being-able-to-Be is brought into proper view. Hence my awareness of my own death as an omnipresent possibility discloses the authentic self—a self that is mine opposed to a they-self. The possibility of my not existing encompasses the whole of

my existence and my awareness of that possibility illuminates me, *qua Dasein*, in my totality.

To return to *The Red Book*, there are so many literary and esoteric allusions running through the text and the footnotes in it, which entailed several forays into the work before I was made aware of the theme of *Parsifal* running through much of the book. These are preceded earlier in the work by Jung's significant dream about *Siegfried*, which he refers to in the following way: "… a mighty dream vision rose from the depths" (Shamdasani, 2009, p. 160). This dream has been much analysed over the years by psychoanalysts, including yours truly.

> I was with a youth in high mountains. It was before day-break, the Eastern sky was already light. Then Siegfried's horn resounded over the mountains with a jubilant sound.
>
> We knew that our mortal enemy was coming. We were armed and lurked beside a narrow rocky path to murder him. Then we saw him coming high across the mountains on a chariot made of the bones of the dead. He drove boldly and magnificently over the steep rocks and arrived at the narrow path where we waited in hiding. As he came around the turn ahead of us, we fired at the same time and he fell slain. Thereupon I turned to flee, and a terrible rain swept down. But after this I went through a torment unto death and I felt certain that I must kill myself, if I could not solve the riddle of the murder of the hero. (1963, p. 173)

Following this dream/vision, Jung seemed to follow a natural process of filling the void left by the death of Siegfried, "the blond and blue-eyed German hero" who "had everything in himself that I treasured as the greater and more beautiful; he was my power, my boldness, my pride" (Shamdasani, 2009, p. 163), and who is sometimes thought of as a storm trooper. Jung gives the following reason for this murder: "I wanted to go on living with a new God" (ibid.), and the rain is "… the mourning of the dead in me, which precedes burial and rebirth … it begets the new wheat, the young, germinating God" (ibid., p. 164).

Before proceeding further with *The Red Book*, it is necessary to retrace our steps and look at what the psychological astrologer and Jungian analyst, Liz Greene, says about the myth attached to Jung's natal sign. My own interest in astrology was piqued through making her acquaintance, and I was particularly drawn to the way she linked mythology to each sign of the Zodiac, which in Jung's case lies in the sign of Leo, the sign that denotes the hero's quest for his spiritual father. The lion is a fiery animal and those born under this sign will have to battle strong instinctual urges in order to begin to *individuate* as Jung expresses it. Liz Greene links the legend of Parsifal to the sign of Leo with its overarching theme of *redemption*, on the face of it a much-lauded quality but one that also has a *shadow* component that will be explored later in this chapter. In the legend of Parsifal, it is the wounded father that needs redeeming, a theme that erupted in and finally destroyed Jung's relationship with Freud. At the start, Parsifal is fatherless, which underlines the lack of a father-principle "although there may be a physical father present" as there was in Jung's life (Greene, 1984, p. 206).

In order to remind ourselves of the story of *Parsifal*, we will now turn to the version of the legend that Wagner chose to use for his last great *oeuvre*. This is well set out in the late Bryan Magee's *Wagner and Philosophy*, a book highly recommended to those who love both Wagner and philosophy as Magee had a profound grasp of both, a combination that is rare indeed. Wagner's late musical dramas owe a huge debt (as he himself acknowledged) to Schopenhauer, with Wagner's *Parsifal* representing the greatest influence of that philosopher, in particular the theme of redemption through compassion. Wagner, of course, also composed and wrote the libretto of *Siegfried*, the third opera of his great opus *The Ring*. It is not entirely fanciful to think of the later works by this incomparable composer as Schopenhauer set to music.

In many ways, the character of *Siegfried* shares quite a bit in common with *Parsifal*, for example, both are bumbling youths when we first encounter them, although *Parsifal* eventually supersedes the fate of *Siegfried*. How much of that might have been in Jung's mind when he was composing his *Red Book* is unknown so let us now remind ourselves of the story of *Parsifal* as it appears in Magee's book.

> The knights of the holy grail are the guardians of the most numinous objects on the face of the earth. These are the grail itself, which is the chalice from which Christ drank at the Last Supper, and the spear that

pierced his side as he hung on the cross. This treasure is guarded by them in Montsalvat, their redoubt in the mountains of northern Spain, the paths to which can never be found by sinners. Here their sublime ritual is a regular re-enactment of the Last Supper in which they themselves drink from the grail. Their fitness for their office requires them to remain pure and chaste. Theirs is an all-male community, except for a dowdy and bedraggled woman called Kundry, a solitary, humble servitor who lives hermit-like in their domain, though occasionally she disappears from the scene for long periods.

At some time in the past a knight called Klingsor has aspired to join the order but been prevented from doing so by his inability to master his sexual desires. In a drastic attempt to kill the lust in himself he castrated himself. This horrendous act, far from giving him entrance to the order, made the order view him with revulsion, and turned him into a permanent outcast from it. His self-mutilation gave him access to magic powers, however, and he set out to use these to gain possession of the spear and the grail. He built a castle in the same mountain range as Montsalvat, and—understanding as he did the disabling power of sexual desire, but being now immune to it himself—drew round him a subject community of gorgeous women with the task of seducing knights of the grail when they sallied forth from Montsalvat. There were plenty of knights who succumbed; and from the moment they did so Klingsor had them in his power. Faced with this mortal threat to the order, its king, Amfortas, set out one day armed with the holy spear itself to destroy Klingsor. But on the way he encountered a fearsomely beautiful woman who seduced him from this aim—only in passing, as he thought. Letting go of the spear to make love to her, he discovered too late that he had fallen into a trap set by Klingsor. The hidden magician, watching the whole scene, rushed in, seized the spear, plunged it into Amfortas's side, and made off with it. So Klingsor had got the spear, and it remained only for him to get possession of the grail.

Amfortas, his life suspended by a thread, managed to get back to Montsalvat, overwhelmed by mortification and guilt, and in physical agony from his wound. The wound never healed and never ceased to agonise, and yet the death for which Amfortas now longed as the only release from intolerable shame never came. He found himself with a mortal wound that was permanent, and he lived on, hanging between life and death. As king of the order he had no choice but to go on leading the regular enactments of the Last Supper—he, the only sinner in the order, conducting the service. He did this under the fiercest protest on account of his sense of unfitness, and had to be dragged to his place by the knights, physically crippled by his wound and emotionally crippled by guilt. The remorse that ate into his soul might be appeased partially if the spear could be returned to Montsalvat, and at least he would be able to die in peace. Year after year, knight after knight rode out to recover the spear and restore the situation; but each of them succumbed to one of Klingsor's temptresses, and none of them ever returned. The order went into a decline which, if not halted, was bound to end in its demise. A prophecy emanating from the grail warned the order that it would be salvaged only by a pure fool whose understanding of the situation was nothing to do with cleverness but had been arrived at through compassion.

This is the background to the moment when a pure fool, killing birds for fun, comes chasing along one of the paths into the knights' domain. As an innocent at large he unknowingly finds ways that are hidden from sinners. This is Parsifal, an abnormally simple and ignorant young man. His father, a knight, was killed in battle before he was born, and his mother, fearful of a similar fate for him, brought him up in ignorance of his father, and of arms in general, and of the dangerous world. But one day he saw a group of men in glittering array ride past on beautiful creatures that he did not even know to be horses. Entranced, he ran after them, but could not run as fast as the horses, and found himself in the end lost and far from home. From then on he wandered aimlessly, living from moment to moment, defending himself with a simple bow against robbers, wild beasts, and giants. His mother, to whom he never returned, died of grief at his loss; but he did not know this, and gave no special thought to her. When he blunders into Montsalvat he has no idea where he has come from; and he is unable to tell questioners what his name is, or who his father was. The wisest of the knights, Gurnemanz, at once seizes on the hope that this person is the prophesied saviour, and intro- duces him as a spectator to the order's ritual and lets him see Amfortas's agony. But Parsifal has no more understanding of any of this, and no more compassion for Amfortas, than he has shown towards his mother. Seeing this, Gurnemanz gives up hope—Parsifal is just a fool, evidently, nothing more. So Gurnemanz turns him out of Montsalvat altogether.

From there Parsifal blunders into Klingsor's domain. There his complete ignorance and innocence make him immune to the seductions of the women; and he routs Klingsor's knights in the same way as he has routed robbers, wild beasts, and giants. To bring him to heel, Klingsor confronts him with his supreme, hitherto irresistible temptress, the very same who had seduced Amfortas. With her characteristic insight she arouses Parsifal's sexuality for the first time in his life by evoking his relationship with his mother. Partly because of this he experiences with her the onslaught of sexual desire in all its ferocity—and realises what had happened to Amfortas. Ravaged by desire at its most terrible and imperious he does not flee from it, despite his terror, but lives it through without evasion, and finally succeeds in overcoming it. The experience constitutes a breakthrough for him in understanding and insight. Through it he achieves compassionate empathy not only with Amfortas but with suffering humankind in general, eternally stretched out on its rack of unsatisfiable willing. He understands its need for redemption, and also what it means to be a redeemer who takes on himself the burden of suffering humanity—and therefore the significance of the re-enactment of the Last Supper which he had witnessed so uncomprehendingly at Montsalvat. All becomes clear to him. But, alas, although he is now able to destroy Klingsor's castle and recover the spear, the temptress has left her curse on him nevertheless: after his experiences with her he is no longer the innocent he had been before, and when he leaves the ruins of Klingsor's castle he can no longer find the path back to Montsalvat—at least not until after many years of wandering and searching, years during which the order of the grail declines almost to extinction. But he does find it eventually. He also finds himself remembered, and recognised, though recognised for what he truly is. He cures the wound of Amfortas by touching it with the point of the spear that caused it, and takes over from a now gratefully released Amfortas the leadership of the order, obviously to restore and surpass its former glories.

The arch temptress too achieves redemption in this final scene. For it turns out that she and Kundry are one and the same person. Through hundreds of years she has been living through a succession of lives in search of atonement for the ultimate sin, the ultimate lack of compassion: she had laughed and mocked at Christ as he was being flogged towards his own crucifixion. At different times in her existence she is both of the faces of the female archetype, on the one hand woman as nurturer and carer, on the other hand woman as temptress and destroyer. When she had been in Montsalvat she had been seeking expiation and redemption as an undemanding, self-sacrificing, barely noticed minister to the needs of others; but during her unaccountable absences she had been in search of self-fulfilment through sexual love, as the ultimately beautiful voluptuary and lover. Having been repudiated in the second of these embodiments by Parsifal it is left to her only to serve him, and through doing so with no longer any possibility of self-gratification she finally reaches her redemption and attains release from the chain of being.

All the characters except Parsifal have been looking for fulfilment or redemption in the wrong place, and therefore would never have found it except through him. Kundry has sought it not through loving but through being loved, or through being needed. Klingsor has aspired to it through power. Amfortas has grasped for it in death. The knights of the order have been hoping to achieve it by belonging to a society whose membership and vitality are in fact declining, and whose rituals, conducted by someone unworthy to do so, are a mockery. Only Parsifal understands that redemption is not to be found through observances and not through any form of self-gratification either, but through its opposite, namely denial of the will in all its forms: if through love, then utterly one-way love; if through power, then mastery over oneself, not mastery over others; if in death, then in death as a fulfilment of life, not as an escape from it; if in ritual, then in enactments dedicated wholly to something outside and beyond the participants, through self-effacement in the transcendental, and hence through self-transcendence in the most literal sense. So the man who brings redemption to most of the other characters, and to the order of knights, himself finds redemption in the process. (Magee, 2000, pp. 265–269)

The Red Book

The themes spelt out in this account appear in *The Red Book* with the figure of *Christ* recurring throughout, including several references to the fifteenth-century religious thinker, Thomas à Kempis's book *The Imitation of Christ:* "There is no one so perfect and holy that he never meets temptation; we cannot escape it altogether" (Shamdasani, 2009, p. 336).

Among several others, there are further allusions to Christ (see pages 137, 331, 343, 356, 357).

The *divine child* symbolised by the pure, innocent fool, *Parsifal*, is another key motif that runs through *The Red Book* (pages 118, 204, 296). The innocence and the potential of the child are both personified by Parsifal. On pages 363–364, there is specific mention of *Parsifal*. At first, Jung finds himself in a magnificent garden and it occurs to him this is *Klingsor's* magical garden. It seems he is in a theatre and that the characters of *Amfortas* and *Kundry* are part of the play. *Klingsor* is also there and Jung says: "How closely Klingsor resembles me! What a repulsive play! But look, Parsifal enters from the left. How strange, he also looks like me" (Shamdsani, 2009, pp. 363–364).

> The scene changes: It appears that the audience, in this case me, joins in during the last act. One must kneel down as the Good Friday service begins: Parsifal enters—slowly, his head covered with a black helmet. The lionskin of Hercules adorns his shoulders and he holds the club in his hand, he is also wearing modern black trousers in honor of the church holiday. I bristle and stretch out my hand avertingly, but the play goes on. Parsifal takes off his helmet. Yet there is no Gurnemanz to atone for and consecrate him. Kundry stands in the distance, covering her head and laughing. The audience is enraptured and recognises itself in Parsifal. He is I. I take off my armor layered with history and my chimerical decoration and go to the spring wearing a white penitent's shirt … I walk out of the scene and approach myself—I who am still kneeling down in prayer as the audience. I rise and become one with myself. (Ibid.)

The dyad of *Elijah/Salome* in *The Red Book* may be linked to *Klingsor/ Kundry*; the male part, *Elijah*, Jung equates with his notion of the *self*, the central *archetype* that is individual to the person unlike the other *archetypes*, that are universal. The female part of the dyad, *Kundry/Salome*, was instrumental in Jung's development of the notion of *anima* in its most ambiguous dual aspect as seducer/destroyer and loving/nurturing mother. Jung's fear of Salome's designs on his head is of course taken from the biblical story wherein she is the cause of John the Baptist's beheading, the latter figure being the herald of a new God just as Jung is seeking one in *The Red Book*. Furthermore, a severed head is another way of talking about castration which, in turn, links back to *Klingsor's* castration.

The figure of the *Magician* has a long chapter devoted to it in *The Red Book* and is represented by *Philemon*, a figure first encountered in antiquity in Ovid's *Metamorphoses*, where he and his wife, *Baucis*, represent the poor ageing couple who welcome into their home the gods, Jupiter and Mercury (Zeus and Hermes in Greek mythology). *Philemon*, who incorporates aspects of *Gurnemanz* and a wise magician, is the prototype for the *mana personality* that Jung developed in his exoteric writing in *Two Essays on Analytical Psychology*. The attainment of this stage of *consciousness* comes about through the subjection of the *mana* (from the Oceanic term meaning magical knowledge and power) of the *anima* daemonic *complex*. Through this process it is possible for *ego* to disengage from entanglements with the *collective unconscious*.

The figure of *Philemon* in *The Red Book* is a benign version of the evil magician *Klingsor*, and represents the *archetypal Wise Old Man* accompanying Jung as a guide on his quest (see pages 395, 397). Jung writes of this figure in *Psychological Types* as follows:

> The magician has preserved in himself a trace of primordial paganism, he possesses a nature that is still unaffected by the Christian splitting, which means he has access to the unconscious, which is still pagan, where the opposites still lie in their original naïve state, beyond all sinfulness, but, if assimilated into conscious life, produces evil and good with the same primordial and consequently daimonic force (Part of that power which would/ Ever work evil yet engenders good).… he is a destroyer as well as savior. The figure is therefore pre-eminently suited to become the symbol carrier for an attempt at unification. (1971, p. 188)

As may be deduced from this long quotation, for Jung it is the ultimate goal of unifying opposites that leads to redemption, a significant theme we shall return to at the end of this chapter. In the meantime, let us press on with identifying other allusions to the *Parsifal* legend in *The Red Book*. A giant Jung encounters is called *Izdubar*, a character from the

Sumerian Gilgamesh epic who has been wounded by the "poison" of science—an allusion Jung lifts from Nietzsche where in *The Gay Science*, Nietzsche argues that thinking arose from several impulses that had the effect of poison—to doubt being one. Izdubar says: "No stronger being has ever cut me down, no monster has ever resisted my strength. But your poison … has lamed me to the marrow" (Shamdasani, 2009, p. 279). Izdubar's wound and Jung's pity for him resonates with the feelings Parsifal has for Amfortas's wound.

Good Friday appears in the play from *The Red Book* previously mentioned and is a direct link to the Good Friday ritual in the Parsifal legend. Jung goes on to say: "This is the Good Friday when we complete the Christ in us and we descend to Hell ourselves … Good Friday on which we moan and cry to will the completion of Christ" (ibid., p. 370). *The Way of the Cross* has its own section in *The Red Book* and begins with the words: "I saw the black serpent, as it wound itself upward around the cross" (ibid., p. 189). The serpent represents the animal soul and appears frequently in the book; this section is also dedicated to the Crucifixion. The *Last Supper* appears in Nietzsche's *Zarathustra*, the *Parsifal* legend, and *The Red Book* (ibid., p. 390). Finally, the magical garden in *The Red Book* has links to *Klingsor's* magical garden and also to the Garden of Eden and the Garden of Gethsemane (ibid., pp. 174, 363, 412, 552), thereby connecting the themes of humankind's fall to that of its redemption. *The Red Book* ends abruptly when Jung abandoned it to focus on his studies on *alchemy*—interest in *alchemy* and the quest for the Holy Grail both have their beginnings in the twelfth century.

Redemption of the father

As a final link to the legend of *Parsifal*, the goal that is being quested for in *The Red Book* is what Jung calls *individuation*, which he views as fulfilment and redemption. In both cases, the theme of redemption was inspired by Schopenhauer, whose concatenation of Platonic and Kantian ideas with the Upanishads was a profound influence in this way and others on Wagner and Jung. Self-renunciation as expressed by Schopenhauer as "… unselfinterested love toward others" is the key to redemption, a notion from Schopenhauer which in turn is adopted by

Wagner and Jung. According to Schopenhauer "All love is compassion" (1819, pp. 434–435).

Jung shares with Parsifal the early experience of the lack of a father, although in Jung's case father was physically present but absent psychologically and intellectually, leaving Jung dissatisfied with their relationship and with a lack of the father principle in his life. Jung came to feel his father was stuck in outworn tradition, taking God as prescribed by the Bible and from the teachings of his own forefathers. When Jung was eighteen years old he had many discussions with his father, when he would try to explain his own feelings about an "immediate living God … omnipotent and free, above his Bible and his Church" (Jung, 1959a, p. 15). His father's response was: "Oh, nonsense, you always want to think. One ought not to think, but believe" (ibid., p. 53).

As already stated in the lengthy chapter on Freud earlier in the book, the resulting father *complex* carried over into Jung's interaction with the creator of psychoanalysis in whom he thought he had found the ideal father figure, as may be readily seen in the following extract from the Freud/Jung correspondence: "… let me enjoy your friendship not as one between equals but as that of father and son. This distance appears to me fitting and natural" (McGuire, 1974, p. 122). This is just one example of the idealised *transference* Jung had onto Freud in their early interaction and, like all such idealisations, it inevitably flipped over into its opposite when Jung berated Freud for patronising him and his other followers. Before that final denouement, one sees evidence of Jung trying to *redeem* Freud from what he views as the error of his ways over psychosexuality, Freud's innovative marriage of *Psyche* and *Eros*.

From Jung's own words it is clear to see that he never worked through his bitter feelings towards Freud, exemplified by the following quotations from the late works *Answer to Job* and *Memories, Dreams, Reflections.*

> With his touchiness and suspiciousness the mere possibility of doubt was enough to infuriate him and induce that peculiar double-faced behaviour of which he had already given proof in the Garden of Eden, when he pointed out the tree to the First Parents and at the same time forbade them to eat of it. In this way he precipitated the Fall, which he apparently never intended. (1958b, p. 375)

> Freud himself had a neurosis … Apparently neither Freud nor
> his disciples could understand what it meant for the theory and
> practice of psychoanalysis if not even the master could deal with
> his own neurosis. (1963, p. 162)

The hubris of trying to *redeem* the father needs to be tempered by humility and compassion, as seen in Parsifal. Attempts to *redeem* the father are not the same as constructive criticism, for example, Wolfgang Giegerich's elucidating critiques of Jung's writings. That is a completely different enterprise to delusional notions of redeeming the founding fathers of psychoanalysis from the error of their ways. Behind that kind of enterprise one may speculate that there are unresolved father *complexes*—and who is ever free from those? The most one can do is to have as much awareness of them as possible so they are not *acted-out* in futile attempts to redeem the *external* father.

Addendum

Michael Fordham, the eminent English psychoanalyst, has written an account of his last meeting with Jung shortly before the latter's death in 1961. Jung had written to an English colleague saying he had failed in his mission and was misunderstood and misrepresented. Fordham visited him in an effort to ease Jung's distress and described the meeting as follows:

> When I came to see him I did not touch on these matters but
> spoke superficially. If I had not done that I would have had to
> convey my thought that it was the delusion of being a world
> savior that made him feel a failure. (1993, p. 120)

CHAPTER 14

Emma Jung's Perceval

This is a fitting juncture at which to introduce Emma Jung, who spent thirty years of her life researching the Parsifal legend that she started to recount in a book entitled *The Grail Legend*. As Emma was unable to finish it before her death in 1955, Jung asked his close associate, Marie-Louise von Franz, to complete the work in order for it to be published as *The Grail Legend*. The result is a 400-page volume based largely on two twelfth-century texts by Chretien de Troyes and Robert de Boron, to which the interested reader is directed, details of which are easily found online, as there is space here for only a brief mention of the main theme running through it, namely, the quest for *wholeness* or *individuation* in Jung's language.

The book is a psychological exploration of the Grail legend set against a backdrop of the Arthurian legend of the knights of the Roundtable—in particular, the story of Perceval's (Parsifal) quest for the Grail. As has been set out in the preceding chapter, it is the story of a simpleton who turns out to be the redeemer which, according to the Grail legend (Magee, 2000), addresses the religious problem of modern humanity. Within its pages, there is also an emphasis on Merlin, the magician, who is put forward as the symbolic vestige of the shaman figure to be found in traditional societies.

Michael Fordham has a touching slant on the book and on Emma Jung, as follows:

> It was when Frieda and I had a meal with the Jungs that we started to make Emma's acquaintance. Both of us liked her and were impressed by her. She was not at first very communicative because her husband tended to take the stage, but she contributed to the conversation in a perceptive and sometimes penetrating way. It was clear that she very much had a mind of her own which was appreciative of but not subservient to that of her husband. Later on Frieda stayed at Kusnacht and I, on a different occasion, went to Emma for a few analytic interviews, and our impression of her was amply confirmed. She made important contributions to analytical psychology, especially in giving the animus a more favourable function as the basis for the logos function in a woman. She also wrote a study of the Grail symbolism which was never published but was swallowed by Marie-Louise von Franz, who made it into a book of her own in which Emma's contribution was destroyed. This was done at Jung's instigation and he will not be forgiven by me for it. Emma was a careful student of the subject, both down to earth and interesting. (1993, p. 115)

This short extract is enlightening in more ways than one; for instance, in its revelation that Fordham had some analytic sessions with Emma Jung though he did not have analysis with Jung himself. I was given first-hand accounts of how perceptive she was as an analyst by Hella Adler, who had also been analysed by her. Emma produced another book titled *Animus and Anima*, which is full of good sense that continues to read well today.

Jung first saw his future wife, Emma Rauschenbach, at her grand house at Schaffhausen when she was seventeen and he was twenty-four years old. She "was heiress to a great fortune" (Bair, 2004, p. 251) and had just returned from a year in Paris where "she learned to speak flaw-less French and to read Old French ... because she had developed an interest in the legends of the Holy Grail and wanted to read them in the original language" (ibid., p. 76). Following her meeting with Jung, she went on to study Greek, Latin, and mathematics, and "a deep and lasting bond formed between them when Emma told him of her interest in the Grail legends, which had fascinated him for years" (p. 78).

The fact of Emma being an heiress meant that Jung's marriage to her relieved him forever of the burden of financial worries—no doubt a major consideration for one who had grown up, as he had, in relative poverty. In addition, it was her money that paid for the construction of a large family house by the Lake at Küsnacht and, earlier than that, provided elegant furnishings for their apartment at Burghölzli Hospital where Jung was practising as a full-time psychiatrist.

The fifty-five-year-long Jung marriage produced five children, four daughters and a son. As a result of Emma's increasing involvement with domestic duties, Jung's *libido* was left free "to spy out of the window" (Jung, 1954, p. 196). It is no secret that Jung did his share of that in having more than one amorous affair—his erotic involvement with Sabina Spielrein, set out in the chapter on *alchemy*, being an example, followed by a forty-year-long affair with Toni Wolff that began after she started analysis with him in 1910. The interested reader is directed to Deidre Bair's biography of Jung for an account of this relationship ("Jung had found a second wife in Toni", Bair, 2004, p. 560). A review of a new book on Wolff acquiesces in its portrayal of her as the prime collaborator on Jung's vast *oeuvre*, an account that appears to be written in the trendy style common today where women of varying talents are resurrected in order to glorify and/or sanctify them. Jung makes no mention of Wolff or Spielrein in *Memories, Dreams, Reflections*, with only brief allusions in it to Emma, one in a footnote on page 205; though "in the protocols of Jung's interviews with Jaffé for *Memories*, there were several significant comments concerning his wife" (Shamdasani, 2005, p. 82). As mentioned earlier, these protocols are currently being worked on by the Philemon Foundation with a view to eventual publication.

When Jung went to visit Freud for the first time in Vienna in February 2007, he was accompanied by Emma Jung. She appears to have developed a warm relationship with Freud as evidenced in the (touching) correspondence between them in 1911 where she poured out her heart to him. This was at a time when she was becoming concerned by what she perceived as a certain strain that was beginning to manifest itself in the interaction between her husband and Freud. The following are brief extracts from four letters to Freud; his responses to her do not appear in the book (*The Freud/Jung Letters*, McGuire, 1974).

> Emma Jung (30th October 1911)
> I don't really know how I am summoning the courage to write you this letter but … I do not know whether I am deceiving myself when I think you are not somehow quite in agreement with "Transformations of Libido".

> Emma Jung (6th November 1911)
> Your nice kind letter has relieved me of anxious doubts, for I was afraid that in the end I had done something stupid. Now I am naturally very glad and thank you with all my heart for your friendly reception of my letter, and particularly for the goodwill you show to all of us.
> And do not think of Carl with a father's feeling: "He will grow, but I must dwindle," but rather as one human being thinks of another, who like you has his own law to fulfill.
> With warm love and veneration

> Emma Jung (14th November 1911)
> You were really annoyed by my letter, weren't you?
> There is one thing, however, I must vigorously defend myself against, and that is the way you take my "amiable ramblings" as you call them.
> Lately Carl has been analyzing his attitude to his work and has discovered some resistances to it. I had connected these misgivings about Part II with his constant worry over what you would say about it …. but now it appears that this fear of your opinion was only a pretext for not going on with the self-analysis which this work in fact means. I realize that I have thus projected something from my immediate neighbourhood into distant Vienna and am vexed that it is always the nearest thing that one sees worst.
> Please write nothing of this to Carl; things are going badly enough with me as it is.

Emma Jung (24th November 1911)

I find I have no friends, all the people who associate with us really only want to see Carl, except for a few boring and to me quite uninteresting persons.

Will you advise me, dear Herr Professor, and if necessary dress me down a bit? I am ever so grateful to you for your sympathy.

Apart from the warm feelings these poignant letters evoke, I feel gratified for confirmation from the highest authority in Jung's life of what I have always maintained about *Symbols of Transformation: An Analysis of the Prelude to a Case of Schizophrenia* (1956) or *Psychology of the Unconscious: A Study of the Transformations and Symbolisms of the Libido*, its original title in 1916, which is that the real patient is Jung himself and the putative patient, Miss Frank Miller, is only the outer hook on which it is hung. The book traces Jung's own struggle for liberation from "the mother" both personal and *archetypal*; whereas his treatise on *psychological alchemy*, as set out in my above account on that vital notion depicts, in part, his struggle to be liberated from "the father". Looked at in this way, both pieces are studies in the struggle for liberation from *incest*. This is a lifelong endeavour as *psychologically incestuous* relationships are potentially there throughout life, and finding oneself caught in one of them endangers psychological and emotional well-being. The so-called *repeating patterns*, cited by psychoanalysts and psychotherapists, are frequently the result of these unresolved *incestuous longings*. The following titles of some of the chapters of *Symbols of Transformation* attest to this quest on Jung's part: *V. Symbols of the Mother and Rebirth*; *VI. The Battle of Deliverance from the Mother*; *VII. The Dual Mother*.

Emma Jung was the most important person in her husband's life throughout the long marriage they shared together. This is attested to by both Deirdre Bair and Sonu Shamdasani—the former writing as follows: "… the only person Jung listened to—his wife" (2004, p. 529). In an interview I conducted with Shamdasani on the contents of *The Red Book* for *The Journal of Analytical Psychology* in 2010, a year after its publication, he mentioned that of the few people who were given privileged access to it at the time Jung was working on it "… the most important person is Emma Jung and not Toni Wolff" (Casement, 2010, p. 41).

The founding of the C. G. Jung Institute in Zürich in April 1948 was marked by Jung's inaugural speech, in which a Curatorium or governing board was proposed by him, with Jung himself as its first president, and C. A. Meier, Kurt Binswanger, Jolande Jacobi, and Liliane Frey-Rohn making up the rest of its five life members. Toni Wolff was not among them, which shocked everyone in Zürich who became convinced that Emma was responsible for this omission as "having moved to the center of her husband's life after his two illnesses, she was not about to jeopardize her status" (Bair, 2004, p. 532).

In an interview I did with the distinguished Jungian psychoanalyst, Verena Kast, for the 2019 *IAAP Newsletter*, she said the following about Jung's inaugural speech: "… he mentioned his merits and he expressed his wish, that members of the Institut will continue his research. It was important for him: the training and also research. But then he left quite soon the board and was replaced by his wife" (Casement, 2019, p. 270).

Emma Jung predeceased her husband by six years and died in her home at Küsnacht in November 1955 from cancer of the stomach. For more information about her death and its sequel, the interested reader is directed to the aforementioned biography of *Jung* by Deirdre Bair, which is an enjoyable read though lacking in intellectual rigour as Jung's concepts are not given the attention they deserve, and which, according to Sonu Shamdasani, contains 600 errors (personal communication). For now, a fitting conclusion to this section is the moving obituary by Michael Fordham for Emma Jung: "Mercifully her end was painless; like an act of divine providence she had scarcely any symptoms till she passed quietly away in a uraemic coma" (1956, p. 112).

CHAPTER 15

Eminent women in analytical psychology

This chapter, as well as those that follow on eminent people, represent my personal choices of individuals in analytical psychology who, in the view of this writer, have made significant contributions to that world. Furthermore, this writer has been and in some cases still is privileged to know many of these people well. The reason for highlighting certain figures in the chapters that follow is in order to demonstrate the extraordinary wealth of personalities who, between them, are or were the repository of in-depth knowledge that goes to make analytical psychology the outstanding discipline it is in the world today. These chapters will be followed by one on some of the historical thinkers whose ideas influenced Jung in the making of his psychology.

Two sources for some of the information included in the chapters on eminent women are Deidre Bair's biography of *Jung* and Thomas "Tom" Kirsch's *The Jungians*. Deidre was a professional biographer whose book on Jung is an entertaining read though noticeably lightweight on his theoretical output. Tom Kirsch was the son of first-generation Jungian analysts, James and Hilde Kirsch, co-founders with Max Zeller of the C. G. Jung Institute of Los Angeles. Tom was a significant presence in the Jungian community throughout his life, serving two terms as president of the International Association for Analytical Psychology (IAAP), which was founded in 1955 and is the professional and regulatory body for analytical psychologists worldwide. Tom was also a prominent figure at the C. G. Jung Institute of San Francisco. He was a walking archive and was generous in sharing his extensive knowledge of all things Jungian over the years, including with the author of this work. His widow, Jean Kirsch, also an MD and Jungian psychoanalyst, accompanied Tom on their first pioneering trip with Murray Stein to China in August 1994, following a suggestion by Heyong Shen, the first individual member of the IAAP in China. Jean has continued her long connection with China through her work at Wuhan. Their joint trip to China led to a visit to Korea, a country in which analytical psychology has since flourished and, in due course, to the opening up of other parts of the *Far East*. Japan, on the other hand, has a long history of analytical psychology, when it was introduced into that country by the eminent Jungian psychoanalyst, Hayao Kawai.

This seems an appropriate place to say more about an important part of the IAAP's work, which is in relation to its establishment of Developing Groups in many parts of the world where there are no IAAP Group Members. One such initiative was in Russia twenty or more years ago when several members of the then four London training groups, including myself, were sent one at a time to St Petersburg to work with a budding Jungian training taking shape there. This was an incredibly emotional experience for each of us as the Russians are soulful people and St Petersburg is one of the most beautiful cities in the world. Moscow, visited by myself for work many years later at the invitation of the psychiatrist of President Boris Yeltsin, is incredible in a different way. Both visits left me with an indelible love for that country, which is now under the yoke of yet another totalitarian regime after its brief glimpse of freedom under the leadership of Presidents Mikhail Gorbachev and Boris Yeltsin.

Unfortunately, there is insufficient space in this book to do justice to the work of the international Developing Groups that are doing creative work in opening up many parts of the world to Jungian psychology, including some countries in Latin America that still do not have a formal IAAP Group Member. The next IAAP International Congress will take place in Buenos Aires in 2022, the first to be held on that continent, yet another part of the world I have had the pleasure to visit many times over the years, particularly Brazil and Mexico. In addition to the personal connections I have with Brazil, I have also worked in Sao Paulo at the invitation of the academic Jungian psychoanalyst, Denise Ramos, and of my friend, Roberto Gambini. I have also worked closely at the IAAP with Paula Boechat from Rio; both she and her husband Walter, are distinguished MDs in that utterly ravishing city (Brazil has two long-standing IAAP Group Members). Patricia Michan is a close friend from Mexico City, for whom I have worked at the *Centro*, now a Group Member of the IAAP, which offers Jungian psychoanalytical training and which was founded by Patricia and colleagues.

ZÜRICH

Jolande Jacobi

As Zürich is the birthplace of analytical psychology, it seems fitting to begin and end this section with an account of two eminent Jungian psychoanalysts in that city, both of whom have left a legacy of their administrative abilities, along with many volumes of written work that attest to their fine intellects.

The first of these, Jolande Jacobi, was not Zürich-born and bred but fled there from Vienna in 1938 to escape the *Anschluss* as she was Jewish by origin though she later converted to Catholicism. In the course of studying psychology at Vienna University, starting in 1934, she went back and forth to Zürich for analysis with Jung though could not complete her degree as a result of the Nazi annexation of Austria. She decided to settle in Zürich but Jung insisted she defend her PhD in Vienna, which she managed to do despite the obvious dangers incurred at the time in that undertaking. This fact alone testifies to the indomitable personality of Jacobi. "After World War II she renewed her connections to Austria and received many honors from the Austrian government. In 1957 she was made an honorary citizen of Austria" (Kirsch, 2000, p. 14).

To celebrate Jung's seventieth birthday in 1945, Jacobi proposed founding a "clinic" which she had been agitating for since 1939. She got the idea "... when she learned about the Menninger Clinic in Topeka, Kansas. She told Jung that, as Menninger was primarily

Freudian, he needed to think about organizing something like a Jungian university … Jung thought it a good idea" (Bair, 2004, p. 506). Jung did, however, add the following caveat: "We have no [medically trained] people. We have all these old ladies here, all sick people … only cured, or half-cured patients but no scientists" (ibid., p. 507). Due to resistance from various quarters, including Emma Jung and the rest of what were referred to as the *Jungfrau*, nothing came of Jacobi's initial idea then, which had to wait until 1948 to come into being.

Jacobi appears to have been an unpopular figure, partly due to what Bair refers to as her "bluntness" but also because she was an *extraverted thinker*, at that time seen in a dim light by the Jungian community. This view prevailed up to the time I entered the analytical psychology world in the early 1960s, when it quickly became apparent that *introverted intuitives* were solely considered to be true Jungians. That attitude, as well as ongoing adherence to what is called the *classical* approach, which increasingly appears dated, has been deleterious to the potential spread and flourishing of Jungian ideas throughout the world that they deserve.

The contentious lead up to the founding of the C. G. Jung Institute came to a head with Jung's insistence that Jacobi be one of the five members of the proposed Curatorium. The outcry against it was countered by Jung giving an impassioned speech in which he said she was the only person who knew how to operate in the world at large, which was evidenced by the detailed reports she had written. "He begged the members to put her on the board because she knew how to liaise with—to give but one example—the Swiss government, with its avalanche of rules and regulations for every educational institution" (Bair, 2004, p. 531). Eventually, "Jung pulled some very private strings" (ibid.) which resulted in her being appointed a member of the Curatorium.

Jacobi's view of that institution is summed up as follows: "The statutes make the *Curatorium* like Stalin, omnipotent! Dictators! Selected for a lifetime! It is impossible to do anything against them. Dispute is guaranteed" (ibid., p. 512). This is a telling example of Jacobi's foresight as disputes and splits continue within and between the various groups that go to make up the analytical psychology world, despite the fact that one of Jung's major contributions to psychology is the concept of the *shadow*.

A further telling example of Jacobi's foresight and clear thinking ("which carried tremendous weight with Jung", ibid., p. 512) is her following communication in 1945 to him about his ambiguous behaviour in the 1930s in relation to the Nazis.

> I myself do not quite understand why all this happened, why you didn't proceed aggressively against Nazism when it was still hidden to the world what kind of devils were at work in it. I understand you because I know you and because I know what it means to be deeply touched by the ambiguities of everything that is archetypal. I also understand the subtleties and the basic ideas which your statements concerning the race problem contained. But the audience does not understand them and cannot understand them, not only because they are too psychological but also because today these problems have the effect of a red rag to a bull, no matter how one approaches them. (Ibid., p. 512)

These lucid comments are as applicable today as they were in the immediate post-war years, and Jung's conduct in the 1930s will most likely forever remain an indelible stain on his reputation. Jacobi's intellect and forthrightness would be welcome today as, too often, "psychoanalytic" presentations contain little in the way of stimulating intellectual content yet evoke clichéd responses such as "seminal", "rich", or "groundbreaking".

NEW YORK

Beatrice Hinkle

There were four women physicians who pioneered Jungian psychoanalysis in the United States. To begin with the first of these, Beatrice Hinkle, she was the translator into English of Jung's 1916 *Psychology of the Unconscious*, the title possibly being the choice of the publishers, Moffat Yard & Co, for its relative lucidity. This remained in print until 1972 despite the appearance of Jung's revision of the originally titled *Symbols of Transformation* as Volume 5 of the *Collected Works*, and was reprinted in 1991 with an informative long Introduction by William "Bill" McGuire. In the Introduction, McGuire includes a brief account of Hinkle, who had attended the 1911 Weimar Psychoanalytic Congress and who followed Jung after the break with Freud.

Born in San Francisco in 1874, her physician father was killed in an accident before her birth. She trained as a medical doctor at Stanford University, graduating shortly before her husband died leaving her with two small children to support. She was then appointed the city physician of San Francisco, the first woman to hold that position. In 1905 she moved to New York and started the first psychotherapy clinic in the country at the medical school of Cornell University.

She moved to Europe in 1909 to study psychoanalysis and have analysis with Freud, though "from her first conversation with Jung, however, she realised she had found the approach to the human psyche she had sought" (McGuire, 1991, p. xxviii). In her lengthy Introduction, Hinkle describes the main thrust of the book as:

> It is this great theme [the self-sacrifice motive] which Jung sees as the real motive lying hidden in the myths and religions of man from the beginning, as well as in the literature and artistic creations of both ancient and modern time, and which he works out with the greatest wealth of detail and painstaking effort in the book herewith presented. (Ibid., p. xxix)

The book received a mixed press, exemplified by the following review:

> … to the scientist who has accepted the general principles of Freud, it will bring much new light. The danger is that its value may be obscured by the almost overwhelming sandstorm of facts which the author found necessary to the support of his tenets. (*New York Times*, Ibid., p. xxx)

A perceptive review indeed!

Hinkle was denied membership of the New York Psychoanalytic Society because she was a Jungian and no New York Jungian body existed at that time.

Eleanor Bertine, Esther Harding, Kristine Mann

Of the above-mentioned three physicians, Esther Harding, Eleanor Bertine, and Kristine Mann, the first was the British-born Esther Harding, who entered analysis with Jung in Zürich after reading *Psychology of the Unconscious.* Her initial Jungian book, *The Way of all Women* (1933), was a best-seller. "She practiced analysis in New York, and every summer Esther Harding, Eleanor Bertine, and Kristine Mann attracted analysands from all over the United States and Canada to their home on Bailey Island, Maine" (Kirsch, 2000, p. 61).

Harding died in 1971 and her estate along with that of Eleanor Bertine, who died in 1970, provided the funds to buy a five-storey brownstone house in midtown Manhattan which, since 1975, has housed the Analytical Psychology Club (modelled on those in Zürich and London), the Archive for Research in Archetypal Symbolism (ARAS), the Professional Association, the Kristine Mann Library, and the Jung Foundation, as well as a book store. In 1941, the Club founded an annual journal, *Spring*, which was bought by James Hillman in 1970 when he moved back from Zürich to the United States, about which more will appear in the section dedicated to him. The New York Association for Analytical Psychology (NYAAP) was formed by the physicians and psychologists grounded in the practice of Jungian analysis. "The NYAAP became one of the founding members of the International Association for Analytical Psychology (IAAP) at its inaugural meeting in Zürich in 1958" (ibid., p. 66).

CAPE TOWN

Vera Bührmann

Vera Bührmann's inclusion here is, in part, a deeply personal choice as I feel an affinity with her based on our backgrounds. As Astrid Berg puts it, Bührmann was "a child of Africa" (2007, p. 95) just as I am a child of India. In her article, Berg goes on to recount Bührmann's professional life that started when she left her family's farm to study medicine and, from there, went to London where she trained as a psychiatrist, child psychiatrist, and Jungian analyst at the Society of Analytical Psychology. She subsequently returned to her black rural roots where she combined her analytic skills with traditional *Xhosa* healers, a practice that has inspired similar work around the world.

It was Bührmann's vision that led to the founding of a Jungian training centre in Cape Town, which was supplemented by the teachings of Jungian psychology by the incomparable Renos Papadopoulos and a couple of other academic psychologists. Arriving in 1989, the Zürich-trained analyst Julian David spent five years in Cape Town where (unusually) all the training candidates had analysis with him and supervision with Vera Bührmann.

> In 1990 a property was donated to the Centre which became home to its administration, public lectures, training seminars, and its library. The latter was established through a bequest from the Frank McMillan Foundation of Texas, arranged by Sir Laurens van der Post. (Kirsch, 2000, p. 203)

As a result of the innumerable creative contributions that Frank McMillan III has carried forward from his father's legacy to the analytical psychology world, he was invited to become an honorary member of the IAAP at the Copenhagen Congress in 2016. His older son, Frank McMillan IV, is the godson of Sir Laurens van der Post and his younger son, Rob, has a special place in my affections since my first meeting with this delightful family in New York in 2009 at the launch of Jung's *Red Book*.

The South African Association of Jungian Analysts (SAAJA), was founded in 1993 and was voted into the IAAP as a Group Member in 1995. Since that time, it has been exceptionally well served there by its representatives, Astrid Berg, whose two terms on the IAAP's Executive Committee (EC) happily coincided with mine, and Fred Borchardt, who has the rare distinction of having served two terms, and then being voted back onto the EC at the Vienna Congress 2019 after the statutory term off.

I shall end this tribute to Vera Bührmann by reproducing a long extract from an obituary that appeared in *The Journal of Analytical Psychology*, Volume 44, No 1, January 1999, which is as empathic and elegant as the obits Dr Ann Wroe skilfully crafts week after week on different subjects for *The Economist*.

> To understand Dr Bührmann's extraordinarily complex personality and the role model she has provided for women world-wide, I would turn to her two powerful, persuasive, and guiding mentors: Dr Robert F. Hobson, her personal analyst, and Dr D. W. Winnicott, her supervising and case analyst. She often spoke to me about what she learned from these two men, who challenged her preconceptions, welcomed

the growing and developing sense of individuation that she exhibited, and, most importantly, assured her that she was no more the victim of the past than she was a creator of the future.

D. W. Winnicott impressed upon Dr Bührmann that "Home is where one starts from" and that with ageing the complexity of the world brings past, present and future into dynamic tension, to paraphrase T. S. Eliot in his poem "East Coker" from *Four Quartets*. Dr Winnicott stressed in his work with her that perfection belonged to machines, but *imperfection* is the one characteristic necessary for human adaptation. What she learned was that in maturity an individual may feel free and independent, despite never really being free of all environmental concerns, for it is the feeling of freedom that makes for happiness and gives a sense of personal identity. Thus, in Dr Bührmann's work with indigenous peoples, she was alert and quick to identify what it was culturally that took the feeling of freedom away: to be in a state of *thwasa*, to be separated from the ancestors, to be lost and alienated, and perhaps worst, to be bewitched. And she spent her career attempting to teach her western-educated African profession-als that first and foremost one had to understand "home" and "culture" before a "feeling" of relief could be attained. I personally witnessed her careful and extraordinary gifts of interpretation with "possessed victims" for whom western psychological nomenclature was inappropriate. Dr Winnicott's finest gift to Dr Bührmann was giving her the courage to be creative, for he stressed with her that life is only worth living according to whether creativity is or is not a part of a person's living experience.

It was Dr Hobson, the personal analyst, who taught Vera, and taught her persuasively, that "darkness lies at the heart of psychotherapy". Vera never shied away from, feared nor ignored darkness, rather she used it as the starting point for analytic exploration. With Dr Hobson, she encountered her aloneness and faced the loneliness that could never be assuaged by what he termed "pseudo-mutuality"; she sought mutuality. Perhaps the most moving aspect of her work with Dr Hobson was learn-ing to say, "I have failed", but never to say, "I am a failure". She knew the difference and used it constructively during difficult times. This is a legacy that is a gift for all of us.

I would like to thank Vera Bührmann for the gifts she has given her country and all of its people, for the example she has given so many of us, and, most of all, for being a true individual.

Lee Roloff, C. G. Jung Institute of Chicago.

ZÜRICH

Verena Kast

A significant part of this section on Verena Kast is based on a lengthy interview I conducted with her for the 2019 issue of the *IAAP Newsletter*. Kast was born at Wolfhalden in Switzerland, and has been active for many years in the analytical psychology world, serving as president of the IAAP from 1995 to 1998. She is currently president of the C. G. Jung Institute Zürich; these are some of her more important administrative roles as she has had several other official positions. The background to these achievements is her training as a clinical psychologist and Jungian psychoanalyst, combined with her career as an academic at the University of Zürich where she was professor of anthropological psychology—an impressive résumé by any standards.

Kast gave the inaugural Fay Lecture in Texas in March 1990 entitled "Joy, Inspiration, and Hope and the Individuation Process". The history of this innovative lecture series is summarised here. Following the death of her husband in 1988, Carolyn Grant Fay endowed an annual lecture and book series in analytical psychology at Texas A&M University, which is ongoing at the C. G. Jung Center at Houston. In more recent times, I was gratified to be invited to be a presenter there on Jung's concept of the *shadow*.

Kast has also produced innumerable other books in German and English on analytical psychology, a short list of which includes: *A Time to Mourn: Growing through the Grief Process; The Creative Leap: Psychological Transformation Through Crisis;* and *Folktales as Therapy.*

A couple of themes that recurred throughout the interview were related to imagination and creativity as evidenced by her response to the question of what drew her to Jung:

> … the image of the human being not seen from the deficits, but from the potentials. This corresponds with Jung's idea, that life is creative, that something creative permeates the whole universe but also the whole individual personality and if you are connected with this creative urge then you can transform, get whole or you can get a good life in a way. (Casement, 2019, p. 266)

Kast has integrated imagination with her grounded analytical insight and turned that union to good use in helping to foster a first-rate Jungian psychoanalytical training at the C. G. Jung Institute Zürich, which she addresses in the following manner: "... we have to be clinically trained so that we can really do therapy. But we have not to forget the soul; the symbols, the imagination and all the other creative methods with transference and countertransference" (ibid., p. 267). I had written an article for the *IAAP News Sheet* some time ago on that rigorous training and had been more than impressed by the clinical demands made on training candidates. This is a minimum four-year training, the least amount of time that should be dedicated to any good quality training to become a psychoanalyst, on top of the university qualifications, psychiatric placements, and previous psychotherapy training that precede it. Kast admitted that only some candidates complete the C. G. Jung Institute Zürich training in four years whilst others usually spend five or six years doing so. It is conducted in both German and English with applicants coming from all over the world.

As president of the IAAP, two of the main achievements of her tenure in that role were changing the organisation's constitution to shorten the president's time in office from two terms to one term of three years—a move I vociferously supported at the Delegates' Meeting of the Zürich Congress in 1998. The other main achievement was "... the development of the Developing Groups especially in Eastern Europe. That was the best thing we have done" (ibid., p. 273).

I have cited the research she conducted on Jung's theory of *anima/animus* in the section devoted to that linked concept, and, true to form, Kast continues to conduct research: "We are discussing research in the German speaking world, we find research—all kind of research—is vital for Jungian psychology" (ibid.). Kast detailed the particular research she is referring to, as follows:

> In Zürich we want to do some research with the association experiment developed by Jung ... This test marks the beginning of Jungian psychology, the complex theory. We have the idea to give this test at the beginning of therapy and at the end. If our theory is correct, the landscape of complexes should change

through therapy—more different emotions, and that means more possibilities to deal with life, more different feelings and so on. (Ibid., p. 275)

One can see from this statement how Kast's academic prowess and intellectual ability result in a much-needed call for analytical psychology to come home to itself through research-based therapeutic work that can keep it from floating ungrounded in a miasma of *participation mystique* and *masked religious* fantasies, on the one hand; and of arid so-called *clinical* presentations on the other. Both approaches usually result in some hapless creature referred to as the "patient" or "client" being dissected according to whichever theoretical construct prevails at that moment. In this way, the magic and mystery that need to be grounded in clear thinking, and that underlie psychoanalysis' unique capacity to engage and transform the sick *soul*, vanish into a black hole of pseudo-theoretical phantasms—what one of my patients scathingly referred to as "supermarket psychology".

A point of note here is that I refer to the people I see for analysis as *patients* and eschew the term *client*, apparently motivated by misguided attempts to be politically correct or to avoid being accused of mimicking the medical profession. The other term I use, when appropriate, is *analysand*—the meaning of both will be clear from the context in which they are used in this book. For my part, I in no way feel demeaned at being called a *patient* on the occasions when I visit my general practitioner or dentist as the term denotes forbearing in the face of suffering—a condition each one of us shares with all human beings. Those who are in denial of their own and of humanity's suffering are the ones most likely to inflict it unwittingly on themselves and others.

CHAPTER 16

Major original figures in analytical psychology

I have borrowed the first three words in the above title from Sonu Shamdasani's Preface to James Hillman's biography wherein he states: "Strikingly in contrast to Freud's legacy, there have arguably only been two major original figures following in the wake of Jung: Michael Fordham ... and (James) Hillman" (Russell, 2013, p. xi). To that short list, I have added two other names, those of Shamdasani himself and Wolfgang Giegerich, for reasons that are spelt out further in this section. The two latter figures are alive so, as a courtesy, I shall not give birth dates for any of the four individuals which, in any case, I do not know, though I will mention the dates of their deaths for two of them. As each of these major figures has produced so much in the way of research, books, articles, and other material relating to analytical psychology that are readily accessible, the current chapter will attempt only brief glimpses of their voluminous professional output.

James Hillman (died 2011)

The scion of a distinguished Atlantic City family, whose life has been well documented in a *warts-and-all* biography by Dick Russell, extracts from which he read, while still working on the manuscript, at Hillman's eightieth birthday celebrations at Pittsburgh in 2006. Interested readers are directed to that work for more personal insights into Hillman's life, whereas this short piece covers some of the theoretical contributions to his chosen discipline. On a personal note, I have met his second wife, Pat Berry, and Margot McLean, his third, both of whom are immensely likeable, creative women.

Hillman's name is most associated with *archetypal psychology* and with the notion of *soul-making*, which are best exemplified in the exchange reproduced here between him and his one-time close colleague, Wolfgang Giegerich. Hillman had invited me to be a participant on his double plenary session panel at the IAAP Congress at Montreal in 2010, to which I agreed with the proviso that I could focus my part of the presentation on Giegerich's work as my actual knowledge of Hillman's was limited. The panel conducted a successful dry run the day before the plenary, but, on the day, Hillman seemed unable to project himself and was downhearted in the short break between the two sessions. I told him it was important that he do the bulk of the talking in the second session as he was the one everybody had come to see. At the back of my mind was the thought that this might be one of his last presentations at a Congress, which turned out to be the case. I asked the other panel members to let James have the floor most of the time to which they agreed; unfortunately, his *daimon* let him down that day and he was unable to be at his charismatic best.

As part of the preparation for the panel, I asked both Hillman and Giegerich to let me know what they thought of the other's work. The following is a summary of extracts from each of their responses—the first is by Giegerich, sent to me for possible inclusion in the plenary; the second was sent at the same time by Hillman. Both were reproduced in a *Journal of Analytical Psychology* article I wrote in 2011 dedicated to Giegerich's thinking (2011a).

Giegerich

1. Hillman started to "Re-Vision" psychology and go beyond Jung. My charge is that he did not go far enough, not all the way.
2. Concerning the style of psychology, his is, basically, an "anima-only" psychology, as I call it. The "animus" and its *negations* have no place in its own form, at least generally.

3. He thinks that the image, the imaginal is the ultimate. I think that the image is merely a form of manifestation of the soul's thought. "The soul always thinks."

4. He eliminated Time, history from his scheme. Ultimately he operates within a scheme of psyche as timeless (his "Platonistic" fallacy).

5. He has a nostalgic agenda. A programme. He does not simply describe and analyse. Hillman rightly attacked the idea that psychotherapy could bring about a bettering of the world, and suggested that there should be a shift from "mirror to window". But by saying "We've had a hundred years of psychotherapy and the world is getting worse" he shows his disappointment, and insofar as a disappointment is the disappointment of a hope or wish, he shows that he wants to be in the business of world-improvement. For me, this is the hope of a prophet, not the job of a psychotherapist.

6. In his style of writing and thinking, he tends to be "impressionistic", merely suggestive (thus also his preference of rhetoric), without thoroughly working out and thoroughly arguing and supporting his case. Some of his interpretations and theses, therefore, are weighed in the balance, and found wanting when one examines them more closely. (Giegerich in Casement, 2011a, pp. 543–544)

Hillman: "Divergences"

For me, the soul's *logos* is *not* a logic, nor is the soul itself a *logos*. The soul's *logos* shows itself in its capacity to word itself, to account for itself, describe itself, tell us truth, and this *logos* is boundless (as Wolfgang already said), and not necessarily only logical, or syntactical. Its *logos*, the *logos* of the psyche, psychology may appear as well in images as in thought.

I like Giegerich's idea that psyche is [also] thought and soul-making is [also] thinking ... [Hillman (2011a, p. 544)] writes that we think in words of language and not in images. I'd say just the contrary. Words are themselves images ... Language can never free us from its primordial mother, the sensory, the natural, the physical ...

Must we prioritize word over image or image over word? If, however, we do make this move in one direction or the other, what could be the consequences? Image first means a psychology that is aesthetic and immersed in cosmos. Word first offers a psychology "cut", as Wolfgang says, from all physicality, save the human mind.

A major divergence is how we look at history … If, however, you look at written work with the lens of image, as paintings or pieces of music, then they may widely differ one from another and not be required to fulfil the idea of chronological consistency. This imagistic, if you will, approach also can apply to Giegerich's attack style. Imagine his using a palette knife, sandpaper, stiff brushes and hard thick black strokes for limning differences, for breaking through conventions. Think early Stravinsky; Shostakovich. Aggressiveness may be a rhetorical necessity; and so his devastations of Freud and Jung, or me, are not to be taken as literally personally nasty. (Hillman, 2011a, p. 544)

Hillman summarises what he means by "the soul of the world" in the following way: "We have to go back before Romanticism, back to medieval alchemy and Renaissance Neoplatonism … to tribal animistic psychologies that are always concerned with the soul of things" (Hillman & Ventura, 1993, p. 51).

The academic, David Tacey, made similar critical comments in his chapter on Hillman's work entitled "Twisting and Turning with James Hillman: From Anima to World Soul, from Academia to Pop", that appeared in a book I put together in 1998. As the title makes clear, the various incarnations Hillman has been through are what Tacey depicts as embodying a " 'Hermes' pattern of fluidity and complexity, combined with an 'anima' emotionality that produces high-flown rhetoric …" (Tacey, 1998, p. 218). What was even more critical was his conclusion that Hillman was largely irrelevant in the analytical psychology world of that time, partly, perhaps, because of his own disdain for Jungians that is apparent in his depiction of them as "second rate people with third rate minds" (ibid.). Tacey's conclusion was that "only his binding commitment to his ruling daimon has supplied security and solidity throughout" (ibid., p. 221).

I had heard James was angry with David and myself over this depiction though he and I repaired some of that damage at the time of his eightieth birthday celebration in Pittsburgh. At that event, I was pleasantly surprised to meet a *Daseinanalyst* and later learnt of James's fascination with Heidegger, which is a joy to me as I become increasingly invested in that philosopher's challenging ideas. While James was director of training at the Zürich Institute in 1959, he reconnected Jungians with *Daseinanalysis*, an enterprise Jung himself had started in the 1930s with the brilliant Medard Boss, the co-founder of that psychoanalytic discipline.

Shortly before his death, I asked James to send me information for an article I wanted to write on the journal *Spring*, the oldest Jungian journal in existence, for the *IAAP News Sheet*, extracts from which are reproduced below. It was one of the very last pieces he worked on which turned into a joint article put together by the two of us. My deep sadness at his loss and appreciation of all that he contributed to Jungian psychoanalysis, including his poetic writing style, courage, intellect, and willingness to embrace his own shadow, is boundless.

1941–1969

Spring was the title in the beginning when it was originally a mimeographed annual largely of translations from German. Its first expansion to print form was in 1960. *Spring* was created in 1941 by the Analytical Psychology Club of New York and published and edited by the Club from 1941 until 1969. The Club had close ties to Jung and Zürich, especially through founding Club members, Kristine Mann and Eleanor Bertine, along with Esther Harding. The early issues of the Journal reflect that close connection, which contain articles by Jung himself and other Zürich Jungians.

1970–2002

In 1970, the editorship and publication of *Spring* was transferred by the Club to James Hillman. It was moved to Zürich where he was living at the time. Hillman had received his analyst's diploma from the C. G. Jung Institute in Zürich. In 1959, he was appointed Director of Studies at the Institute where he also taught. In the first volume edited by Hillman, which was titled *Spring: A Journal of Analytical Psychology and Jungian Thought*, he published his own seminal paper *Why "Archetypal Psychology"?* This was a prelude to his magnum opus *Revisioning Psychology*, which he wrote five years later. Hillman is an author of distinction whose books include: *Suicide and the Soul*, *The Soul's Code*, *Healing Function*, and *A terrible Love of War*. Under Hillman's editorship, the Journal's direction was focused on inaugurating the swerve in the field that has become known as archetypal psychology. A long-time participant in the Eranos conferences, Hillman drew on that sensibility in editing *Spring* emphasizing "image oriented" thought.

When Hillman first moved *Spring* to Zürich, it was located in a small room in the offices of Adolf Güggenbuhl-Craig. Later, Hillman rented a large house, which was called Spring House and contained the *Spring* operations plus rental offices for students and analysts. Murray Stein was Hillman's business manager in 1972–73, followed by Robert Hinshaw. Daryl Sharp also worked at *Spring* during those Zürich years. All three went on to develop their own Jungian publishing houses: Murray Stein: Chiron Publications; Robert Hinshaw: Daimon; and Daryl Sharp: Inner City Books.

Spring's offices followed Hillman from Zürich to Dallas, when he became the Director of Graduate Studies at the University of Dallas in 1978, and then on to Connecticut in 1988. Hillman continued as Senior Editor from 1988 through 1997. *Spring: A Journal of Archetypal Psychology and Jungian Thought* was incorporated in Dallas as *Spring Publications, Inc.* Around 1990, *Spring Journal* and *Spring Publications, Inc.* separated, the latter continuing as the oldest Jungian book publisher under the name *Spring* and James Hillman continues to be Senior Editor.

James Hillman ended his contribution on *Spring* with the following: "It gladdens the old heart to see how much has come from what was obsessing me some forty years ago." (Hillman, 2011b)

James Hillman died in October 2011, shortly after collaborating on this article for the *IAAP News Sheet*—the consummate professional to the end.

Michael Fordham (died 1995)

Michael Fordham was the last person to found a movement in psychoanalysis, his major contribution to that discipline being the uniting of analytical psychology with mainstream psychoanalysis. For that reason alone, the psychoanalytic community owes him a huge debt for creating a new discipline that has come to be called the *developmental* approach. In the course of his life, Fordham's work covered several areas of activity, including being a psychoanalyst, author, leader, creator of the first Jungian training society in the world, founder of a journal—to name the main ones. It is an impossible task to do justice to his vast *oeuvre* in this short encomium—suffice to say it is well documented in books and articles by Fordham and the distinguished Jungian psychoanalyst, James Astor, which will be referenced in this section, as well as by many other psychoanalysts influenced by his work.

I got to know Fordham slightly through attending some of his presentations at the Society of Analytical Psychology (SAP), which he founded, as well as by spending a day with him at Severalls, the family home in Buckinghamshire. This came about as a result of being invited by the editorial committee of the *Journal of Analytical Psychology* to put together an article on the *splits* in the UK Jungian world for its fortieth birthday issue. I was grateful to Fordham for agreeing to that meeting, particularly as he was not in the best of health, which was facilitated by James Astor. For most of that day, he came across as rather chilly with a brusque manner, though we got on well enough, but he mostly kept his distance, only opening up to his true feelings infrequently. One of those occasions was when I asked him what he really thought about Gerhard Adler, at which point he admitted he did not like him because he experienced Adler as being power-driven. He was also dismissive of Erich Neumann's approach to working with children saying that, in his view, Neumann had never encountered an actual child. The other occasions he let his guard down was when he mentioned he was a benign alcoholic and, holding up a cigarette, referred to it as his "best friend"—particularly refreshing to look back on in these neo-puritanical days.

A brief personal account of Fordham's life is that he came from a patrician family from what is known as the Midlands in England, though tragedy struck at fifteen when his beloved mother died as the result of an asthma attack, effectively bringing to an end family life for himself, his father, and two older siblings. This was followed in later life by his father's probable suicide. As is true for many psychoanalysts, their *calling* can arise from early tragedies of this kind, sometimes accompanied by feeling an outsider in their surroundings. Fordham was twice married, the first marriage producing his son, Max, whom it has been my pleasure to meet on a few occasions when he came across as a highly perceptive man; the second marriage was to Frieda, who helped him in his work, in particular his writing, as English was his worst subject at school, where he excelled in mathematics, the sciences, and sports.

There are first-rate accounts easily available of his work by Fordham himself so only brief descriptions of it will be attempted in the following summaries. He was keen to repair the damage done to the psychoanalytic world by the rupture between Freud and Jung in the early twentieth century: "There are those who believe, like myself, that this was a disaster, and in part an illusion, from which we suffer" (Astor, 2007, p. 78), and was keen to repair that damage by promoting discussions and conferences in Britain with speakers drawn from the "Jungian" and "Freudian" communities as well as psychiatry. Furthermore, his interest in Klein was the result of her method of treating children (Fordham being a child psychiatrist as well as a psychoanalyst); it was her practice that he incorporated into his own way of working and that so many of us practitioners now espouse. Fordham was the first to grasp the underlying symmetry between Jung's notion of *archetypes* and Klein's *unconscious phantasies*. "In fact his preference for Klein over Winnicott had been because Klein confronted the destructiveness of human beings and did not place too much optimistic reliance on the goodness of mothers, which was what Fordham [felt] Winnicott did" (Astor, 1995, p. 12)—a view fully supported by the current writer.

Although Jung was the inspiration behind *all* Fordham's work, the latter's massive intellect brought about a much-needed revision of Jung's original thinking in the following areas: shifting the emphasis from over-dependence on the mythical foundations of psyche to a more biological and clinical approach; emphasis on the complementarity between Freud's and Jung's thinking; work with autistic and psychotic children leading to his all-important theory of deintegration/reintegration of early life in the co-creation of the infant's sense of self; reworking Jung's thinking on the latter which resulted in Fordham's seminal work *Defences of the Self* that influenced Donald Kalsched, a best-selling Jungian author; and other creative revisions of Jung's original hypotheses. Above all, he introduced a much-needed noetic stance into the Jungian world as exemplified in the following quote:

> Fordham enjoys thinking about feelings and has lots of thoughts. This is not a characteristic which is common to those attracted to Jung. This difficulty with thinking among Jungians is often presented in the form of denigrating thinking as a defence against feeling. (Astor, 1995, p. 181)

The vital importance of the intellect in psychoanalytic thinking has already featured in the above section on Hillman and will reappear in the entries on Giegerich and Shamdasani further in this section.

Although he was not an atheist, Fordham's work counteracted the "religious" aspect of Jungianism as exemplified by the following:

> My personal relationship with him [Jung] made me aware of a trend amongst some of his followers, and his detractors as well, which he deplored. It hinted that analytical psychology was a sort of religion. It was an error that I also deplored. (Astor, 2007, p. 80)

A significant number of Jungians express this in terms of a "spiritual" quest, behind which lurks the danger of turning analytical psychology into a quasi-religion that can lead to feelings of grandiosity and lack of groundedness among some of its practitioners.

Rumours persist in the analytical psychology world that Fordham harboured ambivalent or even negative feelings about Jung though much of what he wrote about the latter suggests otherwise. "My debt to Jung is so great that I hardly dare to write about him" (1993, p. 111). He defended Jung against accusations of being a Nazi supporter and/or anti-Semitic in stating the following: "Jung was intensely interested in the Nazi uprising and moved by it … and was struggling after objectivity and understanding, using his theory of the collective unconscious and the archetypes to do so" (ibid., p. 112). Fordham came to see Jung's statement that the Jewish people "were not the same as other races" (ibid.) as similar to the way his father would talk outrageously when he was germinating ideas: "… I understand that I loved him … like I loved my father" (ibid., p. 113). And further, "He gave ample evidence of his good opinion of me and it was after all he who suggested that I become editor of his *Collected Works*" (ibid.).

With regard to his interaction with the two other editors of Jung's *Collected Works*, Fordham wrote as follows: "It was also a privilege to know Herbert Read better and to enjoy his sensitive-poetic nature" (ibid., p. 110).

> I should also mention Gerhard Adler … It was rumoured that I could not work with him but that was not the case. The truth was that I could and did work with him but I was not a friend … he was to check on the accuracy of Hull's translations … but … we found ourselves in almost complete agreement as to policy. (Ibid.)

"When Adler was added to the editorial board Jung remarked that it would save me from learning German" (ibid.).

The founding of *The Journal of Analytical Psychology*

The Journal of Analytical Psychology of the SAP made its first appearance on 31st October 1955 under the editorship of Michael Fordham, who remained in office for fifteen years. Jung himself gave his blessings to its founding and had his name on the masthead under the words "In collaboration with" until his death in 1961. Apart from Jung, the earliest issues featured contributions, both on the editorial board and by way of articles, from members of the worldwide Jungian community of every persuasion. The latter included such luminaries as Gerhard Adler, Edward Edinger, Esther Harding, Joseph Henderson, Robert Hobson, James Kirsch, John Layard, C. A. Meier, Erich Neumann, Fred Plaut, Franz Riklin, and Arnold Toynbee.

The advent of the *Journal* ran in parallel with tensions between different orientations to Jung's work, as shown by Tom Kirsch in the following:

> … at the end of the first Congress in Zürich in 1958 … I was at a dinner … with my parents, Marie-Louise von Franz and Barbara Hannah, I remember them discussing Michael Fordham, and the fact that they did not consider him a true Jungian. From this I have always gathered that the tension between the Zürich analysts and London goes back at least that far. (Casement, 2007, p. 192)

The mutual tensions feature in the correspondence relating to the *Journal* between C. A. Meier and Franz Riklin in Zürich, and Fordham in London, when the latter was trying to raise much-needed funds to support the cost of the *Journal* and he was hoping for some contribution from the recently founded IAAP. Riklin's letter of 14th July 1959 stated: "… it was agreed between the London-group and Zürich, that an International Journal should once be edited! You know yourself, that not only Dr Meier, but everybody in this country is disappointed by your autonomous proceeding." To which Fordham responded on 17th July: "I must confess to considerable disappointment at the lack of collaboration exhibited by you people in Zürich, and I frankly do not understand your argument, it being false that there was an agreement between the London group and Zürich" (ibid., pp. 203–204).

A delicate matter arose with regard to an article C. A. Meier had submitted for publication in the *Journal* with Jung writing to Fordham on 16th October 1957, as follows:

> This is a confidential letter, of which I wish you to keep it under your hat … When you study this paper carefully you will discover a considerable snag which I have demonstrated to Meier clearly enough … The author is bringing in the question of synchronicity in an unwarrantable way, according to my view. It is not even quite certain that he understands the term properly. Thus he applies it in places, where one should speak of causality. (Casement, 2007, p. 196)

The correspondence between Jung and Fordham specifically relating to this delicate matter of how to deal with Meier's mistake resulted in Fordham letting the paper be published in the *Journal* as it stood as he was keen to have an article from one of the Zürich analysts. Fordham stated in a letter to Jung of 18th October 1957: "… corrections to it [can be] made in another issue, preferably by Meier himself. I think he might be able to do this without loss of face" (Casement, 2007, p. 200).

The following is an extract from a long letter of Jung's dated 16th February 1954, sent as a result of Fordham's request that Jung write a piece about his interaction with Father White.

> Thank you for your letter and its most amusing report about your philosophical dealings with Father White. Yes, he has a

remarkable mind because it is not only logical, but also a remarkable twister and joker, and you put your foot just right into the
middle of the plate. The question of the privatio boni is or rather
was the favourite subject of discussion with Father White. The
privation boni is not a dogma, but a so-called sentential com-
munis, i.e., a generally recognized doctrine, and a discutable on
principle. Father White thought it necessary—as he obviously did
in your case—not to give way to any doubt about it. The doctrine
is quite obviously a *petitio principii* of the worst kind, and one
can criticize it as you do and in many other ways. One always
comes to the conclusion that it is a nonsense....the privation
boni is one of the main props of the Christian doctrine in general. It hangs together with the necessity to maintain the one way
goodness of the deity, the so-called Summum Bonum. They simply got to make the assertion absolute that God has not created
evil although it is obvious that he has created Satan. (Casement,
2007, pp. 202–203)

The chapter on the *Journal* concluded with a contribution from the
highly regarded Zürich analyst, the late Mario Jacoby, who stated the following about Fordham: "I saw the lack of clinical sophistication over here
in contrast to his attempts to integrate childhood and much more subtle
and differentiated research into the transference–countertransference"
(ibid., p. 214). Barbara Wharton, a former editor of the *Journal*, made
the important related point for the chapter:

Michael Fordham and the others who were involved in setting
up the *JAP* were keen to show how Jung's work could be adapted
to accommodate findings in child development research and in
psychoanalysis. Fordham's aim was not to supersede the classical
Jungian approach, but rather to marry the two, each informing
the other. His theory of deintegration/reintegration is a working
out of this. (Ibid., p. 215)

* * *

At the end of the chapter I wrote that the extensive research required
for it was greatly aided by unstinting help from the following: Jung's

grandson, Ulrich Hoerni, chairman of the Jung Estate, who provided invaluable personal assistance; Leonardo La Rosa of the Jung Archives; James Astor and Max Fordham for permission to use material from the Michael Fordham Archive at the Wellcome Institute; Ann Hopwood, then chair of the Society of Analytical Psychology (SAP), to get permission from the Society's Council to do research in the SAP's Archives; Jean Knox, then editor-in-chief, and Pramila Bennett, then managing editor of the *Journal of Analytical Psychology*, as well as Michael Horne, then North American editor-in-chief; Sonu Shamdasani for his comments on the manuscript of the chapter and for his help in locating documents at the Wellcome Institute Library; and Joe Cambray (a former North American editor-in-chief), Mario Jacoby, Thomas Kirsch, and Elizabeth Urban for their personal contributions. It was important to have input from all these eminent people located in different parts of the world to ensure the chapter was as balanced and unbiased an account of some of the contentious material included in it as it could be. Despite the conflicts and differences in approach between London and Zürich, which are still there to some degree, the collaborative efforts of all the aforementioned people show the generosity of spirit that keeps the Jungian movement alive and relevant in today's world.

Wolfgang Giegerich

The Berlin-based Jungian psychoanalyst Wolfgang Giegerich's contribution to the Jungian psychoanalytical world is summed up by the scholar and honorary member of the IAAP, David Miller, as follows: "If James Hillman's work on 'archetypal psychology' represents after Jung himself second wave Jungianism, the work of Wolfgang Giegerich may well indicate third wave Jungian thinking" (Giegerich, Miller, & Mogenson, 2005, p. x). Noticeably absent from this short list is the name of Michael Fordham, which confirms what has been stated in the entry prefiguring this one about a lack of interaction between different schools of thought in analytical psychology. It was that fact that prompted me to write an article on Giegerich's work for the *Journal of Analytical Psychology*.

A Viennese colleague, Andreas von Heydwolff, introduced me to Giegerich's work at the Cambridge Congress in 2001, sending me three chapters from *The Soul's Logical Life*, though my initial efforts to engage with these produced limited results ("Effort? Yes, Effort!" is the title of one of his chapters in *The Soul Always Thinks*). A couple of years later, Giegerich gave a lecture in London at which I experienced first-hand the depth and clarity of his thinking as well as his humanity and sense of humour. Later, he contributed a chapter to a book I produced, which was followed by working with him from time to time in Berlin, and by a presentation I gave at the first Giegerich conference in Berlin in 2012.

In certain ways, Giegerich himself is an interesting contrast to Fordham, including his typology which I am taking from Jung's typology theory housed in Volume 6, *Psychological Types*, of the *Collected Works*. According to that categorisation of personality types, Giegerich personifies what Jung termed *introverted thinking* and is also an intellectual. Fordham, on the other hand, was an *extraverted thinker* though *not* an intellectual; in that way, he may be seen to be the *shadow* of Giegerich. Fordham's *extraversion* manifested in the fact that he was a leader who, partly, directed his immense capacity for thinking to the founding of entities in the outer world such as an organisation and a journal, as well as in his successful attempts at coordinating relations between "Freudians" and "Jungians" in the UK. Conversely, Giegerich is not interested in directing his fine intellect to outer pursuits as he is a scholar—though he modestly rejects that epithet. Nevertheless, there now exists the International Society for Psychology as the Discipline of Interiority, a group dedicated to taking his work forward.

Any attempt at categorising James Hillman typologically is difficult, in part because he was critical of what he deemed the misuse of Jung's typology and insisted, instead, on the uniqueness of an individual's *calling*. Furthermore, although he was clearly an intellectual, his writing generally lacked clarity of expression akin to the language of poetry, which makes him an unlikely candidate to be situated unequivocally within the spectrum of Jung's "*thinking function*".

Alongside my growing appreciation of the lucidity and depth of Giegerich's writing, I came to the realisation that, unlike Jungian colleagues in Japan, his work was unknown to those UK colleagues who, like me, are from the *developmental* school of analytical psychology and *mainstream* psychoanalysis. This was what led to my writing an account of his work in 2011 for the *Journal of Analytical Psychology*. Several contributions have since appeared by and about him in the *Journal*.

I shall attempt to summarise some of Giegerich's ideas based on that 2011 article. For a start, his entire *corpus* circumambulates the notion of "the *soul*", which he describes as a *mercurial* term that should not be fixed to any one meaning. "For me there is no such thing as a soul. The soul does not exist. It is the depth of the logical life at work in what happens, no more" (Giegerich, personal communication, 2011). In the foregoing, Giegerich is asserting that the *soul* is the ongoing objective thought or logical life *as which* psychic phenomena exist so that there is no substantiated *soul* as a separate producing agent *behind* the *psychic* phenomena. This is a direct example of the influence of Heidegger's phenomenology on his thinking.

The foregoing encapsulates much of what Giegerich is getting at in his critical stance vis-à-vis a good deal of Jung's writings. For example, a 1916 work revised in 1928 has as its title, *The Relations Between the Ego and the Unconscious*, which Giegerich contrasts with the title of the main work of Jung's later period *Mysterium Coniunctionis: An Inquiry into the Separation and Synthesis of Psychic Opposites in Alchemy*. Giegerich says of the first title: "A substantiating or reifying thinking is at work here. We could also call it "ontological" inasmuch as it starts out with the idea of subsisting entities" (Giegerich, 2007, p. 249). Whereas with reference to the second title, Giegerich has this to say:

> He [Jung] is no longer concerned with any substance, any entity. Instead of referring in terms of an ontological or substantiating thinking to the psychic opposites as subsisting entities he simply expresses the abstract notion of the oppositional *structure* or *form* of the psychic. (Ibid.; original italics)

Giegerich tries to penetrate *thinkingly* into psychological phenomena to draw out their internal dialectic. This is a dynamic developmental *process* in which nothing is discarded or destroyed; instead, it is *sublated* or overcome while, at the same time, being preserved but not lost. *Negation* in the dialectic is the negation of a *positivistic*, tangible, demonstrable reality, a taking off deeper into the *interiority* of the phenomenon itself. *Absolute negation* means being absolved or freed from thinking in oppositional terms of, say, *subject* and *object*. The language in which much of this is expressed owes a debt to Hegel as per the following: "The problem, then, is to overcome the separation between *the subject and the object* without *dissolving* their intrinsic characteristics" (Kojève, 1969, p. 201; original italics). A brief acknowledgement is needed here to the effect that I am aware there are criticisms of Kojève's interpretation of Hegel though he does make the latter accessible in a way that Hegel himself does not.

A key aspect of Giegerich's psychological approach is the way dialectical thinking is linked to the *recursive* distillation to be found in *alchemy*. The latter is *contra naturam* in displacing human existence from the biological sphere to the slow path to *mindedness*. This is the relation to or openness for the truth that is the logic of actually lived life at a given historical locus—the releasing of the *Mercurius* imprisoned in the physical-ness of matter through the alchemical *fermentation, corruption, sublimation,* and *distillation* of imagery, which, as a consequence, is transformed into the logical syntax of *consciousness* that is thought.

The *soul's* main alchemical laboratory is history. The development of *soul* as historical process may be exemplified by the evolution of the *Western* mind through myriad changes across the centuries, for example, the Enlightenment and the Industrial Revolution. This development is evidenced in the historical change from polytheistic gods to the one God, and in *Platonic Ideas* giving way to abstract concepts. As a result, the *soul* developed through a series of "killings" or *decompositions* and *distillations* of previously held concepts. As the end product of this processing, the latter are *sublated* or rendered obsolete, and an irreversible increase in *consciousness* has taken place.

In the course of writing the *Journal* article on Giegerich's psychology, I pressed him to send an account of his analytical work. At first, he was reluctant to do so as he did not think it a good idea to include descriptions of that in an account of his published work on psychology. The reason for this is that he makes a strict difference between psychological theory, on the one hand, and work in the consulting room, on the other—a difference with which I fully concur. Finally, he agreed and contributed an account of his way of practising from which I have selected a few extracts as follows:

> I try to be present with a psychologically trained consciousness, but otherwise forget theories and approach the patient

unprejudiced (as much as is humanly possible) in the spirit of Nowness and Eachness ... Great openness. No "technique". No psychological jargon ... By the way: usually chair. But if need be also couch. Or even going for a walk ... I try to be present in the sessions as the concrete ordinary person that I am (human, all-too-human) and to also see the ordinary human being in my patient ... Because of this respect for the ordinary human level, I do not systematically invite transference reactions. I do not offer myself as a kind of guru ... The focus is the soul, the psychology of the situation ... What does the soul, the objective psyche, want? What is the soul content of this dream image or phenomenon ... Not what does the patient want, think, feel ... the basic intention is to enable a patient to get a distance to himself, to see himself objectively ... this helps to avoid the two dangers that go along with a therapeutic approach unaware of the difference, first, the danger of becoming personalistic and positivistic as often in developmental psychology, and secondly, the danger of mystification (unnecessarily inflating the patient's life and experiences with mythic importance ... Mystification is of course also based on positivism: it is the inflation of the positive-factual with "higher" meaning.) (Giegerich, 2011, p. 539)

Giegerich emphasises that abstract thinking is what today's *soul* needs in the shape of more intellect—not more feelings, emotions, body work. He dismisses all those as "ego-stuff". As a psychoanalyst from the developmental school of thought, I have some difficulty with Giegerich's practice in the consulting room, for instance his dismissal of work in the *transference–countertransference* (hence going for a walk would be problematic), and of the concept of the *ego*. The strengthening of *ego* in the process of analysis is vital in the formation and maintenance of *boundaries*. This caveat has already appeared in another part of the book but is worth repeating as disagreements about the role of *ego* are central to the different psychoanalytical approaches that feature in this book.

In another personal communication from Giegerich, he spelt out his main criticisms of Jung as follows. First, Jung hypostasises "the *unconscious*", in this way treating it as if it were some kind of author of dreams, visions, myths, ideas. In the same manner, Jung reifies "the *archetypes*"; here again one sees the influence of Brentano and Heidegger on Giegerich's thinking.

Second, Jung tended to see neurosis ultimately as a sacred disease or religious quest so that *psychic* illnesses are seen as basically valuable, noble, even "sacred".

Third, Jung insisted that the salvation of the world consists in the salvation of the individual *soul*. A psychology that deserves its name cannot take any positive reality, either the individual or the *collective*, as fundamental. What Heraclitus called the existing logos, the *logic* or *syntax* of *being-in-the-world* is not the individual's literalised "*inner*", not his "unconscious", not something "*collective*".

Despite these reservations, Giegerich remains true to Jung's contribution to the discipline of psychology in the following areas: *psychological reality*, the concept of the *soul*, and his later work on *alchemy*.

A version of the above chapter on Wolfgang Giegerich was presented at the IAAP Congress in Kyoto in August 2016

Sonu Shamdasani

I have warm collegial feelings for the three outstanding figures already included in this section whereas Sonu Shamdasani is a friend as well as a respected colleague with whom I share a mutual identity, namely, British Indian. In addition to being a top scholar of the analytical psychology world, Shamdasani is someone of integrity and great personal generosity, of which I have been the recipient on many occasions. I have collaborated with him in a number of ways over the years and will use some of the material from those sources to write about him here. Needless to say, there exists a plethora of books, articles, and interviews he has contributed to the study of Jung over the years, most notably the editing of *The Red Book: Liber Novus*, which is alluded to at various places in the present volume. I shall end this section by citing the work he currently has in hand as the general editor of the Philemon Foundation—all of which is on top of his academic work at University College London as professor in Jung History.

Shamdasani first read Jung when he was eighteen years old visiting ashrams in India—the initial text being *The Secret of the Golden Flower*. This struck Shamdasani as offering the possibility of mediation between

East and *West* psychologically in approaching mysteries without sacrificing reason.

A chapter titled "Philemon Foundation: Ann Casement, in collaboration with Sonu Shamdsani" for the book *Who Owns Jung?* explored the founding of the Philemon Foundation in 2003, which is composed of a governing board and a growing team of scholars. The whole *corpus* of Jung's work will be published by this body in thirty volumes in German and English as *The Complete Works of C. G. Jung*. "The publication of the latter was made possible by the Bollingen Foundation, to which the Philemon Foundation is heir, with the support and contractual collaboration of the heirs of C. G. Jung" (Casement, 2007, p. 170).

The Philemon Foundation was supported, shortly after coming into being, by a $40,000 matching grant from the Andrew W. Mellon Foundation. This sum was met by private donations from Jungian colleagues worldwide, including a grant from the IAAP which announced its intention of collaborating with it in the future. In addition, negotiations between the Wellcome Trust Centre for the History of Medicine and the Philemon resulted in the establishment of the Philemon Readership in Jung History at University College London, initially for ten years. This represents the first recognition of *Jung History* as a formal designation at university level.

A following chapter in the same book by Shamdasani titled "The Incomplete Works of Jung" gives a description of the putting together of the *Collected Works*, some of which has already been elaborated in the section on Michael Fordham. Shamdasani looks at these through the eyes of an historian and concludes that the end result is an edition that is far from satisfactory:

> The level of information provided in the editorial apparatus is far inferior to that present in *The Standard Edition* of Freud's work, let alone in critical historical editions like Harvard University Press' works of William James, or indeed the Bollingen Foundation's exemplary edition of the works of Samuel Taylor Coleridge. (Casement, 2007, p. 181)

The English translation is also far from perfect and Shamdasani's view is that a complete new translation of the English edition of the *Collected Works* is desirable. Jung's patience was tried by the long time it took to produce the first published book, *Psychology and Alchemy*, exemplified by the following:

> Gerhard Adler recalled to Ann Casement that Jung had ambivalent feelings about the book, and placed the following Latin inscription in the copy he gave to Adler: *Omnis festinatio ex parte diaboli est, et sic tam tarde advenit quam pulchre* [all haste is the work of the devil, and so this comes as tardily as it is beautiful]. (Ibid., p. 176)

The Red Book: Liber Novus

I interviewed Shamdasani in September 2009, a month before the publication of *The Red Book* and shortly after he and Maggie Baron hosted a private seminar series in the English countryside to which a few of us were invited. That was a magical time—a veritable *communitas*, in the course of which Shamdasani gave day-long seminars on the book over a period of several days. These seminars turned out to be a godsend as I had to review *Liber Novus* for *The Economist* the actual week in October of its launch in New York, which meant racing through it at lightning speed to get my copy to the books editor from New York—at complete odds with Shamdasani's recommendation in his interview that the ideal pace at which to read the book is a *slow* one.

A brief summary of what Shamdasani said about the book in the course of the interview is set out here for those who have not yet read it as, indeed, I had not at the time of conducting the interview. *Liber Novus* was preceded by the *Black Books* (actually brown) that Jung had written up to 1902 and then taken up again in 1913. He started on the handwritten manuscript of *Liber Novus* in 1914 and worked on it until 1930, the text conveying Jung's prophetic vision of the rebirth of the God image and the image of God. The book is a private cosmology representing Jung's "spiritual biography" (Casement, 2010, p. 43).

In the course of composing the book, Jung formulated his own psychological formulae, namely, "… the concept of the self … the subject imagoes of the persona, shadow, anima/animus, and last but not least, the mana personality" (ibid., pp. 38–39). The whole process delineated in the book shows the genesis of the concept of *individuation*. Prior to undertaking *Liber Novus*, Jung had already developed his *structural theory* that, over time, crystallised into the concepts of *archetypes, collective unconscious, complexes*, non-sexual concept of *libido, introversion/extraversion*, and the notion that dreams were not *wish-fulfilment* but were, instead, *compensatory*.

The key figure of *Philemon* portrayed in the chapter on the *mana personality* is what Jung, in his later works, called the *archetype* of the *Wise Old Man*: "… but that term doesn't convey the richness of this figure—as William James would say, it's a 'thin' language compared to the 'thick' description one finds in *Liber Novus*" (ibid., p. 42).

Philemon foundation

True to its mission statement, the Philemon Foundation has already produced several unpublished works by Jung as follows:

Jung-White Letters (2007)
Children's Dreams: Seminar 1936–1940 (2007)
The Red Book: Liber Novus (2009)
Jung Contra Freud: The 1912 New York Lectures (2012)
Introduction to Jungian Psychology: Notes on the seminar on analytical psychology given in 1925 (2012)
The Question of Psychological Types: The Correspondence of C. G. Jung and Hans Schmid-Guisan 1915–1916 (2012)
Dream Interpretation Ancient and Modern: Notes from the Seminar Given in 1936–1940 (2014)
A Conversation Between Psychology and Theology (2014). In German, the English version came out in July 2020.
Analytical Psychology in Exile: The Correspondence of C. G. Jung & Erich Neumann (2015)
On Psychological and Visionary Art: Notes from C. G. Jung's Lecture on Gérard de Nerval's Aurélia (2015)
The History of Modern Psychology: Lectures Delivered at the ETH Zürich, Volume 1, 1933–1934 (2019)
Dream Symbols of the Individuation Process: Notes of the Seminars given by Jung in Bailey Island and New York, 1936–1937 (2019)
The Black Books (2020)

The works currently being worked on include:

The Original Protocols for Memories, Dreams, Reflections
Jung and the Indologists: Jung's Correspondences with Wilhelm Hauer,
Heinrich Zimmer and Mircea Eliade
C. G. Jung's 1933 Berlin Seminar
On Active Imagination: Jung's 1931 German Seminar
Modern Psychology: C. G. Jung's Lectures at the ETH Zürich, 1933–
1941 (eight volumes)

The huge volume of output by the Philemon Foundation needs funding to continue producing these much-needed books; potential donors are directed to its website online which gives all the necessary information about where to send donations.

CHAPTER 17

Distinguished figures in the contemporary Jungian world

The following list of names is made up of distinguished people whose important work has not featured sufficiently or, in some cases, at all in this volume so far, and whose contributions have enlivened and enlightened the very world this book is about. Many of them are personal friends as I try to have dealings mostly with people I like and/or respect and admire, though that is not the only reason their names appear on this list as there are many other friends in the field who are not mentioned. The people I have selected have had exceptional achievements in that world and made significant contributions to it.

Harald Atmanspacher

The eminent philosopher of science, Harald Atmanspacher, has researched the twenty-year collaboration between Wolfgang Pauli and Jung, one of *the* reasons he was offered honorary membership of the IAAP. He is on the faculty of the C. G. Jung Institute Zürich, the ETH (Swiss Institute of Technology), and the University of Zürich. This is an extremely condensed account of Harald's brilliant *CV*.

John Beebe

John is the doyen of Jung's theory of *Psychological Types* and a prolific author and lecturer. He is a past president of the San Francisco C. G. Jung Institute, who started the Institute's journal now known as *Jung Journal: Culture & Psyche*. His wonderful partner, Adam Frey, is a management consultant helping the San Francisco Institute make a new home for itself. As an undergraduate at Harvard, Adam's concentration was music, following which he went on to take a master's in administration—both John and Adam are Harvard graduates.

Paul Bishop

Paul is William Jacks Chair of Modern Languages at the University of Glasgow whose research has focused on the history of ideas in general and analytical psychology in particular. His most recent publications include *On the Blissful Islands: With Nietzsche and Jung in the Shadow of the Superman* (2016); an introductory study on the thought of Klages titled *Ludwig Klages and the Philosophy of Life: A Vitalist Toolkit* (2017); and *German Political Thought and the Discourse of Platonism: Finding the Way Out of the Cave* (2019). Paul is always a generous personal resource for my forays into German philosophy for which I have a great and ever-increasing love.

Joe Cambray

Joe, a personal friend, is a quintessential *Renaissance Man* who combines intellectual prowess with excellent administrative skills as well as being the creator of the greatest paella dish on the occasions we have been guests at weekend house parties in the USA, or when I have been made welcome in the home he shares with his gifted wife, Linda Carter. Joe, who writes in a similar vein to Harald Atmanspacher about *synchronicity, emergent properties, complex adaptive systems*, and *dark matter*, is a past president of the IAAP, and is currently president and CEO of Pacifica University at Santa Barbara.

Ernst Falzeder

Ernst, a pre-eminent scholar of both Freud and Jung, is also one of the most stimulating conversationalists with whom one can spend hours conversing on psychoanalysis, philosophy, and music. He lives in Salzburg and is enjoyable company on day trips to the Alps, eating venison at one of the food-serving shacks to be found in those famed mountains. Being a native German speaker, he has the advantage of many practitioners and academics in the psychoanalytic and philosophical worlds.

Rosemary Gordon

Rosemary was a close friend and one of the most enchanting people one could hope to meet—the charm belying a first-rate intellect which, combined with her analytic skills, made her an exceptional human being and psychoanalyst. Her death is a loss still felt by her many friends in the developmental Jungian and British psychoanalytical world (Rosemary shared a flat with Pearl King, one-time archivist at the British Society, before she married the lauded BBC documentary maker, Peter Montagnon), as well as by those who knew her only through her writing, for example, *Bridges: Metaphor for Psychic Processes*. She was a former UK editor-in-chief of the *Journal of Analytical Psychology*.

Robert Hinshaw

Bob is a renowned publisher of Jung books from his office high in the Swiss Alps at Einsiedeln. We have worked together on important projects for the IAAP and first met when we jointly chaired its 2001 Cambridge Congress. Following that event, we were asked to do a work assignment for the IAAP in New York and elsewhere in the United States in September of that year which, for obvious reasons, had to be postponed until October. As is easy to imagine, that was an indelible experience, the sharing of which turned us into close friends.

Andreas Jung and Ulrich Hoerni

Andreas and Ulrich are grandsons of Jung as well as architects. Andreas is the only son of Jung's only son, Franz, also an architect, and, like his father before him, lives at Jung's house in Küsnacht. Andreas, accompanied by his wife, Vreni, who has contributed in her own right to scholarly work on Jung, came to New York with Ulrich in 2009 for the launch of

The Red Book along with many other members of Jung's extended family. Both men have contributed extensively to the Jung legacy, with Andreas writing and lecturing on Jung's two houses at Küsnacht and Bollingen; while Ulrich is chair of the *Foundation of the Works of C. G. Jung* that looks after publications of Jung's work, including *The Red Book* to which he contributed the Preface. Both became honorary members of the IAAP at the Copenhagen Congress in 2013. This author has warm relations with Andreas, Ulrich, and Vreni, and been helped by them over the years with her own modest researches into Jung's vast *oeuvre*.

Donald Kalsched

Psychoanalyst, prolific author, and charismatic presenter in the analytical world—Don's influential book published in 1996, *The Inner World of Trauma,* was an outright best-seller. Shortly after its publication, he generously agreed to contribute a chapter, "Archetypal Affect, Anxiety and Defence in Patients Who Have Suffered Early Trauma" to a book I produced with Routledge in 1998, titled *Post-Jungians Today.* Since that time, Don's prodigious output of presentations, articles, and books continues unabated.

Hayao and Toshio Kawai

This cultured father and son duo have contributed immeasurably to analytical psychology over many years, both in Japan and worldwide; Hayao being the one who invited me to work in Japan in 1995 shortly after the devastating Kobe earthquake. Toshio, who was caught up in that earthquake, has done considerable amounts of administrative work for the IAAP and was voted in as its president at the Vienna Congress in 2019. Between them, they have produced a wealth of publications on analytical and clinical psychology and, in Hayao's case, on Buddhism. It has been my good fortune to have had both authors contribute to books I have produced.

Jean Knox

A distinguished former UK editor-in-chief of the *Journal of Analytical Psychology* who did her PhD under the supervision of Peter Fonagy, professor of contemporary psychoanalysis at University College London. Her work in that capacity is a testament to her openness to the diversity of the psychoanalytic community in addition to her long-standing commitment to interdisciplinary work. Her hugely influential book, *Archetype, Attachment, Analysis* wove together theoretical and clinical strands from analytical psychology and attachment theory.

Frank McMillan III

Frank McMillan III is an award-winning author, educator, and speaker, who has been active in international Jungian circles for thirty years. The McMillan Institute for Jungian Studies at the Jung Centre in Houston grew out of the McMillan Professorship in Analytical Psychology at Texas A&M University, the first professorship in analytical psychology founded in 1985 by Frank McMillan Jr. The IAAP awarded honorary membership in 2013 to Frank McMillan III in recognition of his own work and for continuing that of his distinguished father. Frank and his wife, Sheryl, who works tirelessly for homeless individuals and those most in need, live at Corpus Christi, Texas and are dear friends of mine.

Sue Mizen

Sue is a Jungian analyst, who trained at the Cassel Hospital London and the Society of Analytical Psychology, and worked as a consultant medical psychotherapist at Charing Cross Hospital London. She currently lives and works in Devon where she has developed a service for patients with severe and complex personality disorder in an outpatient setting. Sue and I share an interest in neuroscience, being long-standing members of the International Neuropsychoanalysis Association, and are close colleagues of its president, the contemporary Freudian psychoanalyst, Mark Solms.

Renos Papadopoulos

Renos is a friend and generous host at his home located in the same London street where Alfred Hitchcock spent his childhood. He has received many awards for his contributions to the disadvantaged of the world, and is the founder and director of the Centre for Trauma, Asylum and Refugees. Renos combines in-depth scholarship with a dedication to that work—one result of the latter being that he is a consultant to the UN on survivors of torture and political violence. He co-founded the excellent Jungian and post-Jungian master's degree at Essex University with Andrew Samuels and, for that reason alone, analytical psychology owes him a huge vote of thanks (see next entry). Renos and Andrew are among the most charismatic figures in that world.

Andrew Samuels

Andrew, a long-standing friend and inspirer, is an extraordinarily influential figure in the psychoanalytic/psychotherapy world. His many books include the early work *Jung and the Post-Jungians* (1985) that has stood up well to the test of time. Andrew and Renos founded the master's degree in Jungian and post-Jungian studies at Essex University in 1998, with the seminars themselves starting in 1996. These foster a *Socratic* approach to Jungian and other psychoanalytic theory, which makes it a pleasure to work with students in the questioning and constructively critical environment that has been nurtured by these two professors, among the first in the analytical psychology world (David Rosen being the first at Texas A&M—with whom I share a devotion to Elvis). Of equal importance to Andrew is his work as a social activist and political thinker, in which he uses psychoanalytic insights to inform his thinking on the profane world.

Erel Shalit

Erel was a Jungian psychoanalyst at Tel Aviv, past president of the Israeli Society of Analytical Psychology, and founder of the Psychotherapy Programme at Bar Ilan University. He lectured internationally and was a prolific author—his eleven books include two posthumously published volumes edited by his partner, Nancy Swift Furlotti, titled *The Human Soul (Lost) in Transition at the Dawn of a New Era*, and *A Story of Dreams, Fate and Destiny*. He displayed superhuman courage as he battled oesophageal cancer with Nancy at his side until his death; they are the friends everyone dreams of having in life and that I was/am lucky to have.

Murray Stein

Analyst, author, academic, administrator, and publisher—Murray excels in every arena in which he performs. I was fortunate to serve on the Executive Committee at the time he was president of the IAAP; Murray's term in that office was a master class in how to be a president: delegates' meetings started on time and ran smoothly, congresses began to make rather than lose money; and Murray chairing a meeting is a model all chairs should try to emulate. He listens carefully to every view, summarises the business in hand and, finally, comes to a decision. He exudes administrative authority that is rare in the psychoanalytic profession and is an able spokesman for it. (We share a mutual love of Wagner.)

Harry Wilmer

Harry pioneered the use of group psychotherapy at Oak Knoll Naval Hospital to help Vietnam War veterans suffering from PTSD. He was the subject of a docudrama starring Arthur Kennedy as Harry (who does not look at all like him), and Lee Marvin. Harry continued his work at the University of Texas in the beautiful city of San Antonio, home to the legendary Alamo. I was privileged to get to know him and his wife, Jane, late in their lives when they attended the Cambridge and the Barcelona Congresses despite Harry being disabled by then.

Philip and Beverley Zabriskie

Philip was a graduate of Princeton, a Rhodes Scholar at Balliol College, Oxford, and a graduate of Virginia Theological Seminary, being awarded an honorary doctorate from Kenyon College. He and Beverley Zabriskie trained at the C. G. Jung Institute, Zürich, from 1969 to 1973, when Philip graduated. After returning to New York City, Beverley graduated from the C. G. Jung Institute there. Philip was president of the Jung Foundation and served on the IAAP Executive Committee for six years. In 1994 they were founding members of the Jungian Psychoanalytic Association. Each contributed enormously to the Jungian community as teachers, in administrative and trustee roles, as well as through their publications. Philip's calm acceptance of his approaching death was an inspiration to those of us who gathered around him in New York and Maine in the last summer of his life. My book *Who Owns Jung?* is dedicated to his memory.

Beverley cared for Philip throughout his long illness until his death in 2005 on Christmas Day. They were generous and gracious hosts in the Hudson Valley and on the Maine Coast. Beverley has continued their tradition in her New York apartment on Museum Mile after Philip's death.

Luigi Zoja

Luigi is a profound thinker who channels his intellect into his work as a psychoanalyst, scholar, and prolific author of deeply researched books, in some of which he does his own translation of Ancient Greek to elucidate the myths he is exploring. Antiquity is the backdrop to his clinical explorations of pathological states such as greed, addiction, and paranoia. He is a past president of the IAAP and a celebrity in his mother country of Italy, with frequent appearances in the media. I am the fortunate recipient of many of his works, some of which I have managed to review for *The Economist*, a suitable setting for books by one who has an economics degree.

CHAPTER 18

Distinguished figures in the contemporary Jungian world (continued)

There are several other names that deserve to be acknowledged but my publishers have asked me to restrict the word count on this volume so lack of space precludes lengthy encomia on them. In alphabetical order these include: **Edward Edinger** whose "little" book *Encounter with the Self* is a solace in times of need; **Christian Gaillard** past president of the IAAP, and author of the aesthetically and intellectually pleasing volume titled *La Musée Imaginaire de C. G. Jung*; **William McGuire** who collected together many important works by Jung and edited *The Freud/Jung Letters: The Correspondence Between Sigmund Freud and C. G. Jung* (1974); **Erich Neumann** whose *Depth Psychology and a New Ethic* inspired a superb conference at Kibbutz Shefayim outside Tel Aviv in 2015, organised by Erel Shalit and Murray Stein; **Alane Sauder MacGuire**, a close friend who bravely, though only temporarily, triumphed over cancer by producing an in-depth study on the *Persona* before her tragic early death in 2015; **Thomas Singer** able administrator and co-author with Sam Kimbles of the influential book *The Cultural Complex*; **Hester Solomon** past president of the IAAP and prolific author: her writings include *The Self in Transformation* as well as articles and chapters; **Mari Yoshikawa** professor of psychology at the Royal Gakushuin University in Tokyo—her latest book (only available in Japanese) is *The Profession of Psychologist*.

CHAPTER 19

Philosophical, psychological, and scientific influences on Jung's thinking

I was asked by my London organisation, the British Jungian Analytic Association, to put together a piece on some of Jung's precursors in philosophy, psychology, and science for its website. This chapter is an extended version of that original account. Due to the constraints of space left for completion of this book and my own limitations, what I am offering here is, of course, only a truncated study of the many and varied thinkers Jung turned to in his lifetime for inspiration. Sonu Shamdasani's *Jung and the Making of Modern Psychology: The Dream of a Science* (2003) is a rich and reliable source to which the interested reader can turn for more in-depth accounts. Henri Ellenberger's *The Discovery of the Unconscious* and George Makari's *Revolution in Mind* are likewise excellent resources.

Jung's major theoretical contributions were influenced by thinkers reaching back to the pre-Socratic, **Heraclitus**, probably Jung's favourite Greek philosopher. Jung's theory of opposites, central to his psychology, owes a debt to Heraclitus's concept of *enantiadromia*, a psychological law denoting *running contrariwise* which hypothesises that everything eventually turns into its opposite. Heraclitus also posited that everything is in a state of flux which links to the all-important notion of *process* in psychoanalysis. Along with these ideas from Heraclitus, Jung was drawn to the latter's hypothesis that fire was the original creative element.

Plato's theory of the *Forms* is cited as one of the forerunners of Jung's key concept of *archetypes*, inherited patterns in the *psychosomatic unconscious* which, in today's vernacular may be thought of as *psychological DNA*. In this way, Jung linked two sets of opposites: *psyche/soma* and *instinct/image*. The medieval philosopher, Meister Eckhart, amongst others, is a significant influence on this signature concept of Jung's, as he also is of what lies at the heart of Jung's *Answer to Job*, which is a late *working through* of some of the religious ideas explored in *The Red Book*.

From **Aristotle**, Jung derived the all-important notion of *teleology*—the doctrine of final causes. This is an extension of Plato's theory of *Forms* which provided the blueprint that guides the object to its final state or *telos*. The underlying pattern that is there in Aristotle's *teleology* is replicated in Jung's theory of the *individuation process*.

It is, however, rather more recent *Western* philosophy, particularly German *Idealism* and *Romanticism,* that impacted Jung's thinking as much as any other philosophy, for example, **Kant** about whom Jung stated: "Kant is my philosopher" (Shamdasani, 2012, p. 22). Kant's *moral order within* is to be seen at work everywhere in Jung's writing; from my perspective, the former's *starry heavens above* are more evident in Jung's cosmology than in his own. Jung claimed that Kant's epistemology was a major influence, in particular, what he termed the *noumenal* or *thing-in-itself* which underlies the theory of *archetypes*. He mostly links this to Kant's first two *critiques*, but the academic Paul Bishop and I have queried this and suggest, instead, that Kant's third *critique*, viz. *The Critique of Judgement* is closer to Jung's thinking (cf. my chapter "The Complex Pleasure of the Sublime" in *Thresholds and Pathways between Jung and Lacan,* 2021). Nonetheless, Kant's compromise in upholding reason while at the same time making room for faith and belief provided the vital underpinning of Jung's approach to his own psychology.

Hegel synthesised Kantian reason and morality with Herder's ideas on desire and sensibility and was an important, if unacknowledged influence on Jung's dialectical model to be found in *psychological alchemy*. In fact, Jung's dismissal of Hegel is so extreme one wonders if he ever really understood Hegel's as opposed to Fichte's dialectic. The latter is the one who contributed the thesis/antithesis/synthesis model taken up by many writers; whereas Hegel's dialectic is a *spiral* movement, which is what is replicated in Jung's *alchemical* model and which has been elaborated in the section on Giegerich's work. My own thinking about Jung's negative view of Hegel is that he imported this wholesale from Schopenhauer whose diatribes against Hegel (and Fichte) include the following: "Fichte is the father of *pseudo-philosophy*, of *dishonest* method which attempts to deceive through ambiguity in the use of words, through unintelligble discourse and through sophisms ... in *Hegel* as is generally known ... actually ripened into ultimate charlatanism" (Schopenhauer, 1844, pp. 13–14; original italics).

And, further, where he is comparing Hegel unfavourably with his beloved Kant: "These are the fruits of Hegelism. Once the mind is thoroughly corrupted by this senseless gibberish, serious Kantian philosophy no longer gets through" (ibid., p. 39).

Jung, in his turn, is equally scathing about Hegel in accusing the latter of *inflation* in his reductive thinking about God: "... the practical equation of philosophical reason with Spirit ... which achieved such a horrid brilliance in his philosophy of the State." The latter had its culmination in the neo-Hegelian, Karl Marx's thinking. For Jung, Hegel's philosophy is "... reminiscent of the megalomaniac language of schizophrenics, who use terrific spellbinding words to reduce the transcendent to subjective form ... So bombastic a terminology is a symptom of weakness, ineptitude, and lack of substance" (1960b, p. 170).

From my own experience, Hegel is the most turgid writer I have ever struggled to understand and has only himself to blame for the negative reactions he arouses in a writer like Schopenhauer, whose clarity of prose is exemplary. The native German-speaking scholar Ernst Falzeder has assured me that Hegel is even worse to read in the original German. It fell to Giegerich to comprehend Hegel's relevance for psychoanalysis through his historical model and brilliant dialectical method—the latter having its more recent manifestation in Jung's *psychological alchemy*. As elaborated earlier in the book, this is the *recursive* process according to which *neurosis* is transformed into *selfhood* as metaphorical gold is extracted from the base matter of *unconscious* contents.

Following Hegel, later in the nineteenth century, two philosophers who contributed beyond measure to Jung's formation are **Schopenhauer** and **Nietzsche**, the former with his theory of the *Will* and the latter with his theory of the *Übermensch*. This whole book could be dedicated to each of them—important to bear in mind when reading the all-too-brief summaries that follow of a few of their main concepts.

Jung discovered Schopenhauer while he was still at university and the philosopher continued to exert an influence throughout Jung's life, unsurprising in itself as Schopenhauer is one of the forerunners of psychoanalytic thinking as much of Freud's *oeuvre* derives from that great philosopher. Schopenhauer was one of the first Europeans to steep himself in *Eastern* religious writings such as those of Mahayana Buddhism and the Hindu Veda texts, from which Schopenhauer's thinking on *nirvana* derives. Freud borrowed this term to formulate his theory of the *Nirvana Principle*, the tendency of all instincts and life processes to get rid of tension and to seek the equilibrium of the inorganic state, namely, death. This is what underlies Freud's late key notion of the *death instinct*. Freud's *Nirvana Principle* is akin to the principle of *homeostasis*, a central component in the development of the metascience of cybernetics. Norbert Wiener, the so-called father of this new paradigm, defines *homeostasis* as follows: "… an active equilibrium, in which each deviation from the norm brings on a reaction in the opposite direction" (2017, p. 435), which links to Heraclitus's *enantiadromia*, a profound influence on Jung.

Schopenhauer's thinking on the *Will*, also derived from Eastern texts, led to both Freud and Jung adopting it for their own theories of the psychoanalytic *unconscious*, which drives everything the subject does in life that was formerly attributed to *conscious* functioning. Jung, following Schopenhauer, depicted outer reality as illusory or *Maya* as it appears in the Hindu texts. There are many allusions to Schopenhauer in Jung's *Collected Works* so I shall leave the interested reader to pursue further knowledge there about this great philosopher or, better still, to read Schopenhauer himself.

As for **Nietzsche**, his influence on Jung was such that it led to identification with him on Jung's part. The latter's theory of the *self* derives from the *Übermensch*, and Giegerich has pointed to Jung's *Red Book* as his answer to Nietzsche's assertion that God is dead. Jung also conducted a five-year-long series of seminars dedicated to Nietzsche's *Thus Spake Zarathurstra*, which were put together in two massive volumes by James Jarrett in 1988. Jung ended these seminars before their natural conclusion as they were "drowned out by the alarms of war as the fateful summer of 1939 approached" (Jarrett, 1988, p. ix).

Nietzsche was a towering figure who not only was a major influence on Freud and Jung but also on other notable thinkers such as Mann, Shaw, Heidegger, and Jaspers, while his name, though perhaps not his writings, is known everywhere. He himself initially came under the influence of Schopenhauer's *Will to Live* though later renounced that in favour of his own *Will to Power*. To this day he remains a divisive figure for the way the Nazis used his ideas to underwrite their own power-driven philosophy.

Goethe, who chronologically should come before Schopenhauer and Nietzsche, is placed after them as they follow on more naturally from Kant and Hegel, was arguably the greatest of all influences on Jung as he came to see his No. 2 personality being personified by Goethe. Jung's mother suggested he read *Faust* which he found in a handsome edition in the family home.

> It poured into my soul like a miraculous balm. 'Here at last', I thought, 'is someone who takes the devil seriously and even concludes a blood pact with him—with the adversary who has the power to frustrate God's plan to make a perfect world'. (Jung, 1963, p. 68)

Jung came to realise that *Faust* was synonymous with his No. 2 personality, and that his godfather and authority was the great Goethe himself.

> The second part of *Faust* is a link ... which has existed from the beginnings of philosophical alchemy and Gnosticism down to Nietzsche's *Zarathustra*. Unpopular, ambiguous, and dangerous, it is a voyage of discovery to the other pole of the world. (Ibid., p. 181)
>
> I regard my work on alchemy as a sign of my inner relationship to Goethe. Goethe's secret was that he was in the grip of that process of alchemical transformation which has gone on through the centuries. He regarded his *Faust* as an *opus magnum* ... He called it his 'main business' and his whole life was enacted within the framework of this drama. (Ibid., p. 197)

Above all, *Faust* awoke in Jung the problem of opposites: good and evil, mind and matter, light and darkness. "The dichotomy of Faust-Mephistopheles came together within myself into a single person, and I was that person" (ibid., p. 222). The last words of *Memories, Dreams, Reflections* are: "There is, as Goethe puts it in *Faust,* an 'untrodden, untreadable' region whose precincts cannot and should not be entered by force; a destiny which will brook no human intervention" (ibid., p. 345).

A brief summary follows of other significant influences on Jung from the philosophical, psychological, scientific, and religious worlds: **Theodore Flournoy** (non-pathological and creative components of the *subconscious*); **William James** (psychology of religion, *collective uncon-scious*, typology); **Pierre Janet** (the autonomy of *unconscious* contents); **Wolfgang Pauli** (theoretic and quantum physicist and Nobel Laureate, who worked with Jung on the concept of *synchronicity—subjectively meaningful acausally connected events*—that brought together physical and psychic dimensions of reality); **Richard Wilhelm** (East/West con-nections; *alchemy*; *I Ching*); **Wilhelm Wundt** (the *word-association* experiments invented by Francis Galton).

Jung was a religious thinker and the leitmotif that runs throughout his writing is his quest for the dark or *shadow* side of the Godhead. For this, he turned to Eastern and Western religions and to esoterica such as *Gnosticism, Kabala*, and *Manichaeism.*

CHAPTER 20

Orient

O ver the course of many years, I have worked in various parts of the world such as the United States, Brazil, Mexico, several countries in Europe, Japan, Russia, South Africa, and, in more recent years, China. In 2015, Professor Heyong Shen and Professor Gao Lan Shen, both of whom have been friends of mine for many years, invited me to teach in China as some of my writing has been translated into traditional and simplified Chinese. Later that year, I went to Shanghai to give seminars to members of the IAAP Developing Group and of the Sand Play Group. These were large classes of one hundred students during the day followed by one hundred students each evening with an excellent interpreter acting as the liaison.

Prior to my arrival in Shanghai in August 2015, I had been lecturing at Gakushuin University in Tokyo, which I do from time to time. Experiencing them so closely together in 2015, the contrast between the Japanese and the Chinese people was apparent—one obvious feature being that the former do not touch anyone and the latter are uninhibitedly tactile—at least in my experience. I quickly became acclimatised to being hugged, kissed, and touched by many of the people with whom I came in contact whilst I was in Shanghai, which made me feel as if

I were something exotic—almost a being from another world. A further obvious difference between the Chinese and the Japanese is the reverential way the latter treat professors—one manifestation of this is that nobody asks questions in the classroom or at lecture halls as that is considered impolite. I try to get around that by asking a student a specific question to which I usually get an immediate response. Even though the Japanese remain silent during and after a lecture, they are highly intelligent and are taking in every word and thinking about it.

There is a certain amount of being polite to lecturers in China but not to the extent that exists in Japan. In the latter country, I am aware that my natural exuberance and outspokenness is considered to be impolite but that allowances are made for me as a foreigner, particularly by my fellow professor in Tokyo, Mari Yoshikawa, one of the most refined and intelligent people I know. I would find it impossible to be anything other than myself so I do not try to censor every word I speak or act I perform and, instead, remain myself while, at the same time, I do not go out of my way to give offence which, in any case, I would not do in any other culture. Hayao Kawai, the *eminence grise* of Japan, was the first to invite me to meet with the fourteen Japanese Jungian analysts in Tokyo in 1995, and then to lecture at Kyoto University. This initial visit was of huge personal as well as professional importance for me and I have been back several times since to lecture and teach.

CHINA

The following section is devoted to China, for which I solicited entries by some of the people I interact with in that country, so that much of what follows is their own account of who they are and what they do. My input, in the places where it occurs, is easy to discern.

Professor Heyong Shen and Professor Gao Lan Shen

Heyong Shen and Gao Lan Shen, both professors of psychology, were appointed Individual members of the IAAP in 2003 and 2013, respectively, in appreciation of their outstanding work in developing analytical psychology in China. They are also among that country's first batch of internationally qualified psychoanalysts, and are the founders of the Oriental Academy for Analytical Psychology (OAAP), which established the

Research Centre for analytical psychology in the course of the 1998 first session of Analytical Psychology and Chinese Culture. Since that time, they have worked with the IAAP across eight of its international congresses, and have translated many Jung and Jungian books into Chinese, including the twenty volumes of Jung's *Collected Works*, and nine volumes of the *Selected Works of C. G. Jung*. They have also set up the Chinese language *Journal of Analytical Psychology* and *Journal of Sandplay Therapy*. Heyong Shen is a frequent speaker at Eranos (1997, 2007, 2019), and a Fay Lecturer (2018) on the theme: Psychology of the Heart.

The Research Centre has departments in analytical psychology at the Universities of South China Normal, Fudan, and Macau, which support *The Garden of Heart & Soul*, a public welfare master's, doctoral, and postdoctoral degree in analytical psychology, as well as *sand play* therapy. The first workstation of *The Garden of Heart & Soul* was established in 2007 in Guangzhou children's welfare home. Since that time, Heyong and Gao Lan have personally helped raise the money to fund the construction and development of more than eighty such workstations nationwide.

In 2008, a massive earthquake hit Whenchuan County. In response to that terrible event, Heyong and Gao Lan Shen led the Heart & Soul Team that worked on the psychological consequences of that earthquake, setting up seven workstations where the work has continued until the present time. In 2010, a further massive earthquake hit Yushu, situated on the Qinghai-Tibetan Plateau. The Team set up four workstations in the earthquake zone, at which the lead person in charge of the earthquake relief headquarters met with the Team on several occasions to solicit their advice. The Team established a deep friendship with Tibetan friends and were baptised at the Qinghai-Tibetan Plateau, which is the source of three rivers. The psychological healing model developed by the Team has been used in disaster and collective *trauma* work in South Africa, Mexico, Colombia, Chile, and Nepal, and papers on their work have been published in various journals.

The Garden of the Heart & Soul's work on the coronavirus outbreak 2020

When the "new coronavirus" broke out suddenly in Wuhan in 2019 wreaking havoc in the "Divine Land of China" and spreading across the world, *The Garden of the Heart & Soul* launched a volunteer team on 26th January 2020 to organise professional psychological counsellors and therapists recruited from the OAAP and the various Research Centres in China. Over 300 of them have joined in providing psychological aid for frontline medical staff, patients, and their families. The approach generated by *The Garden of the Heart & Soul* is based on the following precepts: wisdom, courage, compassion, and feeling, and is dedicated to pulling together with everyone to overcome the difficulties of this time. I feel privileged to have been appointed a special adviser by Heyong and Gao Lan to the dedicated work of *The Garden of the Heart & Soul*.

Beijing Fateman Psychological Counselling Centre

Following on from my work in Shanghai in 2015, I was fortunate to be invited to work in Beijing by Qin Nan, the owner of the Fateman Beijing Centre, who has since become a good friend. The Centre was founded in 2007 and is listed in the top ten of the capital's counselling agencies providing service to government projects, social welfare, and to Employee Assistance Program projects. It implemented the first large-scale public welfare service for marriage and family counselling in Beijing, along with several other vital public services such as juvenile delinquency prevention within the judicial system.

Since 2012, the Centre has introduced world-renowned international psychologists, psychoanalysts, and psychotherapists to train domestic counsellors and therapists, including Ann Casement from the UK, Mauro Mancini from Italy, and Linda Xiaoqiao from the United States. The Centre itself has contracts with more than fifty counsellors and psychotherapists. It also engages in research and works closely with universities in providing effective mental health guidance.

Qin Nan

The founding owner of the Fateman Centre, Qin, is a psychological consultant and is a guest expert for Chinese media and television channels. She is a China national social worker and has a master's degree in applied psychology from the California Institute of Technology. For nine consecutive years, she has organised the International Psychosomatic

Workshop and Dream Workshop that spans eighteen terms, each lasting ninety days, and fifteen terms of seventy-five days, respectively.

Over the past thirteen years, Qin's distinguished work has resulted in the Fateman Centre being appointed by the Changping District Justice Bureau for the provision of psychological correction for prisoners, and to provide psychological services to the Beijing People's Procuratorate and the Municipal People's Court.

Yuan Lin

At one time, Yuan Lin dreamed of becoming a psychologist, aged fourteen, but she forgot her dream and spent her early career in China as a government diplomatic interpreter. She went on to be an interpreter for the secretary general of the United Nations and many foreign state leaders and diplomats, including Dr Henry Kissinger. Yuan Lin then worked as the assistant to the editor-in-chief of *Caijing Magazine*, then as deputy general manager at the *China Reform Magazine*, part of the Caixin Media Group, that was instituted by Deng Xiaoping. She later acquired her MBA from Fordham University in New York City, following which she ventured into sales and marketing in an IT firm providing outsourcing services to General Electric and Microsoft HQ. Following a series of drastic social changes and personal ups-and-downs, she returned to her dream of psychology and started again from scratch at the age of forty to learn psychotherapy. After meeting Ann Casement in 2018, Yuan Lin is now tirelessly exploring the search for her Self.

The above passage was written by Yuan Lin in the third person, to which I only want to add that she is the best interpreter I have had the pleasure of working with in any country where that has been necessary. This applies both to her language skills as well as to Yuan Lin herself.

Dangwei Zhou

Dangwei and I met seven years ago in London and have become friends and colleagues since then. The range of knowledge and depth of thinking he displays is unrivalled so that conversation with him is a pleasure, in the course of which he is tutoring me in Chinese history and philosophy.

He studied applied psychology as an undergraduate at Kaifeng and at a postgraduate level in Guangzhou, following which he came to University College London where he started his PhD programme under the supervision of Sonu Shamdasani. The title of his dissertation is "Richard Wilhelm (1873–1930): An Alternative Way to Bridge East and West", an historical study of the intellectual history of Richard Wilhelm.

Dangwei has translated into simplified Chinese John Beebe's papers on typology, as well as *The Red Book* in 2016, and in 2019 *The Handbook of Jungian Psychology*, and *Introduction to Jungian Psychology: Notes of the Seminar on Analytical Psychology Given in 1925*.

Dangwei has dedicated himself to spreading Jungian psychology in China and researching the exchange between East and West via depth psychology. His intention is to follow in the footsteps of the Buddhist Monk, Xuanzang (602–664) in the Tang Dynasty, who translated many Buddhist classics into traditional Chinese, and the German sinologist, Richard Wilhelm, who translated a number of Chinese classics into German.

Conclusion

It has been my experience in China, in the course of the lectures and teaching I do either in person or online with participants in that incredible country, that they are eager to add to their growing knowledge of psychoanalytic and psychotherapeutic theory and practice. In particular, it is their embrace of Jung's emphasis on the vital importance of individual creativity that is inspiring and, poignantly, brings back feelings I had when I initially encountered his *thinking* through my first analysis—the joy of finding my own path in life accompanied by Jung's insight and knowledge. I agree with Michael Fordham's moving tribute to Jung that appears earlier in this book and also his critique of the tendency to cultist status in some Jungian quarters. The only way of repaying what one owes Jung is *not* by being a disciple but by *becoming* one's own individual self which was what he was advocating.

Since the advent of Jung in my life in 1964, I have been profoundly affected by his psychological approach, in particular his thinking on concepts such as *shadow* and *psychological alchemy*, chapters on both of which are featured in this book. It is not only Jung's theories, though, that are important for my way of functioning, but also his attitude to work in the consulting room. For instance, Jung's professed approach to analysis is that the analyst is as much in the *alchemical* analytical container as the patient/*analysand*, a fact he conceptualised as *mutuality*. In other words, both participants being jointly in the work of analysis are mutually capable of being transformed by what takes place in the *analytic container*.

Another important dimension of Jung's approach is its light touch when it comes to pathologising patients or *analysands*. For Jung, problems have the potential to open an individual's receptivity to something that has been unavailable to her until she has started to explore them psychologically. This is what Jung means by the prospective *psyche*, so that Jungian analysis does not focus *only* on the patient's past history but also on where this might lead the person in the future. To give a simple example, if a negative parental complex, that has its origins in a patient's past history, can be *worked through* and transformed, that individual will find their own capacity for parenting enhanced.

Jung felt he had benefited enormously from the knowledge he acquired through the sinologist, Richard Wilhelm, of Chinese esoterica such as *I Ching*, the works of *Lao Tzu*, the ancient philosopher and reputed author of *Tao Te Ching*, and the opening up of his interest in *alchemy* through the Chinese alchemical treatise, *The Secret of the Golden Flower*. As a result, he would doubtless have been delighted to see analytical psychology being so well received in China.

Following on from the initial invitation to teach from Professor Heyong Shen and Professor Gao Lan, presidents of the Oriental Academy for Analytical Psychology (OAAP), I continue to work several times a week online with analysands and supervisees in China. As I am Eurasian by birth, it is affording me a great deal of pleasure to be reconnected to the continent of my origin, namely, Asia. As I approach the end, the following words from one of *the* stylish authors of the twentieth century who, himself, spent much time in Switzerland, the birthplace of Jungian psychoanalysis, seem a fitting conclusion: "So we beat on, boats against the current borne back ceaselessly into the past" (Fitzgerald, 1974, p. 188).

References

Astor, J. (1995). *Michael Fordham: Innovations in Analytical Psychology*. London: Routledge.

Astor, J. (2007). *Analytical Psychology and Michael Fordham*. In: A. Casement (Ed.), *Who Owns Jung?* London: Karnac.

Bair, D. (2004). *Jung: A Biography*. Boston, MA: Little, Brown.

Bennet, E. A. (1961). *C. G. Jung*. London: Barrie.

Berg, A. (2007). *Can we prevent colonization of the mind? Traditional culture in South Africa*. In: A. Casement (Ed.), *Who Owns Jung?* London: Karnac.

Bion, W. R. (1965). *Transformations*. London: Heinemann. (Reprinted London: Karnac, 1984).

Bion, W. R. (1967). Attacks on linking. In: *Second Thoughts*. London: Karnac, 1984.

Bion, W. R. (1970). *Attention and Interpretation*. London: Karnac, 1984.

Bion, W. R. (1992). *Cogitations*. London: Karnac.

Britton, R. (2003). *Sex, Death, and the Superego: Experiences in Psychoanalysis*. London: Karnac.

Carotenuto, A. (1984). *A Secret Symmetry: Sabina Spielrein between Jung and Freud*. Foreword by William McGuire. New York: Random House, Pantheon, 1982.

Casement, A. (1995). A brief history of splits in the United Kingdom. *The Journal of Analytical Psychology, 40*(3): 327–342.

Casement, A. (1998). The qualitative leap of faith: Reflections on Kierkegaard and Jung. In: A. Casement (Ed.), *Post-Jungians Today: Key Papers in Contemporary Analytical Psychology*. London: Routledge.

Casement, A. (2007). *Who Owns Jung?* London: Karnac.

Casement, A. (2010). Sonu Shamdasani interviewed by Ann Casement. *Journal of Analytical Psychology, 55*(1): 35–49.

Casement, A. (2011a). The interiorizing movement of logical life: Reflections on Wolfgang Giergerich. *Journal of Analytical Psychology, 56*(4): 532–549.

Casement, A. (2011b). Review of *The Soul Always Thinks: The Collected English Papers of Wolfgang Giegerich. Journal of Analytical Psychology, 56*(5): 715–717.

Casement, A. (2015). Obituaries. *Journal of Analytical Psychology, 60*(5): 753–754.

Casement, A. (2016). Interview with Sonu Shamdasani. *International Association for Analytical Psychology 2016 Newsletter*: 246–261.

Casement, A. (2019). Interview with Verena Kast. *International Association for Analytical Psychology 2019 Newsletter*: 265–282.

Casement, A., & Tacey, D. (Eds.) (2006). *The Idea of the Numinous: Contemporary Jungian and Psychoanalytic Perspectives*. London: Routledge.

Casement, A., Goss, P., & Nobus, D. (Eds.) (2021). *Thresholds and Pathways between Jung and Lacan*. London: Routledge.

Devereux, E., Dillane, A., & Power, M. J. (Eds.) (2015). *David Bowie: Critical Perspectives*. New York: Routledge.

Edinger, E. (1960). The ego-self paradox. *Journal of Analytical Psychology, 5*(1): 3–18.

Edinger, E. (1986). *Encounter with the Self: A Jungian Commentary on William Blake's Illustrations of the Book of Job*. Toronto, Canada: Inner City.

Ellenberger, H. (1970). *The Discovery of the Unconscious: The History and Evolution of Dynamic Psychiatry*. New York: Basic Books.

Escamilla, M. (2016). *Bleuler, Jung, and the Creation of the Schizophrenias*. Einsieden, Switzerland: Daimon Verlag.

Escamilla, M., Sandoval, H., Calhoun, V., & Ramirez, M. (2018). Brain activation patterns in response to complex triggers in the Word Association Test: Results from a new study in the United States. *Journal of Analytical Psychology, 63*(4): 484–509.

Falzeder, E. (2007). The story of an ambivalent relationship: Sigmund Freud and Eugen Bleuler. *Journal of Analytical Psychology, 52*(3): 343–368.

Fitzgerald, S. F. (1974). *The Great Gatsby*. London: Penguin.

Fordham, M. (1956). Obituary to Emma Jung. *Journal of Analytical Psychology, 1*(2).

Fordham, M. (1978). *Jungian Psychotherapy: Study in Analytical Psychology*. London: John Wiley & Sons. (Reprinted London: Karnac, 1986.)

Fordham, M. (1993). *The Making of an Analyst: A Memoir*. London: Free Association.

Freud, S. (1900a). *The Interpretation of Dreams. S. E., 4–5*. London: Hogarth.

Freud, S. (1914d). *On the History of the Psycho-Analytic Movement*. London: W. W. Norton, 1966.

Giegerich, W. (2007). Psychology—The study of the soul's logical life. In: A. Casement (Ed.), *Who Owns Jung?* London: Karnac.

Giegerich, W. (2008). *The Soul's Logical Life*. Frankfurt am Main, Germany: Peter Lang.

Giegerich, W., Miller, D. L., & Mogenson, G. (2005). Conflict resolution, Opposites/ creative union versus dialectics, and the climb up the slippery mountain. In: W. Giegerich, D. L. Miller, & G. Mogenson (Eds.), *Dialectics & Analytical Psychology: The El Capitan Canyon Seminar*. New Orleans, LA: Spring Journal.

Gieser, S. (2005). *The Innermost Kernel: Depth Psychology and Quantum Mechanics, Wolfgang Pauli's Dialogue with C. G. Jung*. Berlin: Springer Verlag.

Graf-Nold, A. (2001). The Zürich School of Psychiatry in theory and practice. Sabina Spielrein's treatment at the Burghölzli Clinic in Zürich. *Journal of Analytical Psychology 46*(1): 73–104.

Greene, L. (1984). *The Astrology of Fate*. London: George Allen & Unwin.

Grotstein, J. S. (2006). Foreword. In: A. Casement & D. Tacey (Eds.), *The Idea of the Numinous: Contemporary Jungian and Psychoanalytic Perspectives*. Hove, UK: Routledge.

Grotstein, J. S. (2007). *A Beam of Intense Darkness: Wilfred Bion's Legacy to Psychoanalysis*. London: Karnac.

Heidegger, M. (1977). *The Question Concerning Technology*. New York: Harper & Row.

Hillman, J. (2011a). Divergences. In: A. Casement, Reflections on Wolfgang Giegerich. *Journal of Analytical Psychology, 56*(4): 544.

Hillman, J. (2011b). Spring: A journal of archetype and culture. *International Association for Analytical Psychology 2011 Newsletter*.

Hillman, J., & Ventura, M. (1993). *We've Had a Hundred Years of Psychotherapy— And the World's Getting Worse*. San Francisco, CA: HarperCollins.

Hoedl, J. (2018). The alchemical 'not' and Marlan's stone that remains a stone. A response to his critique of Giegerich's 'psychology proper'. *Journal of Analytical Psychology*, 63(1): 123–130.

Hogenson, G. (2003). Responses: Archetype theory, evolutionary psychology and the Baldwin effect. *Journal of Analytical Psychology*, 48(1): 107–116.

Jarrett, J. L. (Ed.) (1988). *C. G. Jung: Nietzsche's Zarathustra. Notes of the Seminar given in 1934–1939. Volume 1*. Princeton, NJ: Princeton University Press.

Johnson, S. (2001). *Emergence: The Connected Lives of Ants, Brains, Cities, and Software*. New York: Charles Scribner's Sons.

Jones, E. (1955). *Sigmund Freud's Life and Work. Volume II*. London: Hogarth.

Jones, E. (1959). *Free Associations*. London: Hogarth.

Jung, C. G. (1916). *Psychology of the Unconscious: A Study of the Transformations and Symbolisms of the Libido: A Contribution to the History of the Evolution of Thought*. Beatrice Hinkle (Trans.). Introduction by W. McGuire. New York: Moffat, Yard. Reprinted in 1991 by Routledge and Princeton University Press for the Bollingen Foundation.

Jung, C. G. (1925). Marriage as a psychological relationship. In: *The Development of Personality. Volume 17*. London: Routledge & Kegan Paul, 1954.

Jung, C. G. (1946). The psychology of the transference. In: *The Practice of Psychotherapy. Volume 16*. London: Routledge & Kegan Paul.

Jung, C. G. (1953). *Psychology and Alchemy*. London: Routledge & Kegan Paul.

Jung, C. G. (1954). *The Practice of Psychotherapy. Volume 16*. London: Routledge & Kegan Paul.

Jung, C. G. (1958a). *Psychology and Religion: West and East. Volume 11*. London: Routledge & Kegan Paul.

Jung, C. G. (1958b). *Answer to Job*. New York: Bollingen Foundation.

Jung, C. G. (1959a). *The Archetypes and the Collective Unconscious. Volume 9: Part I*. London: Routledge & Kegan Paul.

Jung, C. G. (1959b). *Aion. Volume 9: Part II*. Princeton, NJ: Princeton University Press.

Jung, C. G. (1960a). *The Psychogenesis of Mental Disease. Volume 3*. London: Routledge & Kegan Paul.

Jung, C. G. (1960b). *The Structure and Dynamics of the Psyche. Volume 8*. London: Routledge & Kegan Paul.

Jung, C. G. (1961). *Freud and Psychoanalysis. Volume 4*. London: Routledge & Kegan Paul.

Jung, C. G. (1963). *Memories, Dreams, Reflections*. London: Collins and Routledge & Kegan Paul.

Jung, C. G. (1966). *Two Essays on Analytical Psychology*. Princeton, NJ: Princeton University Press.

Jung, C. G. (1967). *Alchemical Studies. Volume 13*. London: Routledge & Kegan Paul.

Jung, C. G. (1968). *Analytical Psychology: Its Theory and Practice*. New York: Vintage, Random House.

Jung, C. G. (1971). *Psychological Types. Volume 6*. London: Routledge & Kegan Paul.

Jung, C. G. (1973). *Letters of C. G. Jung. Volume 1*. G. Adler & A. Jaffé (Eds.) (p. 377). London: Routledge.

Jung, C. G. (1977). *The Symbolic Life. Volume 18*. London: Routledge & Kegan Paul.

Jung, C. G. (2001). *Modern Man in Search of a Soul*. London: Routledge.

Jung, C. G. (2009). *The Red Book—Liber Novus*. New York: W. W. Norton.

Kahr, B. (2018). *Coffee with Freud*. London: Karnac.

Kawai, H. (1996). *Buddhism and the Art of Psychotherapy*. College Station, TX: Texas A&M University Press.

Kerr, J. (1994). *A Most Dangerous Method*. New York: Penguin Random House.

King, P., & Steiner, R. (Eds.) (1991). *The Freud-Klein Controversies 1943–45*. London: Routledge.

Kirsch, T. (2000). *The Jungians*. London: Routledge.

Knox, J. (2004). From archetypes to reflective function. *Journal of Analytical Psychology, 49*(1): 1–19.

Kojève, A. (1969). *Introduction to the Reading of Hegel*. New York: Basic Books.

Leach, E. R. (1965). *Frazer and Malinowski. Encounter, XXV*(5): 24–36.

Leeming, D., Madden, K., & Marlon, S. (Eds.) (2010). *The Encyclopedia of Psychology and Religion*. New York: Springer.

Lévi-Strauss, C. (1996). *The Savage Mind*. Oxford: Oxford University Press.

López-Corvo, R. E. (2003). *The Dictionary of the Work of W. R. Bion*. London: Karnac.

Lothane, Z. (2009). Primal curiosity, primal scenes, primal fantasies—and prevarication. *Academy Forum, 53*(2): 17–19.

Magee, B. (2000). *Wagner and Philosophy*. London: Penguin.

McGuire, W. (Ed.) (1974). *The Freud/Jung Letters*. London: Hogarth.

McGuire, W. (1991). Introduction. In: C. G. Jung, *Psychology of the Unconscious*. London: Routledge.

Otto, R. (1917). *The Idea of the Holy: An Inquiry into the Non-rational Factor in the Idea of the Divine and Its Relation to the Rational*. London: Oxford University Press, 1958.

Proust, M. (1913). *In Search of Lost Time*. New York: Chatto & Windus and Random House, 1992.

Roberts, A. (2018). *Churchill: Walking With Destiny*. London: Penguin Random House.

Russell, D. (2013). *The Life and Ideas of James Hillman: Volume 1: The Making of a Psychologist*. New York: Skyhorse.

Safranski, R. (1999). *Martin Heidegger: Between Good and Evil*. Cambridge, MA: Harvard University Press.

Samuels, A., Shorter, B., & Plaut, F. (1986). *A Critical Dictionary of Jungian Analysis*. London: Routledge & Kegan Paul.

Sauder MacGuire, A. (2017). *Embodying the Soul: Toward a Rescuing and Retaining of Persona*. Jung Journal: Culture & Psyche, *11*(4): 45–80.

Schopenhauer, A. (1819). *The World as Will and Representation. Vol. 1*. London: Pearson Longman, 2008.

Schopenhauer, A. (1844). *The World as Will and Representation. Vol. 2*. London: Pearson Longman, 2008.

Schwartz-Salant, N. (1982). *Narcissism and Character Transformation: The Psychology of Narcissistic Disorders*. Toronto, Canada: Inner City.

Segal, R. A. (2018). Merkur on Jung, on ethics, mysticism and religion. *International Journal of Jungian Studies*, *10*(2): 147–154.

Shamdasani, S. (2003). *Jung and the Making of Modern Psychology: The Dream of a Science*. Cambridge: Cambridge University Press.

Shamdasani, S. (2005). *Jung Stripped Bare by His Biographers, Even*. London: Karnac.

Shamdasani, S. (2009). *The Red Book: Liber Novus. A Reader's Edition*. S. Shamdasani (Ed.), M. Kyburz, J. Peck, & S. Shamdasani (Trans.). New York: W. W. Norton.

Shamdasani, S. (2012). *C. G. Jung: A Biography in Books*. New York: W. W. Norton.

Shamdasani, S. (Ed.) (2020). *The Black Books, 1913–1932*. New York: W. W. Norton.

Solms, M. (2021). *The Hidden Spring: A Journey to the Source of Consciousness.* London: Profile.

Solms, M., & Friston, K. (2018). How and why consciousness arises: Preliminary communication. *Journal of Consciousness Studies, 25*: 202–238.

Stark, T. (2015). 'Crashing Out with Sylvian': David Bowie, Carl Jung and the Unconscious. In: E. Devereux, A. Dillane, & M. J. Power (Eds.), *David Bowie: Critical Perspectives.* New York: Routledge.

Stein, M. (1998). *Jung's Map of the Soul.* Peru, IL: Open Court.

Stepansky, P. (1992). The empiricist as rebel: Jung, Freud and the burdens of discipleship. In: R. Papadopoulos (Ed.), *Carl Gustav Jung: Critical Assessments* (pp. 169–199). London: Routledge.

Stevens, A. (2006). The archetypes. In: R. Papadopoulos (Ed.), *The Handbook of Jungian Psychology.* Hove, UK: Routledge.

Tacey, D. (1998). Twisting and turning with James Hillman: From anima to world soul, from academia to pop. In: A. Casement (Ed.), *Post-Jungians Today: Key Papers in Contemporary Analytical Psychology.* London: Routledge.

Urban, E. (2005). Fordham, Jung and the self. *Journal of Analytical Psychology, 50*(5): 571–594.

Vermote, R. (2005). *Bion's Critical Approach to Psychoanalysis: Volume One.* London: University College London Press.

Whan, M. (2018). Disavowal in Jungian psychology: A case study of disenchantment and the timing of shame. In: L. Hinton & H. Willemsen (Eds.), *Temporality and Shame: Perspectives from Psychoanalysis and Philosophy* (pp. 242–260). London: Routledge.

Wiener, N. (2017). *Norbert Wiener—A Life in Cybernetics. Ex-Prodigy: My Childhood and Youth, and I Am a Mathematician: The Later Life of a Prodigy.* Cambridge, MA: Massachusetts Institute of Technology.

Wittels, F. (1934). *Sigmund Freud.* London: Allen & Unwin.

Wittgenstein, L. (1933). Remarks on Frazer's *Golden Bough.* In: *Philosophical Occasions, 1912–1951* (p. 137). Indianapolis, IN: Hackett, 1993.

Index